World Openness Report 2022

Institute of World Economics and Politics, CASS
Research Center for Hongqiao International Economic Forum

Paths International Ltd

中国社会科学出版社
CHINA SOCIAL SCIENCES PRESS

Foreword

Ever since our ancestors could communicate with each other, they formed communities. Small communities developed into villages, towns, cities, and eventually whole countries. The limits to society size are organizational and technical, not a human desire not to mix with each other. Sanitation, disease, and inability to transport ourselves and our goods across large spaces brought an end to city growth; inability to control large populations brought an end to empires. But as we progress, larger size communities are becoming possible, to humanity's advantage.

There is a very simple reason why we seek proximity to other human beings: we benefit socially and economically; economists call it economies of scale, a benefit that the father of modern economics, Adam Smith, already pointed out. Others call it benefits from agglomeration; and in the context of this Report, we can call it benefits from openness.

We are still not ready to make the whole world one single community, with the obvious advantages that well-run single communities enjoy. One day we will be in that position. Europeans have been warring each other for centuries. Who would have guessed that most of them today would be living in a large Union without borders? The next best thing to a single country, which allows us to enjoy many of the advantages of a unified world, is openness.

Society's ultimate objective is to improve the well-being of its people. Well-being derives from our social, cultural and economic life;

above all, the objective is – or should be – to fight poverty and misery, which do not allow those unfortunate enough to suffer it to live beyond subsistence. Social and cultural well-being are achieved through the development of legal and moral systems that protect the rights of the individual and enable him or her to flourish free of oppression from others. Economic well-being comes from the efficient organization of production and the development of technologies that help eliminate poverty and improve the quality of life. There is no doubt that a world that engages in free social, cultural and economic interaction, including exchange of ideas and travel across borders, is one that stands above a system of recluse and warring nations.

Openness is the best way to advance well-being across national borders. Understanding each other's cultures and social conventions is a prerequisite to peaceful coexistence; exchange of goods and ideas opens horizons that cannot be unlocked in single isolated countries. The World Openness Report is a valuable tool to advance this aim: it informs countries of the benefits of openness; it tells them where they stand, and it helps them achieve more. We have rankings of countries by international organizations that address competitiveness, innovation potential, transparency and corruption and many others that influence economic and social well-being. But we do not have one on openness. This Report fills this gap.

Welcome additions to the factors that it considers in the construction of the World Openness Index are the social and cultural pillars. It is rare to find economic indices that consider social and cultural factors, despite their importance in promoting good relations between nations. Good relations encourage better economic exchange too.

The bulk of the World Openness Index is given to economic indicators. Each indicator is first made independent of units of measurement by dividing it by a normalizing aggregate (as, for example, dividing imports by gross domestic product) and is then given a weight that captures its importance in the overall index. The weights were calculated from questionnaire responses of 41 Chinese experts in international economics and add up to one.

Amongst the three pillars in the Index, economic factors dominate with a weight of 0.799; social openness follows with weight 0.134 and cultural openness with a weight of 0.067. The main economic indicators are trade barriers, as measured by the World Bank and the World Trade Organization, and imports of goods and services. A question that would be good to address in this connection is the implication of country size. For example, China has many regions, each of which can be the size of a large European state. Trade between Sichuan province and Guangdong is classified as internal, and it doesn't contribute to openness. But trade between Belgium and the Netherlands is external trade, and it contributes to the openness of the two countries. Dividing exports by the GDP of all countries except for the exporting country corrects this imbalance to some extent – Belgian exports are divided essentially by world GDP, whereas Chinese exports are divided by about 80% of world GDP. But this probably does not totally correct for the fact that Chinese regions (and American States and German Lander) enjoy several of the benefits of openness through domestic trade, whereas Belgian regions need to trade internationally to enjoy them.

The social pillar is dominated by the movement of people – students, tourists, and immigrants, in that order of importance – which is a good way of capturing it. Cultural factors, however, include scientific outputs, such as science papers and patents, and just one set of items that would be considered truly cultural: the UNESCO measure of cultural goods imports and exports. These two get a rather low weight of 0.012, or 1.2%. As with the social pillar, I would love to see in a future edition more discussion of this pillar, and the implications of attaching more weight to it. As I pointed out, the weight attached to this pillar was derived from a survey of Chinese experts. Personally, I would have given this pillar more weight than 0.067, which is more than ten times less than the economic weight, but that is a matter of judgement, and judgments amongst economists are as famous for their differences as they are for their similarities. It should also be borne in mind that cultural factors are notoriously difficult to quantify and this might explain the low over weight to this pillar.

I devoted my discussion so far to the World Openness Index, because of its importance in informing us of the openness across countries and of recent changes. But there is a lot more in the World Openness Report. The special features, appearing as self-contained essays in individual chapters, are informative in important aspects of openness; for example, in the current Report there is discussion of the Belt and Road initiative and its implications for opening, and the war in Ukraine and its implications for trade.

Openness and globalization have been on upward trend since the large-scale industrializations of the twentieth century, but their growth has been checked in more recent times. This is to a large extent due to one-off factors, such as the financial crisis of 2008, the COVID-19 pandemic and the war in Ukraine, all of which increased international tensions and let countries repatriate many activities. Repatriation of the production of goods and services without big losses was made possible by new digital technologies, which enabled meetings without travel and production without reliance on expensive labour. Indeed, labour costs, which in the past were behind much of the openness associated with the location of production, feature less and less in business location decisions.

Geopolitical tensions and disagreements about the role of international organizations, such as the World Trade Organization, create uncertainty about the future; and uncertainty is a deterrent of investment in activities that involve collaborations with foreign countries for supply chains or direct trade. Unfortunately, this uncertainty is also a barrier to enjoying the benefits of more interaction with the rest of the world. Nations need to realise this truth and maintain their efforts to iron out their disagreements about economic openness. The coming of artificial intelligence and automation can be a catalyst in resolving disputes, but only if used correctly in humanity's efforts to defeat poverty and achieve good levels of well-being for all.

I conclude by warmly congratulating the Hongqiao International Economic Forum and the Institute of World Economics and Politics at the Chinese Academy for Social Sciences for the initiate that they have taken and the quality of the Report that they have produced. It should become a standard reference for anyone interested in economic development and international economic relations and I look forward to future editions.

Sir Christopher Pissarides

Regius Professor of Economics at the London School of Economics and Nobel Laureate in Economic Sciences, 2010

Contents

Figures

Tables

Boxes

Preface: Common World Openness
—The Right Path to the Future

The original intention of the *World Opening Report* is to build a global consensus on openness, promote the common opening of the world, and enhance the well-being of all people on the earth, just as President Xi Jinping pointed out, "**Let Spring Breeze of Openness Warms the World**".

Over the past year, the world has experienced a chilly spring, with the specter of the COVID-19 pandemic lingering on, wars and conflicts breaking out one after another, and such headlines as "The global economy enters an era of chaos" and "Globalization is behind us" emerging from time to time. As the world enters a new period of turbulence and transformation and is once again at a crossroads, it is time to ask such questions as "What happened to world openness?" and "What about future openness?" This also endows us with a new mission to compile *World Openness Report 2022* in the new year.

Retrospect and reflection: Economic globalization is encountering headwinds and a chilly spring

The world today is undergoing profound changes unseen in a century. These changes are not the changes limited to specific time, a single event, one country or one region, but profound and far-reaching changes of the times. The pandemic, geopolitical tensions sparked by the Ukraine crisis, and disrupted supply chains have brought new variables and sudden changes to the world economic pattern, with more uncertainties and more contradictions and conflicts exposed.

——In the past, efficiency was given priority and globalization developed rapidly, but now some countries pay more attention to security, protectionism and populism are on the rise, economic problems are politicized, and globalization is encountering adverse currents.

——In the past, developed countries were the driving force of world openness and played a leading role in the development of globalization, but now emerging economies are very involved, and the interests of openness are more diverse.

——In the past, capital, technology and population served as stronger and more dynamic support of globalization, but now the new-added "cake" is shrinking, and resistance to globalization is on the increase.

——In the past, multilateralism was based on rules and orderly governance, but now unilateralism is on the rise to injure others and oneself, institutions are failing. The four major deficits of governance, trust, peace and development are posing increasingly obvious challenges, and interactions between politics, economy, security and ideology are intensifying.

——In the past, economic globalization was once regarded as Alibaba's cave, but now it is regarded as Pandora's box and is in the most difficult time since the end of the Cold War.

But there is nothing new under the sun. Through the telescope of history, we can see that without contradictions, there would be no world, and without unity of opposites, there would be no advancement of the times. In the three rounds of ebb and flow of globalization, contradictions have always existed and never been eliminated. Today's anti-globalization, games among big countries, and decoupled and disrupted chains can all find answer in the analysis of the contradictions in the process of world openness. Through the measure of openness index, Chapters 1-4 of this report make a long-term scanning of the openness trend of 129 economies in the past 11 years, and make a close-up of the status of world openness under the background of the pandemic and the Ukraine crisis, so as to explore the "logic of openness" in the unity of opposites.

——**Pushing or resisting? Various forces are still seesawing.** The results of the openness index show that the trend of world openness is consistent with the real challenges. On the overall level, the World Openness Index continued to show a downward trend in 2020, decreasing 0.02% and 4.1% compared with

2019 and 2008, respectively. As far as the fields of openness are concerned, the overall pattern of "the most open in economy, relatively open in society and relatively less open in culture" continues, but the pace of social and cultural openness has been accelerated in recent years, narrowing the gap with the economic openness. The lates ratio of world economic openness index, social openness index and cultural openness index was 2.8:1.6:1, but 3.5:1.5:1 in 2008. Openness policy index reflecting the government's willingness to open up and openness performance index reflecting openness performance have both declined. Compared with last year and 2008, the latest world openness policy index decreased by 0.2% and 8.1% respectively, while the world openness performance index decreased by 0.09% and 0.9% respectively during the same period. From a regional perspective, the most open regions in the world are Europe, North America, East Asia and the Pacific. Only two regions --- East Asia and the Pacific, and North America --- expanded their openness compared with the previous year, while the remaining five regions all saw shirking openness. Both theory and practice indicate that the evolution of world openness shows not a linear but an oscillating trend, while at present it is still in a turbulent downward stage.

——**Conservative or reformist? The order is being reshaped.** Although the process of globalization has gone against the current in the short term, it will still follow the general trend of history and roll forward in twists and turns in the long term. In the face of challenges and obstacles, we really need to respond to urgent needs, **divide the cake well**, and let different economies, strata and groups share the fruits of globalization. The most fundamental thing is to jointly **make the cake bigger**, make the flow of goods, services, capital and people freer and more convenient, and create greater opening dividends. To make the cake bigger and share it better, we need a more just and reasonable international order and a more effective governance mechanism. Although the overall openness level of developing countries was lower than that of developed countries, the openness index of many developed economies showed a downward trend, which reduced the global opening momentum. In sharp contrast, economies involved in the Belt and Road Initiative continues to broaden openness, and the openness index of the BRICS countries has significantly increased, both releasing positive effect of wider openness. This makes us rethink: to solve the problem of anti-globalization, we need to consider the transformation of the original unbalanced and unequal world order; to achieve more just global governance, we need to better leverage the role of emerging forces; to share the opportunities of global common development, we need to resort to a more inclusive global approach. **Globalization is not Westernized or Orientalized, but makes each other meet halfway**.

——**Opportunities or challenges? The perspective needs to be changed.** Whether openness is warranted or not is an important issue facing the development of an open world economy. An economy's openness should match its own development stage, basic national condition and the general trend of the world to find the optimal openness. We study simply the causal relation between openness and development then conclude that one percentage point increase in openness index will increase the development index by 0.512 percentages. For all stakeholders of opening-up, the opportunities and challenges brought by opening-up always coexist. To make full use of the opportunities and properly deal with challenges brought about by opening-up, both require the relations to be effectively balanced between the degree of openness and the level of development, between the course of openness and the upgrading of competitiveness, between openness skill and governance capability, between openness power and responsibility shouldering, and between openness benefit and inclusiveness and sharing, and the "middle way", i.e., **the most suitable "degree"**, to be found during different times and at different development levels. For developing economies, actively and steadily expanding openness and maintaining the continuity and stability of their opening-up policies are more conducive to seizing the opportunities of globalization and better promoting their own modernization process. **The issue of openness is not a dilemma of 0 or 1, but a choice of "golden bonding point".**

Exploration and outlook: The spring dawn of world common openness is in sight

Where is globalization going? To answer this question we should "look out into the sea at a ship whose pointed masts are already visible". Although the world economy is struggling amid turbulence and the international economic landscape is facing profound adjustments, the theme of our times **has not changed**, the direction of economic globalization **has not changed**, and the historical mission of the international community to work together and achieve win-win cooperation **have not changed**. This is why our world has made positive progress in opening-up.

Focusing on the new trends and new features of global openness, Chapters 5-9 of this report make in-depth analyses of such areas as the reform of the WTO, global economic governance, regional trade agreements, the global manufacturing pattern and resilience of industrial supply chains, financial openness, and digital and green openness. We are concerned that the common security challenges faced by all economies in the world are stern, the trend of oversecuritization is intensifying, the linkage, transnational and diversity of security issues are more prominent, and new vulnerabilities, poverty zones and sources of instability are constantly emerging. If we only care about our own absolute security and ignore the security of other countries, we will eventually fall into a prisoner's dilemma in which everyone is insecure. We should transcend the zero sum thinking of "you lose and I win", pursue self-reliance and excellence, seek peace through openness and inclusiveness, promote security through win-win cooperation, and jointly create a globalized future from the perspective of human destiny and common development.

——**New consensus gathers opening-up momentum.** In the multilateral scope, the 12th WTO Ministerial Conference (MC12) was held in June 2022, reaching a package of 10 outcome agreements on fishery subsidies, food security, e-commerce and other issues. This has not only rescued the WTO from the ICU and given it new life, but also greatly boosted the international community's confidence in the multilateral trading system and injected a strong warm current into the effort to deal with global challenges and promote world economic recovery. From a regional perspective, on January 1, 2022, the Regional Comprehensive Economic Partnership (RCEP) formally took effect, forming an integrated market with one-third of the world's economic share, which has released the institutional dividends of strengthening regional trade and investment cooperation, and transmitted the positive signal of opposing unilateralism and trade protectionism, supporting free trade, and maintaining the multilateral trading system.

————**New impetus has eased the difficulties.** The pandemic has profoundly changed human life and consumption modes, and accelerated the development of digital economy. From agricultural civilization to industrial civilization and to the surging "digital civilization" in today's world, the new generation of digital economy will become an irreversible and truly global economy that is free from geopolitical influences. In 2020, the scale of digital economy in 47 countries reached $32.61 trillion, about 43.7 percent of the sum of their GDP. In June 2022, the 14th BRICS Summit reached important consensus on deepening BRICs digital economic cooperation with an agreement on the BRICS Digital Economy Partnership Framework, which launched a new process of digital economy cooperation among BRICS countries. The "hard connectivity" and "soft connectivity" brought about by digital technology have been vigorously advancing all the way, being a new driving force for the opening up and globalization of the world.

————**New ideas lead the way to prosperity.** Accelerating low-carbon transition and promoting stronger, green and healthy global development will help the world economy achieve "green recovery". The *G20 Sustainable Finance Roadmap* adopted at the 2021 G20 Summit and the *Report on the Common Classification of Sustainable Finance -- Climate Change Mitigation*, issued by the United Nations Climate Change Conference and jointly compiled by China and the EU, have established a globally consistent system of sustainable disclosure standards and guided cross-border climate investment and financing activities, making them two important outcomes in regulating global cooperation on green standards. Countries have successively joined and implemented the *Mission Innovation Initiative* (MI) to promote investment in clean energy technologies and achieve global clean energy technology cooperation, and brought green development onto a "fast track".

Adherence to integrity and sense of responsibility: China's high-level opening up forwards together with spring

China's development is inseparable from the world, and the prosperity of the world needs China. This is a portrayal of China's relations with the world in the new era, also a reflection of China's worldview. **Opening up allows Chinese people to look at the world, discover gaps and differences, learn from and catch up with gaps, and compare and learn from differences.** We not only focus on the internal affairs, focusing on "China in the world" and adjusting ourselves to integrate into the world, but also care about the external affairs, looking to "the world where China is in" and promoting healthy interaction between China and the world.

China adheres to the basic national policy of opening up and unswervingly promotes high-level opening up. The past decade is a decade during which China has **made vigorous efforts** for opening-up. It has pursued a more proactive opening-up strategy, promoted institutional openness, and fostered a new pattern of all-round openness, making it a major stabilizer and source of power for world economic growth. The past decade is a decade during which China's opening-up has **achieved fruitful results**. China's openness index jumped from 0.7107 in 2012 to 0.7507 in 2020 with an growth of 5.6 percent, and its ranking jumped from 47th to 39th, becoming a key variable for economic globalization. The past decade is a decade of China's openness, **mutual benefit and win-win cooperation**. China has taken an active part in global economic governance and firmly upheld the multilateral trading system, making it a clear banner and pioneer of the times. As Chapters 10-12 of this report show, **China's opening-up is irreversible and irreversible, and the road to national rejuvenation will be the road to wider opening-up**.

——**Stronger openness confidence.** In 2021, China's trade in goods exceeded $6 trillion, the world's only country with more than $5 trillion countries in trade in goods, the foreign capital it utilized exceeded 1 trillion yuan for the first time, ranking among the world's top three in foreign investment stock for five consecutive years, its general tariff level was lowered down to 7.4%, and the negative list at a national level was reduced from 93 items in 2017 to 31. All this shows China has taken solid and resolute steps toward high-level opening-up. Standing at a new starting point, we more believe opening-up is the key to China's development. The wider China opens, the more developed it will be and the more open it will become, and China's opening up is always on the way. China will continue to pursue a more proactive, higher-level and more shared opening-up. It will follow the path of emancipating minds and deepening reform, the path of breaking barriers, innovate and break through, and the path of mutual learning among civilizations.

——**More solid opening-up institutions.** In 2021, the Hainan Free Trade Port launched the first negative list for cross-border service trade, along with 19 percent increase in their utilization of foreign investment. Free trade zones, free trade ports and other open platforms aimed at expanding pilot opening-up of the service sector have continuously launched investment liberalization and facilitation measures, with continuing improvements of institutional openness. Standing at a new starting point, the new development pattern has set higher requirements for the level and quality of opening-up. China will make better use of both international and domestic markets and resources to achieve stronger and sustainable development, promote deep-seated reform and high-quality development with high-level opening-up, and with "unchanged" confidence and will of reform and opening-up, respond to the "ever-changing" world political and economic pattern.

——**More evident opening-up determination.** The number of China's free trade partners increased to 26 and is actively promoting its accession to the CPTPP and DEPA. In August 2022, the working panel on China's accession to DEPA was officially established. The CIIE has been successfully held for four consecutive years, providing the world with international public goods that share China's opportunities. In the past two years, President Xi Jinping has put forward the *Global Development Initiative* and the *Global Security Initiative*, which have contributed China's wisdom to reduce the deficits of human development and world peace. Standing at a new starting point, China, with a more open approach and more opening-up initiatives, will promote mutually beneficial and win-win economic cooperation, mutual learning and reference in cultural exchange, and mutual assistance and sharing in global governance, to contribute its efforts to world common prosperity.

Some 530 years ago, Columbus sailed to the New World and told King Ferdinand II and Queen Isabella I of Spain that **"the earth is round"**. Seventeen years ago, Thomas Friedman, an international affairs columnist for *New York Times*, launched his next book on globalization trends, declaring unambiguously that **"the world is flat"**. With the rapid development of the world, our understanding is not what it used to be. No matter how we interpret it, it is an expansion of consensus in communication, and also a joint creation under the condition of openness and mutual learning. Today, we are willing to follow the path of world peace and development and continue to explore the truth of world openness and development in the cause that concerns the destiny of mankind.

"Don't say it's hard to get the spring light. It's a sunny day after the floating clouds". It is hoped that *World Openness Report 2022* will provide a more objective and comprehensive perspective, inspire more reflection, build bigger consensus and explore more effective strategies for opening-up and cooperation. Regardless of wind and thunder, we are ready to forge a bright future with firefly glimmer, and jointly hold the banner of building an open world economy even higher and more steadily.

Chapter 1   World Openness Index 2020

In 2020, as the COVID-19 pandemic was still raging, how open was the world, and how open will it be? What characteristics have been shown compared to 2019? This chapter will attempt to offer an answer to these questions.

I. World Openness Index

1. The world is not as open as it used to be

In 2020, the World Openness Index was 0.7491, down 0.02% from 2019, 4.1% from 2008, and 1.5% from 2015.

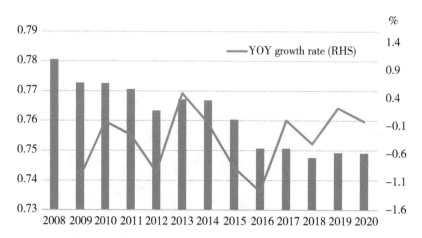

Fig. 1.1   World Openness Index, 2008-2020

2. Top 20 most open economies

Singapore was the most open economy in the world in 2020. Its Openness Index ranked top among the 129 economies gauged. In the 13 years after 2008, Singapore ranked top in six years and second in the remaining seven years.

Germany and China's Hong Kong SAR ranked second and third in 2020. The two economies have perched in second to fourth place in recent years.

Ireland, Switzerland, the Netherlands, Canada, Malta, France, and the United Kingdom ranked fourth to tenth.

The economies ranking eleventh to twentieth were, respectively, Belgium, South Korea, Luxembourg, Hungary, New Zealand, Czech Republic, Australia, Austria, Cyprus, and Denmark.

Table 1.1　　　　**Top 20 most open economies in the world, 2020**
(G20 members are shown in bold)

	2020	2019	2008
Singapore	1	1	2
Germany	**2**	**2**	**3**
Hong Kong, China	3	3	4
Ireland	4	4	11
Switzerland	5	6	10
The Netherlands	6	7	8
Canada	**7**	**9**	**7**
Malta	8	10	6
France	**9**	**8**	**9**
The UK	**10**	**5**	**5**
Belgium	11	12	16
South Korea	**12**	**14**	**51**
Luxembourg	13	20	41
Hungary	14	25	26
New Zealand	15	28	14
Czech	16	19	27
Australia	**17**	**16**	**25**
Austria	18	23	21
Cyprus	19	15	19
Denmark	20	24	23

For the openness index numbers and rankings of the 129 economies, see the Appendix I & II of this report.

II. World Openness: Specific Indexes

1.The world was more open economically and culturally, yet less open socially in 2020 than in 2019

a. Slightly more open economically than in 2019

Economic openness refers to the degree to which cross-border trade in goods and services, direct investment, and securities investment are registered. The World Economic Openness Index (WEOI) in 2020 was 0.8805, up 0.5% from 2019, and down 8.4% from 2008 and 4% from 2015.

The most open economy was Singapore, followed by Germany (2nd), Hong Kong, China (3rd), Ireland (4th), South Korea (5th), Malta (6th), Switzerland (7th), Belgium (8th), Hungary (9th), and France (10th). China, the United States, and Japan ranked 69th, 110th, and 50th, respectively.

In terms of the economic openness index, South Korea registered the greatest cumulative growth (13.3%) from 2008 to 2020, followed by Ireland (5.2%), Singapore (2.6%), Hong Kong, China (1.3%), and Germany (0.2%). The number for China, the United States, and Japan was 1.6%, -24.6%, and -6.1%, respectively.

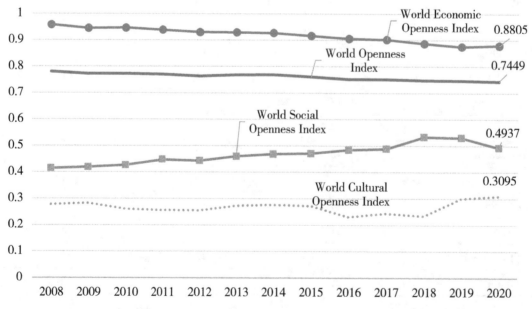

Fig. 1.2 World Economic, Social and Cultural Openness Indexes, 2008-2020

b. Significantly less open socially than in 2019

Social openness refers to the degree to which cross-border movement of people, i.e. the movement and migration of tourists and international students, are registered.

The World Social Openness Index (WSOI) in 2020 was 0.4937, down 7.1% from 2019, and up 18.4% from 2008 and 5.3% from 2015. The top ten most socially open economies were: Macau, China (0.4521, 1st), Germany (0.4299, 2nd), Australia (0.3972, 3rd), the United States (0.3911, 4th), Singapore (0.3897, 5th), Canada (0.3779, 6th), United Kingdom (0.3756, 7th), Switzerland (0.3744, 8th), Luxembourg (0.3703, 9th), and France (0.3675, 10th).

c. Slightly more open culturally than in 2019

Cultural openness refers to the degree to which the cross-border flow of cultural products is registered, mainly including cross-border trade in cultural goods and intellectual property services, cross-border patent applications, and international citations of literature.

The World Cultural Openness Index (WCOI) in 2020 was 0.3095, up 2.9% from 2019, 16.4% from 2008, and 17.8% from 2015. The top ten most culturally open economies were: the United States (0.4437, 1st), Hong Kong, China (0.2438, 2nd), Singapore (0.24, 3rd), Ireland (0.2231, 4th), Japan (0.197, 5th), Cambodia (0.1904, 6th), China (0.1882, 7th), Guyana (0.1867, 8th), Canada (0.185, 9th), and Vietnam (0.1824, 10th).

The situation in which the economic openness index is higher than, the social openness index, which in turn is higher than the cultural openness index, has remained since 2008, although the latter two have grown faster than the former to narrow the gaps between the three. The ratio between the WEOI, WSOI, and WCOI was 2.8:1.6:1 in 2020, 2.9:1.8:1 in 2019, and 3.5:1.5:1 in 2008.

2.Slightly lower openness performance and policy indexes

Openness performance refers to the cross-border flow of carriers of economic, social, and cultural openness (goods, services, capital, personnel, knowledge, etc.). It indicates the direct results of openness. Openness policy refers to the government's standardized regulations on economic, social, and cultural openness. It indicates the willingness of a sovereign government to open up.

a. The openness performance index declined amid fluctuations

In 2020, the World Openness Performance Index (WOPerI) was 0.7445, down 0.09% from 2019, 0.9% from 2008, and 1.8% from 2015. The top 10 economies in terms of openness performance index were: the United States (0.8815, 1st), Singapore (0.8693, 2nd), Germany (0.8445, 3rd), Hong Kong, China (0.8428, 4th), China (0.8228, 5th) , Ireland (0.8107, 6th), Luxembourg (0.7729, 7th), Macau, China (0.7505, 8th), Canada (0.7369, 9th), and Netherlands (0.7364, 10th).

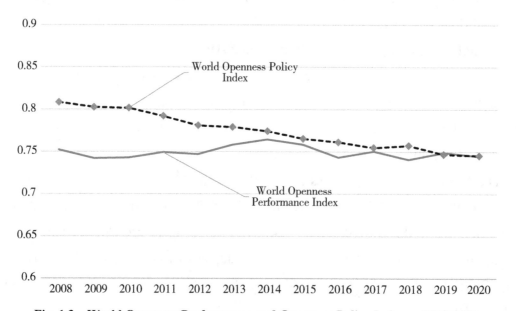

Fig. 1.3   World Openness Performance and Openness Policy Indexes, 2008-2020

b. The openness policy index dropped consistently

In 2020, the World Openness Policy Index (WOPolI) was 0.7453, down 0.2% from 2019, 8.1% from 2008, and 2.6% from 2015. The top 10 economies in terms of openness policy index were: Singapore (0.9093, 1st), South Korea (0.8924, 2nd), Switzerland (0.8866, 3rd), Czech Republic (0.8764, 4th), Australia (0.874, 5th), Lithuania (0.8739, 6th), Latvia (0.8732, 7th), Germany (0.8729, 8th), Estonia (0.8716, 9th), and Romania (0.8697, 10th).

3.World inbound and outbound openness Indexes

For an economy, there are two types of openness: one is its openness to other economies ("inbound openness"); the other is the openness of other economies to it ("outbound openness"). The corresponding indexes are the "inbound openness index" and the "outbound openness index". The inbound and outbound openness indexes of each sample economy are weighted according to their share in the total GDP of all sample economies to get the world inbound and outbound openness indexes. The inbound and outbound openness indexes of each economy are not necessarily equal. The same applies to the world inbound and outbound openness indexes.

a. World Inbound Openness Index

In 2020, economies were opened wider to other economies than in 2019. The World Inbound Openness Index (WIOI) was 0.8306, up 1.2% from 2019, but down 10.5% from 2008 and 4.3% from 2015. The YoY growth rate of the WIOI was negative in 12 of the 13 years from 2008 to 2020.

In 2020, the top 10 economies that were most open to other economies were: Hong Kong, China (0.9299, 1st), Singapore (0.9231, 2nd), Ireland (0.897, 3rd), Malta (0.8756, 4th) , Bahrain (0.8711, 5th), Cambodia (0.8546, 6th), Macau, China (0.8523, 7th), Luxembourg (0.8509, 8th), Australia (0.8497, 9th), and Jordan (0.8479, 10th).

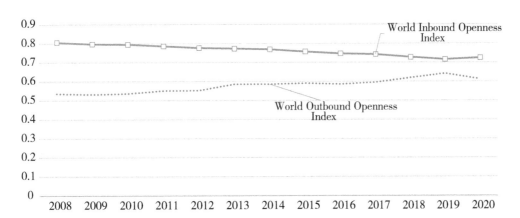

Fig. 1.4   World Inbound and Outbound Openness Indexes, 2008-2020

b. World Outbound Openness Index

In 2020, the world was less open to other economies than it was in 2019. The World Outbound Openness Index (WOOI) was 0.5719, down 4.6% from 2019, but up 13.8% from 2008 and 4.8% from 2015. In the 13 years since 2018, there were ten years when WOOI achieved positive YoY growth.

In 2020, the top ten economies in terms of outbound openness index were: the

United States (0.8555, 1st), China (0.7368, 2nd), Germany (0.7151, 3rd), South Korea (0.6204, 4th), Japan (0.6179, 5th), Singapore (0.5973, 6th), France (0.555, 7th), Switzerland (0.5534, 8th), United Kingdom (0.5477, 9th), and the Netherlands (0.5469, 10th).

III. Regional Openness Index

1.High-income and upper-middle-income economies continued to open wider, while those in other income groups became less open

In 2020, the most open economies were still high-income ones (with 49 sample economies, the same below), the least open were lower-middle-income economies (30), and in between the two were upper-middle-income economies (39) and low-income economies (11).

The groups with a higher openness index in 2020 than in 2019 were high-income and upper-middle-income economies, and those with lower openness were lower-middle-income and low-income economies.

The openness index for each group in 2020 was as follows.

The openness index of economies in the high-income group was 0.7804, up 0.01% from 2019, and down 5.6% and 2.33% from 2008 and 2015, respectively.

The openness index of upper-middle-income economies was 0.712, up 0.61% from 2019, 5.83% and 2.11% from 2008 and 2015, respectively, marking the fifth consecutive YoY growth.

The openness index of lower-middle-income economies was 0.6033, down 0.31% from 2019, and up 5.93% and 0.1% from 2008 and 2015, respectively.

The openness index of low-income economies was 0.6381, down 1.63% from 2019 and 0.46% from 2015, and up 0.27% from 2008.

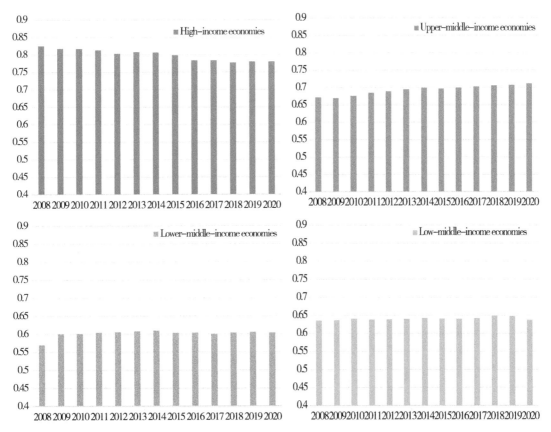

Fig. 1.5　Openness index by income group, 2008-2020

2.Openness index of the seven geographic regions

In 2020, the three regions with the highest openness index were Europe and Central Asia (0.7745), North America (0.7699), and East Asia and the Pacific (0.7538).

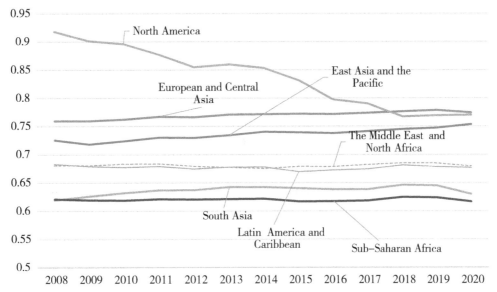

Fig. 1.6　Openness index by geographic region, 2008-2020

Only two regions opened wider in 2020 than in 2019, that is, East Asia and the Pacific, and North America, with their openness index up by 0.86% and 0.08%, respectively. The remaining five regions became less open in 2020: the region with the largest drop was South Asia (-2.34%), followed by Sub-Saharan Africa (-1.13%), Latin America and the Caribbean (-0.26%), Europe and Central Asia (-0.55%), the Middle East and North Africa (-0.82%).

3.Openness index of the "Belt and Road" economies

As of February 6, 2022, there are 149 signatory economies under the *Belt and Road Initiative* (BRI), of which 99 were subject to the gauging of the World Openness Index. This paper takes these 99 economies as a sample to calculate their openness indexes, which indicate the degree to which these 149 economies are open (see Appendix IV for details).

In 2020, the openness index of the BRI economies was 0.7218, up 0.4% from 2019, and 5% and 1.7% from 2008 and 2015, respectively. In the 12 years from 2009 to 2020, except for the YoY decline in 2009, each of the subsequent years saw YoY growth. This indicates the widening openness of the "Belt and Road" economies and the huge potential for greater openness brought about by the BRI.

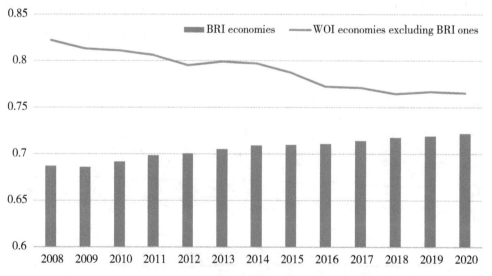

Fig. 1.7   Openness Index in BRI and non-BRI economies, 2008-2020

The BRI economies have been opened wider, in stark contrast with the other 30 economies (hereinafter referred to as "non-BRI economies", unless otherwise specified) gauged by the World Openness Index. Firstly, the degree of openness for the non-BRI economies has long been higher than the BRI economies. From 2008 through 2020, the openness index of the BRI economies was between 0.7646 and 0.8221, while that of non-BRI economies was between 0.6869 and 0.7218. Secondly, the degree of openness for non-BRI economies has been shrinking, with their openness index down by 7.1% from 2008 (down 0.2% from 2019), a cumulative decrease exceeding that of the BRI economies. The gap between the two has been narrowing, from 20% to 6%.

4. Openness index of G20

In 2020, the openness index of the G20 countries (exclude the EU, unless otherwise specified) was 0.7526, down 0.1% from 2019, down 5.6% and 2.2% from 2008 and 2015, respectively.

The openness index of the remaining economies gauged by the World Openness Index was 0.7347 in 2020, up 0.3% from 2019, and 2.2% and 1.4% from 2008 and 2015, respectively.

Thus, the gap between the openness of G20 members and that of the remaining economies is shrinking. In 2008, the openness index of G20 members was 10.7% higher than that of other economies. The number was 6.1% in 2015 and merely 2.4% in 2020.

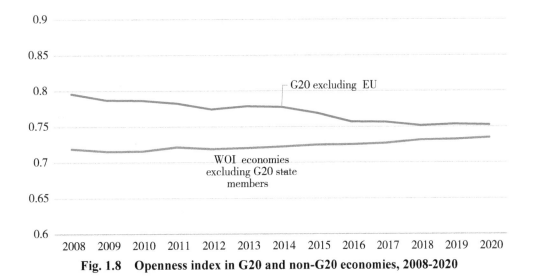

Fig. 1.8   Openness index in G20 and non-G20 economies, 2008-2020

5. Openness index of BRICS countries

In 2020, the BRICS openness index was 0.7091, up 0.2% from 2019. Non-BRICS economies, i.e. the 124 economies measured by the World Openness Index, have an openness index of 0.7617 in 2020, roughly the same as in 2019.

Since 2008, the openness of the BRICS countries has been on the rise, but that of non-BRICS economies has shown a downward trend. The openness index of BRICS countries in 2020 grew by 6.3% and 1.6% over 2008 and 2015, respectively, while the numbers for non-BRICS economies were -5.3% and -2%, respectively.

In other words, BRICS countries are less open than non-BRICS economies, but the gap is narrowing. The openness index of BRICS countries was 17.2% lower than non-BRICS economies in 2008, 10.3% lower in 2015, and 6.9% lower in 2020.

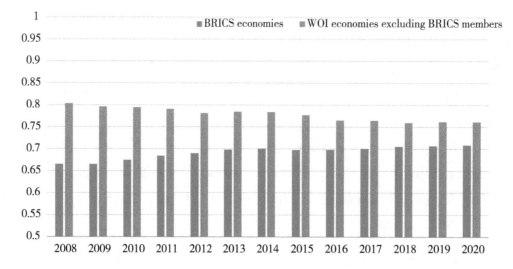

Fig. 1.9   Openness index, BRICS and non-BRICS economies, 2008-2020

6. Openness index of developed economies

Among the 129 economies gauged, 36 are developed economies (40 developed economies in total, see Appendix IV for details), and the remaining 93 economies are emerging markets and developing economies, which are collectively referred to as "developing economies" in this chapter.[①]

---

① The 36 economies are listed in alphabetical order as follows: Australia, Austria, Belgium, Canada, Cyprus, Czech Republic, Denmark, Estonia, Finland, France, Germany, Greece, China's Hong Kong SAR, Iceland, Ireland, Israel, Italy, Japan, Latvia, Lithuania, Luxembourg, Macau China, Malta, Netherlands, New Zealand, Norway, Portugal, Singapore, Slovakia, Slovenia, South Korea, Spain, Sweden, Switzerland, United Kingdom, United States. The other four developed economies not gauged by the Openness Index are Andorra, Puerto Rico, San Marino, and Taiwan Province of China. See IMF (2022): World Economic Outlook, April 2022, https://www.imf.org/en/Publications/WEO/weo-database/2022/April/select-country-group

In 2020, the openness index of developed economies was 0.783, a slight decrease from 2019, and a decrease of 5.9% and 2.5% from 2008 and 2015, respectively.

The openness index of developing economies was 0.6963, an increase of 0.2% over 2019, and an increase of 4.4% and 1.5% over 2008 and 2015, respectively.

In other words, the openness gap between developed and developing economies is shrinking. The openness index of the former was 24.7% higher than that of the latter in 2008, 17% in 2015, and only 12.4% in 2020.

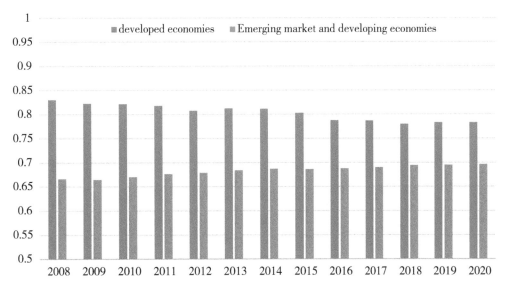

Fig. 1.10   Openness index in developed and developing economies, 2008-2020

The EU has continued to open wider over the past 13 years. In 2020, the openness index of the EU was 0.7974, surpassing that of non-EU economies (0.7371), an increase of 0.2% over 2019, 1.7% over 2015, and 3.3% over 2008.

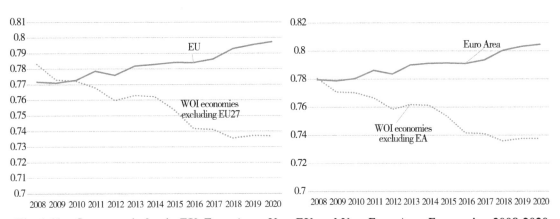

Fig. 1.11   Openness index in EU, Euro Area, Non-EU and Non-Euro Area Economies, 2008-2020

In 2020, the openness index of the 19 countries in the euro area was 0.8047, higher than that of the non-euro area (0.7378), up 0.2% from 2019, 1.7% from 2015, and 3.2% from 2008. The gap between the euro area and the non-euro area is widening. In 2008, the openness index of the former was 0.1% lower than that of the latter, but it was 5% higher in 2015 and 9.1% higher in 2020.

The degree of openness of Group 7 (G7) continued to shrink. In 2020, its openness index was 0.7824, down 8.7%, 3.7% and 0.2% from 2008, 2015 and 2019, respectively.

The non-G7 countries have continued to open wider. In 2020, its openness index increased by 3.6%, 1.3% and 0.3% compared with 2008, 2015 and 2019, respectively. The openness gap between the G7 and non-G7 economies has been narrowing. The openness index of the former was 23% higher than that of the latter in 2008, 14.3% higher in 2015, and 8.7% higher in 2020.

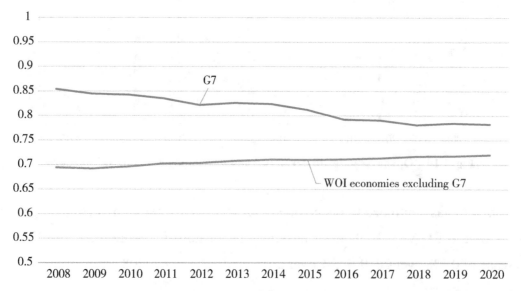

Fig. 1.12 Openness index in G7 and non-G7 economies, 2008-2020

To sum up, The openness of the world in 2020 is slightly lower than that in 2019. This is mainly due to the strengthening of cross-border social isolation caused by the COVID-19 pandemic. The world's opening policy and performance both declined slightly, and the decline of opening policy was bigger than that of opening performance.

Chapter 2   Warranted Openness: An Analysis Based on Some Countries

Whether openness is warranted or not is an important issue facing the development of an open world economy. Openness brings both opportunities and challenges to all parties concerned. To make full use of the opportunities and properly deal with challenges brought about by openness both require the relations to be effectively balanced between the degree of openness and the level of development, between the course of openness and the upgrading of competitiveness, between openness skill and governance capability, between openness strength and responsibility shouldering, and between openness benefit and inclusiveness and sharing, and the "golden junction" to be found during different times and at different development levels.[1]

I. The Problem of Warrantedness of Openness

1. An diversity analysis of country openness

Take the Group of 20 (G20) countries as a sample. From 2008 to 2020, the openness index of the 19 state members of the G20 was between 0.6189 and 0.9328, and the simple arithmetic average was 0.7271. Of the 129 economies in the World Openness Index 2020 list, the highest openness index of the G20 countries is 0.8591 (Germany) and the lowest is 0.6189 (Brazil), ranking 2nd and 107th, respectively.

Based on a simple arithmetic average of the openness index between 2008 and 2020, the 19 members of the G20 can be divided into the following three groups.

---

[1]   The Institute of World Economics and Politics of Chinese Academy of Social Sciences & Research Center for Hongqiao International Economic Forum (2021). *World Openness Report 2021.* Beijing: China Social Sciences Press. Page 5.

First group: three countries with the highest average degree of openness --- the United States, Germany and the United Kingdom, whose simple arithmetic average openness index is 0.843, 0.8365 and 0.805, respectively. They are the only three G20 members whose openness index exceeds 0.8, as shown in Fig. 2.1 (a). The openness index of these three countries is between 0.7653 (US, 2018) and 0.9328 (US, 2008), with a simple arithmetic average openness index of 0.8282. The coefficient of variation[①] of US' openness index is 0.0712, which is the G20 member with the largest fluctuation in openness.

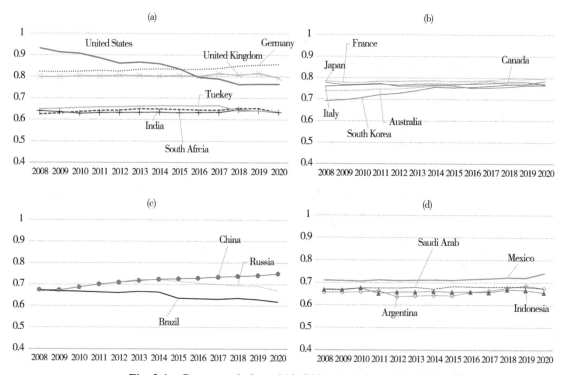

Fig. 2.1   Openness index of 19 G20 countries, 1980-2020

Second group: eight countries with an average degree of openness between 0.7 and 0.8. According to the simple arithmetic average openness index from 2008 to 2020 and in a "from high to low" order, they are France (0.7879), Canada (0.7876), Italy (0.7718), Japan (0.7658), Australia (0.7608), South Korea (0.7422), China (0.717) and Mexico (0.7165). The openness index of these eight countries is between 0.6747 (China, 2009) and 0.7998 (Canada, 2020), and the simple arithmetic average openness index is 0.7562.

---

① The coefficient of variation in openness index is equal to ratio of the standard deviation of openness series to its average, where a higher result indicates a greater fluctuation of openness index, and vice versa.

Among them, the degree of openness of South Korea and China has fluctuated greatly, and the coefficient of variation in openness index is 0.0405 and 0.0346, respectively.

Third group: eight countries with an average of openness index between 0.6 and 0.7. According to the simple arithmetic average from 2008 to 2020 and in a "from high to low" order, they are Russia (0.6981), Saudi Arabia (0.6779), Indonesia (0.6623), Argentina (0.6596), Turkey (0.6558), Brazil (0.649), India (0.6431) and South Africa (0.635). The openness index of these eight countries for each year is between 0.6189 (Brazil, 2020) and 0.7241 (Russia, 2013), and the simple arithmetic average openness index is 0.6601. Among them, Brazil, Russia and Argentina had the largest fluctuations in openness degree, with a coefficient of variation in openness index between 0.0229 and 0.0291.

Of course, the above grouping method is simple, but the results are intuitive. The G20 members include almost all the countries with the largest economies and populations in the world, but their openness degree is diverse, varying from high to low in world rankings.

——There are 10 high-income countries (Australia, Canada, France, Germany, Italy, Japan, South Korea, Saudi Arabia, the United Kingdom, and the United States), and their highest world ranking in openness index is 2nd (Germany), the lowest is 71st (Saudi Arabia). Except for Saudi Arabia, the remaining nine countries are all developed economies, with the highest and lowest world ranking in openness index being 2nd (Germany) and 27th (United States), respectively.

——There are 7 upper-middle-income countries (Argentina, Brazil, China, Mexico, Russia, South Africa, Turkey) and 2 lower-middle-income countries (India, Indonesia), and their highest and lowest world ranking in openness index are 37th (China) and 107th (Brazil), respectively.

So, did openness index for each of the 19 countries from 2008 to 2020 satisfy themselves and their partner economies? This requires an assessment of their "warrantedness of openness".

2. Theoretical analysis of warranted openness

The term "warranted" is used in law, linguistics and economics. In economics, there are related concepts such as "warranted growth rate", which refers to economic growth rate warranted by the savings rate. The definition of "warranted openness" in this chapter has reference from the concept of "warranted growth rate".

a. Concept of "warranted openness"

The "warrantedness" of openness refers to the characteristic that openness is warranted by the openness capacity of the subject concerned. This definition includes the following keywords.

The first keyword is the "subject of openness", that is, the state carrying out the act of openness or the subject as a component of the state.[1] The basic unit of this chapter is the economy, so it takes the economy as the subject of openness.

The second keyword is "openness capacity", which refers to the comparative advantages/disadvantages of an economy compared with its partner economies in terms of openness, as well as realistic ability to govern openness dimensions, intensity, speed, and order. The stronger the ability to open up, the higher openness can be, and vice versa. The main determinant variable of openness capacity is the endowment of the economy, including innate endowment and acquired endowment, with the former including such elements as geographical location and natural resources, and the latter including such elements as population, production technology, labor quality, capital, institution, culture, etc. Some endowments can increase openness, while others can decrease openness, and ultimately, all endowments together determine the strength of openness.

The third keyword is "warrant". The specific openness of an economy needs to be supported by the corresponding openness capacity. If the latter does not exceed the maximum openness capacity of the economy, then its openness can be defined as warranted openness, otherwise its openness can not be defined to be warranted.

To sum up, the warranted openness of an economy refers to openness warranted by the capacity of the economy to open up.

Theoretically, warranted openness has the following characteristics.

---

① The components of one economy include institutional sectors or industrial sectors. According to the definition of the *System of National Accounts*, resident institutions can be divided into the following five institutional sectors: the general government sector, the non-financial corporate sector, the financial corporate sector, the non-profit sector serving households sector, and the household sector. Non-resident institutions that interact with resident institutions are collectively referred to as the foreign sector. Another common concept is industry sector. Each industry sector corresponds to each industry in the international standard industrial classification, including the most detailed industry classification levels and higher levels based on aggregations (such as medium category, large category and final category). "Individual businesses" refers to the economic agent doing business, that is, the operator (See SNA 2008, Para.4.24, 5.46).

Firstly, there can be multiple values of warranted openness. As long as the openness of an economy does not exceed its maximum openness capacity, corresponding openness can be called "warranted openness". Openness that requires maximum openness capacity to warrant is the greatest "warranted openness" of the economy. Obviously, there must be more than one value of openness below maximum warranted openness capacity, and they all belong to warranted openness. Openness that exceeds maximum warranted openness capacity is not warranted openness, that is, unwarranted openness.

Secondly, while remaining relatively stable in the short term, maximum warranted openness may change significantly in the medium and long term. This is because the endowments of an economy may change more slowly in the short run, and therefore openness capacity determined by it and corresponding maximum warranted openness are more stable. Given that changes in an economy's endowment over the medium to long term may be more pronounced, openness capacity determined by it and corresponding maximum warranted openness may also see significant changes as time goes by.

Thirdly, given that maximum warranted openness is achieved under the utilization of openness capacity to a maximum degree, it should become the main goal of all economies to explore openness practice.

b. Relations with optimal openness

The openness of an economy is determined by its demand for openness (hereinafter referred to as "openness demand") and its supply of openness (hereinafter referred to as "openness supply"). The "authentic openness" formed when openness demand equals openness supply is "equilibrium openness", which includes low-level equilibrium openness and high-level equilibrium openness. When openness demand is low, openness supply with which it forms a state of equilibrium is clearly below maximum openness capacity, at which point only part of openness capacity is utilized. When openness demand is high, if openness supply with which it forms a state of equilibrium is also at a higher level, most of openness capacity is fully utilized.

When openness demand is high enough to reach maximum openness capacity, "equilibrium openness" promoted by it is "optimal openness". Obviously, whether openness is optimal depends on whether openness capacity is maximally utilized and whether openness demand is high enough to form equilibrium with maximum openness capacity.

Warranted openness is not necessarily optimal openness, but optimal openness must be warranted openness. When openness is in an optimal state, the utilization of openness capacity would reach its maximum level, and corresponding openness is maximum warranted openness.

If the openness supply level matching with openness demand exceeds maximum openness capacity, it is excessive openness, which means openness is not sustainable. This is because excessive openness requires more openness supply than its maximum openness capacity, resulting in a gap in openness supply. As a result, openness supply and demand will be at an unbalanced state, pushing openness demand back to the scope that can be warranted by openness capacity.

3. Warrantedness of openness should take development as fundamental direction to achieve optimal openness

If openness is warranted, does it mean that the effects of openness are satisfactory to the economy concerned? The specific objectives served by an economy's opening up to the outside world belong to the "result" of openness. The "result" of openness is quite rich in connotation and extension, and the concept that can best summarize it is probably *development*.

Development is the basis and key to solving all problems. As Chari & Corbridge (2008)[1] puts it, *development* has become one of humanity's most quoted words since its creation, but also one of the most controversial words. In the existing massive literature, the word *development* has been widely applied to many fields, such as economic development, social development, cultural development and political development. This corresponds to the "openness" as defined by the "Openness Index" in this report: cross-border openness likewise covers economic, social, cultural, political and other dimensions.

Just like the concept of *openness*, the concept of *development* is also applicable to all economies: No matter whether the starting point of development is high or low, or the current level of development is high or low, any economy is always on the road to development, its development in economic, social, cultural, political and other fields is endless, and there is always a need for it to have sustainable development.

An example is that the research subject of development economics was for a

---

① Chari, S., & Corbridge, S. (2008). Introduction of Part I: The Object of Development. In *The Development Reader*, Routledge, The 1ˢᵗ edition., pp. 3-8.

long time poor economies, later it expanded to backwards economies, or developing economies, and now it covers almost all economies, because the research purpose is to "explore ... a way to enjoy growing prosperity" for these economies (Clive Bell[①]). Clearly, under the concept of a community with a shared future for mankind, all economies are entitled to "growing prosperity" for themselves and the world.

The development of an economy has both macro- and micro-level connotations.

On the macro level, development refers to the growth of some specific macro targets and the structural transformation of the economy (Summer &Trible, 2008[②]). In both development economics and economic history literature, "structure" refers to the relative importance of sectors in the economy (in terms of production and factor use), that is, the subdivision of the economy as a whole, which can be extrapolated from technical or behavioral relationships into certain ratios (the former, such as input-output coefficient, the latter, such as aggregate savings rate); "structural transformation" refers to the process of the change of numerous interconnected structures (Syrquin, 1988[③]).

On the micro level, development is "related to individual life and death, well-being and illness, happiness and misery, freedom and vulnerability, etc." (Sen, 1988[④]; Meier, 2001[⑤]). It refers to increasing behavioral choices, growing capabilities, and improving well-being of individuals in this economy, specifically represented by "material prosperity" and "dignity, freedom, and satisfaction in the workplace" (Clive Bell).

The macro and micro connotations of development may or may not coincide. When the two coincide, the economy is at an optimal level of development.

Openness is a means of development and aims at promoting development. Development achieved through openness is "development under openness", referred to as "open development". Openness is one of the many means of

---

① Clive Bell. Development Economics. In *The New Palgrave Dictionary of Economics and The Law* (Edited by John Eatwell, Murray Milgate, Peter Newman), Vol. 1, Chinese version, Economic Science Press, 1992, pp. 884-891.

② Pansera, M, & Owen, R. (2018). *Innovation and Development: The Politics and the Bottom of Pyramid*. ISTE ltd. and John Wiley & Sons. Chapter 1, pp. 1-9.

③ Syrquin, M, (1988). Patterns of structural change. In *Handbook of Development Economics*, edited by Chenery, H., & Srinivasan, T. (1988), ScienceDirect, Chapter 7, pp. 203-273.

④ Sen, A. (1988). The concept of development. In *Handbook of Development Economics*, edited by Chenery, H. & Srinivasan, T. (1988), Chapter 1, pp. 9-26.

⑤ Meier, G. (2001). Introduction: Ideas for Development. In *Frontiers of Development Economics: The Future in Perspective*, edited by Meier, G, & Stiglitz, J. (2001), The World Bank & Oxford University Press, pp. 1-11.

development, which aims to promote high-quality development through internal and external connectivity, that is, it is necessary to improve the ability to make good use of both international and domestic markets and resources, and it is also necessary to strengthen the ability to use international economic and trade rules to fight for international economic narratives. In China, "open development" is an important part of the new development concept.

Box 2-1　China's New Development Philosophy

Development philosophy is the precursor of development actions. It is something of overall, fundamental, directional, and long-term management, and a concentrated embodiment of development thinking, development direction, and development priorities.

New development philosophy refers to innovative, coordinated, green, open and shared development. Among them, innovative development focuses on providing the driving force of development, coordinated development focuses on solving the problem of unbalanced development, green development focuses on solving the problem of harmony between man and nature, open development focuses on promoting the internal and external connectivity of development, and shared development focuses on solving the problem of social equity and justice.

New development philosophy conforms to the needs of the times, and it is of great guiding significance to eliminating development difficulties, enhancing development impetus and building up development advantages.

If the development effect of an economy is ideal, it indicates that its openness is warranted or even optimal. If the development effect of an economy is not ideal, it indicates that there may be some following problems with openness.

Firstly, when, openness is warranted, but equilibrium between openness supply and demand is at a low level, the utilization of openness capacity has not reached its maximum, and the development effect of openness and even the overall development effect are not maximized.

Secondly, although openness is not only warranted but also optimal, the development effect of openness does not achieve the best synergistic effect with the development effect of other ways, which may result in unsatisfactory effects of overall development.

Thirdly, openness is not warranted, that is, openness exceeds the scope that maximum openness capacity can warrant, or excessive openness.

II. Typical Case Analysis of Warranted Openness

1. Methods, variables and data

With "openness" as the center, if the reasons of openness are linked directly to the its effects, it will form such a causal chain:

Openness capacity → openness → development effect of openness.

Clearly, one of the manifestations in this process is "openness", which is located at the center of the causal chain described above. The causal relationship between the first two of the chain shows that since the warrantedness of openness is guaranteed by openness capacity, then it can be evaluated based on openness capacity.

The causal relationship between the latter two of the chain shows that since openness will form a development effect, then the warrantedness of openness and whether it is optimal can be evaluated based on the effect.

From the perspective of methodology, the warrantedness of openness can be defined and measured either from the development effect of openness or from the determinants of openness capacity on openness. However, in both theory and practice, as the determining force of openness, the connotation of openness capacity is easy to define, but its extension is difficult to define and measure. Similarly, the determining forces of development effect are also diverse, and openness is only one of them. It is also difficult to accurately identify the development effect of openness from it.

In the following part, this chapter attempts to directly link openness and development effect, preliminarily explore the closeness of this relationship, and make a concise and intuitive judgment on the "warrantedness" of openness, in order to form a complementary causality study between them.

As mentioned above, development is reflected by "total growth and structural transformation" on the macro level, and "increased individual behavioral choices, growing ability and improved well-being" on the micro level. Therefore, this chapter applies "development index" to measure the performance of development.[1]

---

[1] The composite index method has a defect, that is, the development index of each year cannot reflect the dynamic effect between economic variables across years.

Table 2.1 **Basic indicators of development index**

	Indicators	Specification	Data sources	Weighting
1	Real GDP growth rate	Measuring real economic growth rate of the previous year in the reporting year.	*International Financial Statistics,* IMF	0.5
2	Gini coefficient of income, YOY change	Income Gini coefficient measures income distribution among individuals or households within an economy, and in some economies it is a gauge of consumption distribution.	*World Development Indicators,* World Bank	0.3
3	Human development index (HDI), YOY change	Measuring individual choice opportunity, ability and will-being level in an average sense.[1]	UNDP[2]	0.2

Development index is the weighted composite value of YOY changes of the following three basic indicators: real GDP growth rate; Gini coefficient of income (the difference in income distribution between households or individuals); Human Development Index (HDI). See Table 2.1 for definitions, specifications and data sources of each indicator. There are also upgraded versions of the HDI sub-indices adjusted for their respective distribution gaps. The upgraded HDI version based on the weighting of these adjusted subdivision indicators can replace the weighting of income Gini coefficient and HDI, but its data time series is limited to 2010-2019, which does not meet the requirements for calculating development index as above.

When creating development index, the weight of its basic indicators is as follows: the weight of real GDP growth rate is 0.5, the weight of income Gini coefficient is 0.3, and the weight of HDI is 0.2. Before weighting, the dimensions of these three basic indicators were all unified as 0-100, among which the income Gini coefficient and the HDI were already between 0-100, and the real GDP growth rate was converted to the value between 0 and 100 with 100 as the benchmark in 2008. The principle of weight determination embodies the following understandings of development.

Firstly, growth is the basis and key to solving all problems, including structural evolution and changes in individual choice opportunities, well-being and abilities.

---

[1] The HDI is the weighted mean of three sub-indicators: life expectancy index (based on life expectancy at birth); education index (based on two indicators: average years of schooling for people aged above 25 years old and expected years of schooling for school-age children); gross national income index (based on GNI per capita ppp$).

[2] https://hdr.undp.org/data-center/human-development-index#/indicies/HDI.

Secondly, the income structure is one of the most important among many structures, which is mainly determined by production structure, especially production input structure, and determines consumption structure. The structure of production is more fundamental to development than the structure of income, but it is difficult to measure because many economies lack consistent and long-term subdivision data. As a measure of individual will-being structure, consumption structure is more suitable than production structure and income structure, but its basic data are not easy to obtain in most economies, and even are greatly affected by the development of consumption finance in some economies.

Thirdly, human development is not only the source of economic development, but also the result of economic development. In order to reduce the circular causal effect between HDI and GDP growth rate and income Gini coefficient, the weight of HDI is set by this paper the lowest among the three indicators.

Of course, even based on these three points of understanding, the weight distribution of the three indicators can still choose other schemes for which readers can have a try.

Because the basic data of some indicators in the sample period are not complete, the development index values of some countries are not available in some sample years, among which all development index series values of Russia and Saudi Arabia are not available.

As for the relationship between openness and development, this paper adopts an indirect evaluation method, taking development as the "result" and "openness" as the cause, and applies ordinary least squares (OLS) to estimate the effect of openness on development. The alternative method is, with openness capacity as the "cause" and openness as the "result", apply corresponding econometric methods to estimate the determining effect of openness capacity on openness, but the measurement of "openness capacity" also faces a higher difficulty. The common deficiency of these two methods is that the relationship between openness and development has not been fully elucidated by scientific and rigorous professional theoretical models[1], resulting in the

---

① The relationship between the openness in specific field and the development in specific term has been elucidated by some professional theoretical models, such as "trade-growth" theory and "direct investment-growth" theory, but it is still necessary to further integrate economic (including trade, investment, finance), social and cultural openness, and set up the theoretical models on interactive relationships between these openness and development (such as growth, structure transformation, increased individual ability and will-being improvement).

causal relationship identified by the aforementioned empirical method may not be the causal relationship elucidated by the theoretical model.

2. Judgment of openness warrantedness

Table 2.2 shows the results of the econometric analysis based on the "openness-development" relationship of the 17 G20 members from 2008 to 2020. The econometric estimation takes into consideration two scenarios: (1) country heterogeneity is not considered; (2) country heterogeneity is considered. The results of the former are given in the first column of the upper panel of the table, and the results of the latter are given in the lower panel of the table.

Table 2.2   Econometric estimates of the "openness-development" link for 17 G20 countries, 2008-2020

	Openness significantly promotes development									Openness may drag foot on development
	17 members	UK	France	Germany	China	Mexico	Australia	India	South Korea	US
Openness	0.5124***	6.9454***	6.4932***	5.7774***	4.2446***	4.096***	3.4549***	3.4119***	1.6732***	-0.8524***
	(6.58)	(2.46)	(7.03)	(6.02)	(11.80)	(2.20)	(9.51)	(8.02)	(14.55)	(-14.11)
Constant term	0.3726	-4.808	-4.3045	-4.0118	-2.3664	-2.2139	-1.8362	-1.6221	-0.4378	1.4982
	(6.51)	(-2.11)	(5.93)	(-5.02)	(-9.21)	(1.66)	(-6.66)	(-6.01)	(-5.23)	(29.13)
Sample number	178	10	11	11	12	13	11	4	9	12
R^2	0.1974	0.4311	0.8471	0.8008	0.933	0.3065	0.9095	0.9708	0.9678	0.9522
F	43.29	6.03	49.46	36.2	139.24	4.86	90.37	64.26	211.77	199
Openness does not significantly affect development										
	Canada	Brazil	Turkey	Japan	South Africa	Indonesia	Argentina	Italy		
Openness	6.7852	-0.8682	-0.8241	-0.9050	-2.8403	-2.6999	-0.7518	-2.0181		
	(1.80)	(1.36)	(-0.25)	(-0.47)	(-0.58)	(-0.68)	(-0.76)	(-1.09)		
Constant term	-4.5546	1.3053	1.2385	1.5029	2.4488	2.4840	1.2853	2.3512		
	(-1.53)	(3.15)	(0.56)	(1.00)	(0.79)	(0.94)	(1.97)	(1.65)		
Sample size	10	13	12	6	7	13	13	11		
R^2	0.2873	0.1442	0.006	0.0513	0.0625	0.0402	0.0500	0.1165		
F	3.23	1.85	0.06	0.22	0.33	0.46	0.58	1.19		

Notes: *$p < 0.1$, **$p < 0.05$, ***$p < 0.01$. In parentheses is the t-statistics.

Econometric analysis based on sample data reveals that openness has a significant impact on development. Taking development index as dependent variable, openness as independent variable, and the practice of 17 G20 member countries from 1980 to 2020 as the sample (except for Russia and Saudi Arabia which lacks of development data), and using ordinary least squares (OLS) and STATA software, we can get parameter estimation results as shown in Table 2.2. The analysis based on these results is as follows.

From 2008 to 2020, the results without considering country heterogeneity show that a one percentage increase in openness increases the development index by 0.512 percentage (see Column 2 in the upper panel of Table 2.2). After taking account of country heterogeneity, openness does not necessarily have a significant impact on the development of all countries. In nine countries the opening-up has significantly affected their own development, while the opening-up in the other eight countries has not significantly affected their development.

——There are eight countries where openness promotes their development. The following eight countries (in a "from big to small" order in terms of influence) whose openness has significantly boosted their development: UK, France, Germany, China, Mexico, Australia, India and South Korea.

——There are eight countries where the relationship between openness and development is not statistically significant. As shown in the lower half of Tables 2-2, the impact of openness on development is insignificant in Canada, Brazil, Turkey, Japan, South Africa, Indonesia, Argentina, and Italy.

For the eight above-mentioned economies where openness has considerably promoted their development, the value of their development index can be fitted well based on above econometric results. If the actual development index is greater than the fitted development index, then corresponding openness is considered to have higher warrantedness, and the corresponding year is a year with a higher level of warranted openness. Based on this criteria, the annual statistics of openness warrantedness for the eight G20 countries in the sample period are shown in Table 2.3.

Table 2.3   Years of higher warranted openness for the eight G20 countries, 2008-2020

(Only for years with available development index data, in a descending order in the proportion of years with warranted openness)

No		Years of warranted openness	Total (years)	Development index time series	Total (years)	Percent of years with warranted openness
1	China	2008-2010、2016-2019	7	2008-2019	12	58.3
2	South Korea	2010-2012、2015-2016	5	2008-2016	9	55.6
3	France	2010-2012、2015-2017	6	2008-2018	11	54.5
4	Mexico	2013-2019	7	2008-2020	13	53.8
5	India	2008、2011	2	2008-2011	4	50.0
6	UK	2008、2014-2017	5	2008-2017	10	50.0
7	Germany	2008、2012、2015-2017	5	2008-2018	11	45.5
8	Australia	2012、2013、2018	3	2008-2018	11	27.3

As shown by Table 2.3, during the sample period, among the years with available development index value, China has the highest proportion of the years with high-level warranted openness (58.3%), followed by South Korea (55.6%) and France (54.5%), then by Mexico (53.8%), India (50%), the UK (50%), Germany (45.5%) and Australia (27.3%). As shown in Fig. 2.2, the years of warranted openness at a higher level for China, South Korea, France, and Mexico are marked.

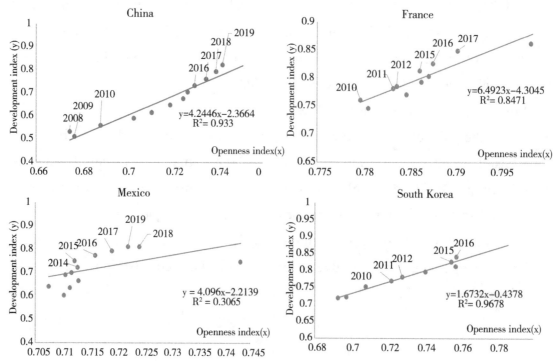

Fig. 2.2   Years of higher-level warranted openness for China, France, Mexico and South Korea, 2008-2020

The years of higher-level warranted openness for India, the UK, Germany and Australia are shown in Figures 2-3.

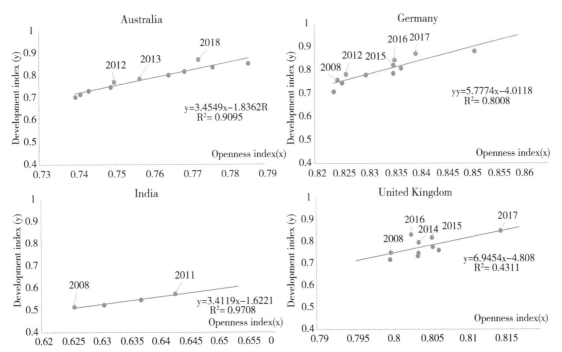

Fig. 2.3   Years of higher-level warranted openness for Australia, Germany, India, and the United Kingdom, 2008-2020

III. Conclusions and Policy Implications

So far, the evaluation of openness warrantedness is not a mature topic in theory, method and data. This paper tries to put forward some views on these aspects, in order to "throw a brick to attract jade", looking forward to further discussions of readers from all walks of life. From discussions on warranted openness, this paper obtains the following conclusions and policy implications.

1. Warranted openness is not difficult, but optimal openness is not easy

To judge whether specific openness is warranted, we only need to see whether openness capacity matching it exceeds the maximum of actual openness capacity. Any openness that does not exceed this maximum is warranted openness. To maximize the utilization of openness capacity, achieve maximum warranted openness, and then achieve equilibrium between openness supply and demand and optimal openness should be the policy goal of openness practice. But this requires the best "time", "place" and "people" conditions inside and outside an economy. No matter in theory or practice, it is difficult to achieve maximum warranted openness.

2. Cultivating openness capacity to improve warrantedness of openness

What determines the warrantedness of openness is openness capacity, while the latter in turn depends on an economy's innate and acquired endowments. Innate endowments, such as geographical location and natural resources, have strong exogeneity and are difficult to change in a short period. It often takes several generations to persevere and work for a long time to form some certain inmate endowments. Acquired endowments, including population, production technology, labor quality, capital, system, culture, etc., should not only balance dynamic relationship between quantity increase and quality improvement of each of them, but also need to carefully plan organic combination of all of them, so as to provide a solid foundation for strong openness capacity. Among them, improving national governance, especially cross-border openness governance, is one of institutional prerequisites for maximizing openness capacity.

3. Openness must take development as fundamental guidance

Openness is the means to achieve development, while the core of development is to put the people at the center. This makes it necessary not only to accelerate economic growth and make a bigger economic pie, but also to realize structural transformation, especially to optimize the structure of production and income, and to increase the opportunities for the majority of individuals to make behavioral choices, boost their main abilities and improve their material will-being.

When the development effect of an economy is not ideal, it may need to improve its development philosophy in time. Development philosophy is the forerunner of development actions that guides overall, fundamental, directional and long-term development, and the concentrated embodiment of development thinking, development direction and development priorities. Even if a country's development philosophy is appropriate, it still needs to explore its own development path suited to its concrete conditions.

4. Building a new cross-border openness landscape of mutual benefit and win-win result

The core of warranted openness is the full and even maximum use of openness capacity of an economy. However, in an open world economic system, an economy's openness capacity is often affected by its open partner economies. Therefore, the openness of an economy should be coordinated with the openness of other economies in the world under the principle of mutual benefit and win-win results, so that they can both share the development benefits of opening-up and shoulder the responsibility for building openness capacity, to upgrade their warranted openness to an optimal level and build a community with a shared future for mankind.

Chapter 3   U-Shaped Evolution of Openness: Cases of Typical Countries

For post-industrial countries, the level of openness usually shows a U-shaped evolution, in which it first falls before it rises. The United States and Germany had seized the opportunity window of the industrial revolution through trade protection policies to grow into industrialized powers; Latin American countries mostly had implemented an Import Substitution Strategy in the early stage of industrialization, but after that, they had generally been trapped in economic difficulties, and forced to pursue opening-up; the East Asian economies had at an early stage started to transition from a domestically-oriented development mode to an export-oriented development mode and actively received industrial capacities transferred from the developed economies, thus achieving a growth miracle. China's recent and modern opening-up process still conforms to the law of U-shaped evolution. According to the U-shaped evolution law, China's pace of opening-up will not stop in the future; it will continue to advocate economic globalization, while supporting the establishment of more inclusive international economic and trade rules that are more tolerant of developing countries.

I. Law of U-shaped Openness Evolution

It is generally believed that with the improvement of the level of economic development, the level of openness also gradually increases. But in reality, changes in an economy's openness are often non-linear. On the one hand, the opening-up policy will change in a wave-like pattern with the change of factors such as regime change and external environment; on the other hand, for countries in the process of industrialization, the level of opening-up usually shows a U-shaped evolution, in which it first falls before it rises.

Trade openness is the most important measure of a country's openness, and it is also the most complete and continuous indicator to meansure openness. Some countries had finished industrialization dozens or even a hundred years ago, but were yet to have a complete statistical system. To summarize the U-shaped evolution law of openness in each historical period, in addition to using the World Openness Index, this chapter uses the level of trade openness in the historical data of some earlier stages for research. The level of trade openness is measured by the ratio of total imports and exports to GDP, to be exact.

Traditional industrial powers, Latin American countries, East Asian, and South Asian countries have all proved the law of U-shaped evolution in their opening-up process. The following is a detailed analysis of the opening-up process of the above-mentioned countries amid the U-shaped evolution, and then the U-shaped distribution in the 2020 World Openness Index will be analyzed.

1. Traditional industrial powers

a. Britain

As the most dominant old imperialist power that took the lead in completing the first industrial revolution, Britain began to adhere to a free trade policy in the mid-to-late 19th century. But before that, Britain still experienced a U-shaped evolution from free trade to trade protection and back to free trade again. In the 15th century, with the great geographical discovery and the development of European industry and commerce, a global market began to emerge, leading to the rapid development of European foreign trade, and the level of British trade openness increased during that period. Since the 16th century, to meet the needs of primitive accumulation of capital, Britain began to pursue a mercantilist policy and adopted a series of trade protection policies, which reduced its level of openness. The early mercantilist policies emphasized the deep intervention of the government. After the Glorious Revolution, Britain mainly carried out trade protection through tariff policy. In the mid-19th century, Britain completed its industrial revolution and achieved an absolute dominance in the world market, so it abolished the Corn Laws and other mercantilist policies, and began to move towards laissez-faire.

Box 3-1   Corn Laws: Mercantilism Vs. Laissez-faire

The Corn Laws, promulgated in 1815, prohibited importing foreign grain when the domestic grain price fell below 80 shillings per quarter. The Corn Laws were in nature trade protectionist policies under the guidance of mercantilism, aiming at protecting the interests of the British landed aristocracy.

During the Napoleonic Wars (1803-1815), the price of British corn rose rapidly. With the advent of peace time, the price of corn began to drop significantly. To protect their traditional interests, the British landlord class passed the Corn Laws in 1815 to resist competition from foreign traders selling low-priced grains and maintain domestic grain prices. The Corn Laws, in the first place, harmed the interests of urban factory owners, who hoped to reduce wages and raw material costs through grain imports. The Corn Laws also harmed the interests of workers and peasants, and call for free trade of grain had grown ever stronger. In 1836, the Anti-Corn Law League was established and since then, it had gradually won the support of all classes in the UK.

The Corn Laws were ultimately repealed in 1846, marking the UK's full entry into laissez-faire.

b. United States

After the War of Independence, the United States began to try to get rid of its trade dependence on suzerain Britain and implement an independent tariff protection policy. However, at the early stage of independence, the US' federal system of government resulted in the lack of unified trade policy and the federal government cannot sign trade agreements with foreign countries. Tariffs varied greatly among states, and some states even implemented tariff exemptions. After the Constitutional Convention, Alexander Hamilton's trade protectionism had had a profound impact on the country's trade policy formulation at that time. The Tariff Act and the Duties on Tonnage statute came into effect in 1789, clearly stating that the purpose of tariffs was for "the encouragement and protection of manufactures". In 1816, the United States promulgated a new tariff bill, and the average tax rate on manufactured products soared to 25%, which was obviously aimed to protect its infant industries. In the mid-19th century, the United States vacillated between trade protection and free trade. In the latter part of the 19th century, when the second industrial revolution began, that the United States ultimately passed the McKinley Tariff Act in 1890, with the import tariff rate exceeding 48%. At the turn of the 20th century, the United States became one of the most important industrial powers, and it began to expand globally, proposing the "open door" policy and starting advocating free trade. At that time, the tariffs of the United States were still higher than those of European countries, and only after the implementation of the Reciprocal Trade Agreements Act in 1934 did the United States truly start to embark on the road of free trade.

c. Germany

Germany is a typical country that has achieved industrialization through a U-shaped opening-up path. After its reunification in 1871, Germany first implemented trade liberalization reform, and reduced tariffs several times from 1873 to 1877. As a result, its average tariff level of the manufacturing industry was much lower than that of France, a major industrial power at that time. In the late 19th century, imports from major industrial powers seriously affected Germany's domestic industries, especially the steel industry. In 1879, the Otto von Bismarck government revised the tariff law, sharply raising tariffs on agricultural and industrial products, and Germany began to embark on the road of trade protection. Since then, Germany had maintained high tariffs, consciously supporting the domestic industrial sector; it had levied lower tariffs or even exempted taxes on raw materials and intermediate products, while levying higher tariffs on industrial final goods. Through protecting domestic industries, Germany quickly established its international competitiveness in some fields, such as heavy industry. After the 1890s, Germany signed reciprocal trade agreements with European countries, and the average tariff level had continually declined.

In addition, during the same period, Japan also completed the industrialization process and achieved economic catch-up; its level of openness also showed a U-shaped trajectory (See Fig. 3.1).

Box 3-2   Friedrich List's Infant Industry Protection Theory

German economist Friedrich List (1789-1846) put forward the theory of infant industry protection, which was the first economic theory to describe the U-shaped evolution of openness.

List was originally a supporter of the free trade theory. He migrated to the United States in 1825 and was deeply influenced by Alexander Hamilton's thought on trade protectionism. In 1841, he published The National System of Political Economy, which systematically expounded his economic theory. List divided national development into five stages: primitive undeveloped stage, pastoral life stage, agriculture stage, agriculture united with manufactures stage, and the stage where agriculture, manufactures and commerce are combined.

To promote the development of national productivity, different trade policies need to be adopted at different stages. List believes that trade policies should also be divided into three stages. First, free trade policies should be adopted to pass through the primitive undeveloped stage, the pastoral life stage, and the agricultural stage; then it is necessary to adopt trade protection measures to protect the domestic infant industry as it advances from the agriculture stage to the agriculture united with manufactures stage; finally, the free trade policy should be restored so that the country can actively participate in international competition at the agriculture, manufactures and commerce stage.

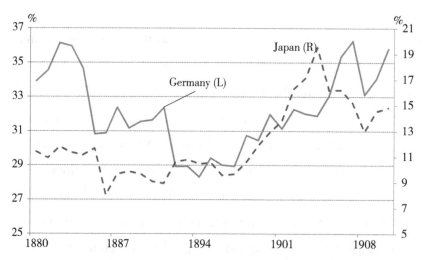

Fig. 3.1   U-shaped evolution of trade openness in the 2nd Industrial Revolution of Germany and Japan, 1880-1910

Sources: International Historical Statistics: Europe, International Historical Statistics: Asia. In the figure, the left axis refers to Germany's level of trade openness, while the right axis refers to Japan's level of trade openness.

2. Latin America countries

The opening-up of Latin American countries has generally gone through a U-shaped evolution trajectory. From the 19th century to the first half of the 20th century, Latin American countries had a relatively high degree of openness. Most Latin American countries had shaken off the colonial rule and achieved independence in the 19th century, becoming relatively open regions in the world. During that period, Latin American countries had a low level of industrialization and their exported products were very limited; they mainly exported primary products, such as agricultural products and mineral, in exchange for industrial manufactured goods from developed countries. After the World War II, the surging wave of national independence worldwide also had a bearing on Latin American countries. In 1949, Latin American countries jointly initiated the United Nations Economic Commission for Latin America and the Caribbean, marking the start of Latin American countries in their pursuit for an independent development path.

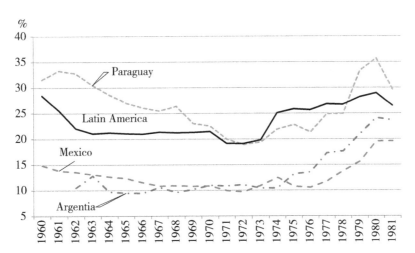

Fig. 3.2   U-shaped evolution of trade openness of Latin American countries, 1960-1981
Source: World Bank WDI database

In the middle and late 20th century, Latin American countries gradually adopted trade protection measures. Reforms in Latin American countries had been deeply influenced by Argentine economist Raul Prebisch. Prebisch found that since the 1930s, foreign trade conditions of Latin American countries had continued to deteriorate, and prices of their exported primary products in comparison with those of developed countries' manufactured goods had moved on a long-term downward trajectory. On the basis of that finding, he put forward the "Centre and Periphery Theory", arguing that the international division of labor at that time was unequal, and the developed countries "in the centre" have enjoyed the dividends of international trade for a long time, while the vast number of developing countries "in the periphery" can only be attached to developed countries; with their productivity levels locked, they can only provide primary products to industrialized countries. To get out of such a predicament, it is necessary for the developing countries to actively develop the import substitution strategy and take trade protection measures to protect domestic industries. Influenced by his theory, major Latin American countries, such as Argentina, Brazil, Chile, Colombia, and Mexico, had generally adopted the import substitution strategy from the late 1960s to the late 1980s, and they had once achieved good economic results. Brazil, for example, created an economic growth miracle in the 1960s.

In the latter half of the 1960s, the drawbacks of the import substitution strategy gradually surfaced and became obvious, and the national competitiveness of the Latin American countries stagnated, which hindered the development of export enterprises and led to continually declining foreign exchange earnings. In the 1970s, due to the impact of the oil crisis, some Latin American countries tried to carry out trade liberalization reform, but most of the Latin American countries still continued to implement the import substitution strategy.

After the start of the 1980s, the Latin American countries gradually shifted to economic liberalism. In early 1980s, the debt crisis that originated from Mexico spread rapidly to the Latin American continent; meanwhile, the East Asian economies, which had adopted an export-oriented strategy, performed well in terms of economic growth. As a result, the Latin American countries started to reflect on and reform their development strategy. To alleviate the debt crisis, they accepted the advices from the IMF and started to open up their economy to the outside world. In the middle and late 1980s, they partially opened up their economy, and then in the 1990s, they carried out comprehensive, full-scale economic opening-up. In 1989, the "Washington Consensus", which serves to guide the reform and opening-up of Latin American countries, came into being, marking the systematic establishment of economic liberalism in the economic reform policies of Latin American countries. Since then, the trade openness of Latin American countries had continually improved. They had successively joined the World Trade Organization and actively pushed forward regional trade liberalism. In 1995, the Southern Common Market, or Mercosur, was officially launched, becoming the first common market launched and organized entirely by developing countries.

Box 3-3   Washington Consensus

Pushed by the US-based Peterson Institute for International Economics, some international organizations, such as the International Monetary Fund, the World Bank, and the US Treasury Department, and relevant countries held a conference in Washington in 1990 to reach the Washington Consensus, which focuses on the economic reform of Latin American countries.

The Washington Consensus includes ten main contents:

1). Strengthening fiscal policy discipline, with focus on reduction of fiscal deficits and inflation to stabilize macroeconomic situation;

2). Redirection of public spending toward fields with high economic returns and those that contribute to fair income distribution, such as primary education, primary health care and infrastructure investment;

3). Carrying out tax reform to lower marginal tax rates and broaden tax base;

4). Implementing market-determined interest rates;

5). Adopting a competitive exchange rate regime;

6). Trade liberalization and market opening-up:

7). Liberalization of inward foreign direct investment;

8). Privatization of State enterprises;

9). Deregulation;

10). Legal security for property rights.

The Washington Consensus was later widely used in guiding reforms in developing and transition countries. Joseph Stiglitz summarizes it as "minimization of the role of government, rapid privatization and liberalization".

3. East and South Asian economies

East Asian economies, represented by the "Four Asian Tigers", have attracted widespread attention due to their success in export-oriented strategy. However, those economies have also undergone a transition from an import substitution strategy to an export-oriented strategy, with their openness still first declining before moving upward.

Unlike Latin American countries, East Asian economies have long been affected by colonization and invasions, and were not able to adopt independent economic policies until after the World War II. To get rid of the control from their former suzerain countries, those East Asian economies had usually adopted an import substitution strategy in developing their economy. For instance, South Korea began to implement an import substitution strategy in 1953, levying high tariffs on, or directly prohibiting imports of, products that can be made domestically. Its economy quickly recovered to pre-war levels and continued to grow. However, such a domestically-oriented development model limited South Korea's ability to utilize overseas markets and resources, which later affected, to an extent, its economic development. Other economies in East Asia that adopted the import substitution strategy were also caught in trade and balance of payments predicament, and so they quickly turned to adopt the export-oriented strategy. In the 1960s, South Korea and Singapore had already started to move towards an export-oriented economy. In the 1970s, some ASEAN countries, such as Malaysia, Indonesia, the Philippines and Thailand, began to implement the export-oriented strategy. Laos and Vietnam, which had long adopted the planned economy model, began to open up their economy in the 1980s.

The East Asian economies has seized the opportunity window of labor-intensive industry transfers by the developed economies and achieved economic growth miracle through adopting an export-oriented strategy. Now much headway has been made in regional trade liberalization. In 2022, the Regional Comprehensive Economic Partnership (RCEP), led by major economies in the region, came into effect, becoming the world's largest free trade agreement in terms of population and economic scale.

India, a major South Asian economy, has also gone through a process in which its openness first decreased before starting to move up in the post-independence era. Although it was one of the earliest members of the GATT, India still practiced trade protectionism for a long time. It is committed to the development of a mixed economy combining capitalism and socialism. In 1951, it started to implement its first five-year plan, putting the economy and trade under strict control while establishing the development strategy of import substitution. The import substitution strategy has provided India with a relatively independent and complete industrial system, but it has also increasingly put it in a growth dilemma. After the 1980s, India began to explore new opening-up policies. In 1991, India abandoned its former development model and began to embrace a free market economy, marking the start of the historical process of gradual opening-up.

4. U-shaped distribution of openness of various countries in 2020

The U-shaped evolution trend of the level of trade openness is reflected not only in the process of economic development of various countries, but also in the comparison of countries with different economic development levels under the same time section. The distribution of the World Openness Index in 2020 is in line with the above-mentioned U-shaped evolution trend.

As shown in Fig. 3.3, an economy with a population of more than 20 million, after its per capita GDP reaches $2,700, would see its economic openness performance index first fall before rising following the increase in its per capita GDP; and the U-shaped bottom is somewhere between $3,000 and $10,000, which falls into the category of lower-middle and upper-middle income economies under the World Bank criteria. As the economy enters the upper-middle and high-income stages, its openness level begins to increase steadily. Among the middle-income economies, Vietnam has the highest level of openness, with its openness performance index reaching 0.246. However, Morocco and the Philippines, which have higher per capita incomes, have lower levels of openness, standing at 0.185 and 0.178, respectively, and Argentina has the lowest level of 0.163. Then after a country's per capita GDP reaches and exceeds $10,000, its openness index begins to gradually increase following the increase in per capita GDP.

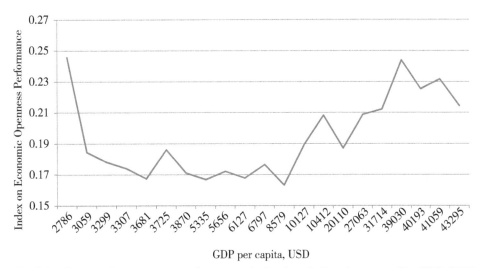

Fig. 3.3   Economic openness performance index in relation to per capita GDP, 2020
Source: World Openness Index 2020 Annual data.

II. Causes of the U-shaped Evolution Law

The law of U-shaped evolution of openness prevails in the process of a country's industrialization. The main reasons are as follows.

1. Choice of development strategy

The main purpose of a country's trade protection is to promote its development of industrialization. The choice of development strategy in the process of industrialization has a direct bearing on the level of openness. At the early stage of economic development, a country exports agricultural products, raw materials, and primary products in exchange for industrial manufactured products from developed countries, and its productivity increases at a relatively slow pace. To eliminate its disadvantage and gain an edge in international trade, it is necessary for a country to promote its domestic industrial development. To that end, it is necessary to reduce the impact of foreign competitors on domestic infant industries; therefore, at such a stage of development, a country usually adopts an import substitution strategy and implements trade protection policies. When a country has had a quite solid domestic industrialization foundation and, as its international competitiveness increases, been able to make profits from overseas markets, then generally it would reduce trade barriers and improve its level of openness.

Box 3-4   Import substitution strategy and export-oriented strategy

The import substitution strategy and the export-oriented strategy are two main economic development strategies in opposite directions.

Import substitution strategy: It refers to a country taking various measures to restrict the import of certain foreign industrial products, promote the production of domestic related industrial products, and gradually replace imported products with domestic products in the domestic market, so as to create favorable conditions for the development of its own industry and achieve industrialization. . It is an inward-looking economic development strategy.

Export-oriented strategy: It refers to the strategy implemented by the governments of developing countries to encourage the export of processed products to replace the original export of primary products, improve the industrial structure, and increase foreign exchange incomes, thereby promoting domestic economic development. It is an export-oriented economic development strategy.

2. The difference of international division

At the initial stage of economic development, a country, based on division of labor of comparative advantages given their different resource endowments, exchanges its abundant domestic resources for the scarce industrial products from developed countries, and its gains from trade are relatively significant; the process of industrialization is actually one of division of labor of "reverse comparative advantages"; to cultivate its domestic industries that are at a disadvantage compared with foreign industries, a country needs to artificially distort prices through necessary trade protection measures; with the further completion of industrialization, the comparative advantage division of labor based on global value chains or the intra-industry division of labor based on economies of scale and differentiation becomes more profitable, and its level of trade openness increases accordingly.

3. International bargaining powers

Economically less developed countries are often put in a disadvantage in international trade and their early-stage opening-up is often a passive move made under the pressure of developed countries; some of them even become de facto economic colonies or vassals of developed countries. As its industrialization process continues, a country will see its international competitiveness improve, and, therefore, it will become more independent in the choice of its trade policies, so that it can be capable of adopting a more independent opening-up strategy. For instance, the North American Free Trade Agreement was first negotiated between the United States and Canada, and on that basis, Mexico joined in. The United States and Canada are both developed countries, and the trade agreements they have formulated have a relatively high level of openness, and Mexico has no choice but accept them.

4. Influence of domestic interest groups

At the early stage of economic development, a country's domestic commerce and trade groups are relatively weak, but as its international trade grows continually, some vested interests would come into being. They generally pursue trade surplus, call for the protection of domestic enterprises, and promote the introduction of trade protection policies. Once that country's productivity increases significantly and becomes relatively strong international competitiveness, its domestic interest groups often change their stance and support free trade to facilitate their efforts to grab profits in overseas markets.

5. Influence of major global powers.

The concepts and trends of free trade and trade protectionism are generally influenced by the leading powers at that time. For instance, Britain had influenced the modern European thought of trade liberalization and the United States' influence had given rise to Germany's theory of protecting infant industries. After the World War II, the Soviet Union became an important pole in the "bipolar" structure and the global influence of socialist countries increased day by day; some developing countries at that time opted to achieve fast industrialization through planned economy and import substitution strategy. After the 1980s, the United States gradually gained an upper hand in the competition between the United States and the Soviet Union, and market economy and free trade, advocated by the United States, began to become the international norm, which affected the adjustment of opening-up policies of the developing countries.

The above-mentioned factors combine to shape the U-shaped evolution in the opening-up process, but they are not the only elements to influence an economy's level of openness. Some economies, due to other factors, may deviate from the U-shaped openness evolution trajectory. For instance, in terms of cross-sectional comparison, large countries tend to have a larger domestic share, and their level of openness, measured by the proportion of trade in GDP, is significantly lower than that of small countries; in terms of time scale, the anti-globalization trend has become apparent in recent years, and the openness level of various countries tends to decline. Those adverse factors, however, are not typical in the process of economic development, and generally do not change the U-shaped evolution trajectory.

III. China's Opening-up Process and Law of Evolution

1. China's opening process and law of evolution since 1840

Since 1840, China has undergone dramatic changes and it has not had consistent trade policies. However, during different historical periods, China has been faced with the issue of modernization and opening-up, and the law of U-shaped evolution of openness has remained applicable to China's modern development process since 1840. Before the founding of the new republic in 1949, China had been forced to open up under the oppression of foreign powers; after the founding of the new republic, the West imposed economic blockade on China and the latter started to pursue an independent development and industrialization strategy; since the start of reform and opening-up in late 1970s, China has actively embraced economic globalization, and its level of openness has continued to rise.

a. Before the founding of the new republic

China became a semi-colonial and semi-feudal society after the opium wars, and the Western powers forced China to sign a series of unequal treaties, which led to China opening up to the outside world. China opened up trade ports and established a modern customs system. Judging from the tariff rate, the import tariff rate of ordinary goods at that time was only 5%, which was even lower than the average tariff level of countries in Europe and America in the same period. However, it must be pointed out that the opening-up of the Qing Dynasty government at that time was passive and the government did not independent in the formulation of the opening-up policy. After the Treaty of Peace, Amity, and Commerce, between the US and the Qing government, and the Treaty of Whampoa, between France and the Qing government, were signed, China accepted the principle of "agreement on tariffs" and lost the right to tariff autonomy. Even China's customs were taken over by foreigners. Although such passive opening-up brought massive fiscal revenues to the Qing government, it had failed to bring the prosperity of the Chinese economy. China continued to mainly export primary products, such as agricultural products, and its terms of trade continued to deteriorate.

In the wake of the 1911 Revolution, or the Xinhai Revolution in 1911, China was yet to complete its industrialization process, and gradually lost its traditional comparative advantages in agricultural products. Although the customs at that time were still managed by foreigners, China had obtained the right to formulate tariff policies. From 1921 to 1928, China's import tariff rate was 3%-5%, and it rose to 8.5% in 1929, and eventually to 25-27% in 1934-1936. However, the protectionist measures during that time failed to bring about an increase in exports and economic prosperity.

b. Pre-reform and opening-up period

After the founding of the new republic in 1949, Western countries began to block and impose embargo on China, and China was forced to adopt a "lopsided" trade model, engaging in trade with socialist countries, such as the Soviet Union. To catch up with and emulate the industrialized powers within a short period of time, China adopted a development path that prioritizes heavy industry, which, in essence, remained an import substitution strategy. During that period, China was at the bottom of the U-shaped openness evolution, and it established an independent and complete industrial system, laying a solid foundation for the economic take-off after the start of the reform and opening-up initiative.

c. Post-reform and opening-up period

After it started its reform and opening-up drive in late 1970s, China actively integrated into economic globalization, achieving a miracle of economic development and trade growth through bringing out its comparative advantages and participating in international division of labor. Unlike the "shock therapy" advocated by the developed countries, China's opening-up is a gradual process. On the one hand, it has maintained economic and social stability, and, on the other hand, it has gradually opened up different regions and sectors. China's level of openness has been continuously improved, and the total tariff level has dropped significantly from 43.2% in 1992 to 15.3% in 2001. After joining the World Trade Organization in 2001, China expanded its opening-up in an all-round way and deeply integrated into the global value chain. Since the 18th National Congress of the Communist Party of China in 2012, China has further expanded its opening-up, and its overall tariff rate has declined to 7.4% in 2021. China has deeply integrated into the global industrial chain and supply chain, and has become the center of regional division of labor. It is the main trading partner of more than 120 countries and regions, and the largest trading partner of more than 50 countries and regions. It plays a pivotal role in the global division of labor and trade.

2. The U-shaped evolution of openness and prospect of China's future opening-up pattern

In recent years, economic globalization has continued to suffer setbacks, and the world openness index has been in a descending channel. Since the outbreak of the novel coronavirus pandemic, or COVID-19, trade, investment, and personnel flows across different countries have suffered serious setbacks. In the new historical era, where will China's opening-up head for? Based on the law of U-shaped evolution of openness, this paper looks into the future trend of China's opening-up.

a. China will not stop the pace of opening-up

General Secretary of the Communist Party of China Xi Jinping has reiterated that no matter how the international situation changes, China will unswervingly expand its opening-up. From the perspective of theoretical support, the law of U-shaped evolution of openness shows that China has completed its accumulation of industrialization basis, gained quite strong global competitiveness, and become a beneficiary of, and contributor to, economic globalization. China now is in the ascending channel of the U-shaped openness evolution trajectory, and there is no reason for it to turn back in the future.

b. It is the common feature of any country with a large population or economic size to mainly focus on "domestic economic cycle"

The U-shaped openness evolution theory emphasizes that only by examining countries with similar characteristics can scientific and reasonable laws be concluded. The degree of openness, measured by trade as a share of GDP, is not suitable for comparisons between countries with large differences in economic size. For a country with a large population or economic size, due to its vast domestic market, even if its level of openness is high, it will not maintain a high degree of trade dependence for a long time. If we take the ratio of trade to GDP in the US and Japan as a benchmark, then China's trade-to-GDP ratio is still too high (see Fig. 3.4)[①], indicating that China's past development has mainly relied on "external cycle", and a reduction in its trade-to-GDP ratio in the future does not mean China's level of openness will decline, but a normal adjustment to achieve a more rational trade dependence.

---

①   Fig. 3.5 shows that the US and Japan each have a stable trade-to-GDP ratio, which has been kept between 20% and 30% in recent years. China's trade-to-GDP ratio gradually peaked after it joined the WTO and has declined gradually and shown a stabilizing trend in recent years, although it remains higher than that of Japan and the US. As a major country whose economic size is close to that of the US and whose population is multiple times that of the US, it is reasonable for China to have a higher ratio of "domestic economic cycle".

Fig. 3.4   Comparison of trade-to-GDP ratio in China, United States and Japan, 1978-2020

Source: World Bank WDI database

c. The level of openness, as a country's choice, is highly related to the stage of its economic development, and international economic and trade rules that are more inclusive to developing countries should be established.

The law of U-shaped evolution of openness shows that it is necessary for economies that have not yet completed industrialization to protect their infant industries, and should not go beyond its capabilities to pursue the same level of openness as developed countries; meanwhile, the objective laws of economic development, such as that of comparative advantages, should be respected. The protection of a country's infant industries should be conducive to promoting the development of productivity so that the country can become able to integrate into the global division of labor as soon as possible. China will continue to advocate economic globalization, encourage and help developing countries improve their level of openness; at the same time, it will safeguard the interests of developing countries in the international economic and trade system, and call for the establishment of more inclusive international economic and trade rules for developing countries.

Chapter 4　Evolution of World Pattern and Megatrend of Global Openness

Economic globalization is the megatrend of world development. In the wake of the Cold War, globalization has advanced rapidly, featuring fast-paced integration of almost all economies. In recent years, the world has undergone accelerating changes that are "unseen in a century", to which the COVID-19 pandemic has brought new possibilities; meanwhile, the development imbalance of various countries has worsened, and the anti-globalization sentiment has been rampant. In general, however, economic globalization is an objective requirement of the development of productivity and an inevitable outcome of scientific and technological progress. It is an irreversible trend of the times. In history, plagues, wars, and crises have once hindered the development of economic globalization, but the general direction of globalization has not changed. With the vigorous development of the digital economy in the post-pandemic era, new technological innovations will promote globalization to ensure it embarking on a new journey amid twists and turns.

I. Global Openness at A Crossroads

From the exploration of the Silk Road to the formation of the world market and then the rapid advancement of globalization in the wake of the Cold War, economic globalization, with multi-dimensional and complex characteristics, has been constantly evolving, and, in its development process, has experienced many "counter-trends" and setbacks. In recent years, the world economy has suffered great shocks caused by the pandemic. In addition, while promoting economic development, governments of various countries have paid more attention to national security. As a result, protectionism and unilateralism have been on the rise, and economic globalization has once again faced challenges. Where is the world heading for? It is the question of the times that we must answer.

1. Despite anti-globalization sentiment, economic globalization advances amid twists and turns

Today's world has entered an era of high-level division of labor, and the global allocation of resources for the purpose of improving productivity is still the megatrend of economic development. Multinational corporations, the carriers of globalization, continue to establish footholds globally, and science and technology, the driving force of globalization, are still advancing; meanwhile, and the established international norms and mature international mechanisms will also further strengthen the foundation of globalization development and continue to give impetus to economic globalization. Economic globalization will continue to move forward amid twists and turns.

a. Anti-globalization sentiment increases resistance against globalization

As the global political and economic environment changes, the anti-globalization sentiment has kept resurging, and the world economy is facing many complex challenges; the economic globalization has encountered resistance.

Protectionism is on the rise. In recent years, some countries have begun to prioritize their own interests domestically, and, when it comes to foreign relations, adopt protectionist policies. For example, some Western developed economies have begun to reduce foreign trade and investment, and some countries have successively introduced policies that require their enterprises to move back their production capabilities from other countries. According to the Global Value Chain Development Report 2021, jointly released by the WTO and other organizations, from 2018 to 2020, the average level of participation in global value chains showed a downward trend[1].

Unilateralism worsens. The global multilateral trading system, represented by the WTO, is facing challenges. The willingness and strength of support from some developed economies for multilateral institutions, such as the IMF and the World Bank, are seriously insufficient, leading to weakening multilateralism. The foundation

---

[1] *Global Value Chain Development Report 2021: Beyond Production*, jointly released by the WTO, University of International Business and Economics and other institutions, 16 November 2021; http://rigvc.uibe.edu.cn/docs//2021-11/2808a0a300af4f11aba55bd3a9dfa777.pdf.

of global cooperation and common development has been damaged, thus seriously affecting the development of globalization.

Populism prevails. Economic globalization has seen many multinational companies transfer capital and production lines to developing countries, resulting in rising unemployment in their home countries, which, together with the depressing domestic economic situation, in turn triggers political and social turmoil in the developed economies. Meanwhile, in the era of globalization, the personnel flow has accelerated and a large number of refugees have poured into the developed countries, which has increased the domestic burden of those economies. Against such a backdrop, populism in some countries has intensified and some populist politicians have even begun to call for changes in the rules and values of world politics, arguing that the globalization process under the framework of neoliberal order has trampled on national sovereignty, traditional values and local culture; the anti-globalization sentiment has become increasingly strong.

b. Digital economy injects fresh impetus into globalization

A new round of scientific and technological revolution and industrial transformation is advancing by leaps and bounds, and the in-depth integration of science and technology with economic and social development has accelerated, leading to the formation of new growth engines for economic globalization.

The digital economy has prompted a shift in consumption patterns in the post-pandemic era. In the wake of the outbreak of the pandemic, governments around the world have taken measures to limit the movement of people to stem the spread of the virus, spurring demand for digital products and services. Major online social platforms have reported significant growth in online messaging, voice and video calling services, and mobile network communication traffic has increased by more than 50%. The pandemic is changing people's habits and consumption patterns, and their reliance on the Internet has become prominent.

The digital economy has become a new engine for the economic development of various countries. From the first set of artificial intelligence intergovernmental policy guidelines, officially approved by 42 countries in 2019, to the advocacy and exploration of global data governance policies and structures, the global digital economy has achieved stable development despite the many negative forces hindering its development. To keep up with technological progress and the pace of the times,

Italy and other EU countries have taken the digital economy as an important engine for recovery of development and accelerated the region's digital transformation. Statistics show that in 2020, the value added of the digital economy in 47 countries around the world reached $32.6 trillion, a nominal increase of 3.0% year-on-year, accounting for 43.7% of their GDP in total[①]. In contrast, the overall global GDP growth rate in 2020 was -3.6%. With the global economic growth falling into the negative territory, the digital economy has become a strong tool to promote global economic recovery and a key force driving growth of the global economy.

Box 4-1　Digital Economy

The digital economy A new-type economic form that takes digital knowledge and information as the key production factors, uses digital technology as the core driving force, and takes modern information network as an important carrier to achieve in-depth integration of digital technology and the real economy to continually improve the level of digitalization, networking, and intelligence of the economy and society and accelerates the reconstruction of economic development and governance models. Specifically, it comprises four major parts: first, digital industrialization, that is, the information and communications industry, including electronic information manufacturing, telecommunications, software and information technology services, and the Internet industry; second, industrial digitization, that is, the application of digital technologies in the traditional industries that brings about output and efficiency improvement, including, but not limited to, integration-based new industries, new models and new business forms, such as industrial Internet, the integration of industrialization and digitization, intelligent manufacturing, the Internet of Vehicles, and platform economy; third, digital governance, including, but not limited to, diversified governance, the combination of technology and governance featuring "digital technology + governance", and digitalized public services; fourth, data value, including, but not limited to, data collection, data standards, data rights confirmation, data labeling,

---

① China Academy of Information and Communications Technology, *Global Digital Economy White Paper — New Hope for Recovery against the Pandemic Shocks*, August 2021, http://www.caict. ac.cn/kxyj/qwfb/bps/202108/t20210802_381484.htm.

data pricing, data transaction, data flow, and data protection. The digital economy is developing rapidly, has a wide range of coverage, and has a profound impact. It is driving profound changes in production methods, lifestyles, and governance methods, and has become a key force in reorganizing global factor resources, reshaping the global economic structure, and changing the global competition landscape.

c. Regional integration becomes the main feature of globalization

Globalization has shifted significantly to regionalization and multilateralism and become more group-based in recent years. Such a change has become the dominant trend of economic globalization.

Globalization is showing a trend towards regionalization. Compared with globalization, regional integration further reduces transportation costs, achieves higher levels of tariff reduction and exemption, and highlights the advantages of intra-industry division of labor of trade. The latest statistics from the World Trade Organization show that as of 2022, the number of effective regional trade agreements has amounted to 354 in total, of which 82 are effective regional trade agreements that appeared between 2019 and 2021[①]. Although global trade has suffered setbacks, the pace of regional integration has not stagnated, and the level of intra-regional economic and trade liberalization and facilitation has continued to improve.

Regional integration promotes in-depth development of globalization. As the Regional Comprehensive Economic Partnership (RCEP), which covers the largest scale of economy and population and the highest level of openness in the Asia-Pacific region, formally entered into force, tariff and non-tariff barriers will be significantly reduced in the region. Meanwhile, the dependence of Asian economies and countries signing the RCEP and CPTPP on Asian trade of goods will continue to increase. The signing of the RCEP also marks a major breakthrough of East Asia in terms of method to achieve regional integration, which is of great significance for further promoting free trade and stabilizing the supply chains in the region. Regional integration facilitates relevant countries to bring out their respective advantages, improves their economic development efficiency, and accelerates establishment of economic development

---

① WTO (2022). Regional Trade Agreements Database. May 9. http://rtais.wto.org/UI/charts.aspx.

alliances among relevant countries; at the same time, it also changes the political and economic landscape of the world and promotes the continuous development of economic globalization.

Box 4-2   China's stance towards CPTPP

In September 2021, China officially applied to join the CPTPP. The move marks an important measure for China to expand its opening-up in the new era.

CPTPP is a high-standard international economic and trade agreement. The high standards are consistent with China's direction of further deepening reform and opening-up. Regarding joining the CPTPP, China is willing to fully meet the CPTPP standards through active efforts to deepen reform and expand opening-up. **In terms of market access**, China will make an opening-up commitments that exceed all existing commitment-fulfilling practices, further expand opening-up, promote in-depth domestic reforms, and achieve high-quality development; **in terms of market reform**, China has the capacity to implement the CPTPP rules on State-owned enterprises; **in terms of e-commerce**, China has passed the Data Security Law, the Cybersecurity Law, and the Personal Information Protection Law, and relevant departments are formulating relevant implementation regulations or detailed rules. China will work with all parties to promote regional trade and economic integration and make efforts to contribute to regional economic development and world economic recovery.

2. New trends in global trade and investment cooperation

Open cooperation in trade and investment caters to the common interests of all countries in the world. For more than half a century, more and more countries have reduced the barriers to cross-border flow of goods, capital, information, personnel and other factors through bilateral and multilateral negotiations, thus becoming promoters, participants and beneficiaries of open cooperation. In 2022, the world economy will face intensified risk of uncertainty and some economies have begun to pursue "localization" and "decoupling", and international trade and investment will face increasing uncertainties.

a. Weakening international grade growth momentum

Throughout the history of international trade, there has been a long-term game between free trade and trade protection. Since the GATT took effect, trade liberalization and facilitation, after decades of evolution, have entered the track of institutionalized development, and an open and cooperative multilateral trading system has gradually become the main trend of world trade development. However, in the wake of the global financial crisis, especially since the outbreak of the COVID-19 pandemic in 2020, the momentum of global economic development has weakened, and trade in goods and services has inevitably been affected.

In terms of trade in goods, the negative impact of the pandemic has somewhat eased, and the overall trade in goods has shown a new trend of slow growth amid fluctuations and rising proportion of trade in industrial products. In terms of overall trade volume, the level of trade in goods has somewhat recovered, but its growth is expected to slow and fluctuate drastically. In 2020, due to the impact of the pandemic, the total import and export of international trade in goods fell by 7.3% to $35.5 trillion. In 2021, following the global economic recovery, the total import and export volume of international trade in goods increased remarkably by 26.1% to $44.8 trillion, and the ratio of trade in goods to global GDP rose from 41.8% in 2020 to 46.6%. In 2022, the Ukraine crisis, to an extent, affected trade in goods, especially that in primary products, such as food, fuel and energy. Using a global economic simulation model, the WTO has predicted that in the short term, the global trade growth may drop by nearly 50% to 2.4%-3% in 2022; in terms of long-term impact, conflicts and sanctions may further exacerbate the global economy, restrain international industrial competition, dampen global scientific and technological innovation, and result in the global GDP growth rate reduced by 0.7-1.3 percentage points to between 3.1% and 3.7%[1]. In terms of sectors, with the development of science and technology and the improvement in the level of industrialization, global trade in goods has gradually been dominated by the trade in manufactured goods, and the share of trade in agricultural, fuel and mining products has been small. In 2020, the trade value of industrial goods was $25.16 trillion, accounting for 70.8% of the total value of global trade in goods[2].

---

[1]   WTO (2022). The Crisis in Ukraine: Implications for the War for Global Trade and Development. April. https://www.wto.org/english/res_e/booksp_e/imparctukraine422_e.pdf.

[2]   WTO STATS: accessed on 2 July 2022, https://stats.wto.org/.

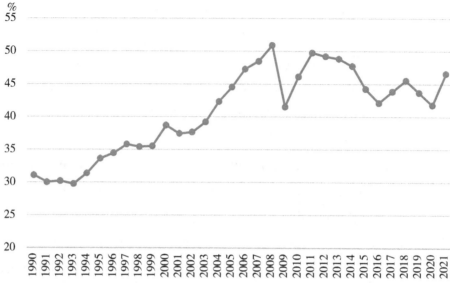

Fig. 4.1 Ratio of total global trade in goods to GDP, 1990-2021

Source: WTO STATS: accessed on July 2, 2022; Wind database, accessed on July 2, 2022, https://stats. wto.org/.

In terms of services trade, the adverse impact of the COVID-19 pandemic has continued to ferment, featuring shrinkage of total trade volume and adjustment of trade structure. In terms of total volume of services trade, in 2020, the total global services trade dropped by 19.8% to $9.89 trillion. In 2021, the total volume of services trade increased moderately to 11.42 trillion yuan, up by 15.4%, reaching the pre-pandemic level in 2020. In terms of composition, knowledge-intensive services trade has grown strongly. In 2021, the total volume of trade in the knowledge-intensive services, such as construction, insurance, finance, technical services, intellectual property, and personal culture and entertainment, already reached $7.34 trillion, accounting for 64.3% of the total global trade in services, up from 53.2% in 2018; China has gradually been playing a dominant role in global services trade[①].

In terms of North-South cooperation, the international market landscape is being reshaped, with the proportion of developing countries participating in world trade increasing and the North-South development becoming more balanced. From 2000 to 2021, in terms of trade in goods, the share of trade of the developed countries had decreased gradually, while that of the developing countries had increased year by year. In 2020, the total volume of trade in goods of the developed countries reached $20.9

---

trillion and that of the developing countries amounted to $14.7 trillion, accounting for 58.7% and 41.3% of the total global trade in goods, respectively. The gap between the two groups of countries was not very big. In 2021, the total trade in goods of the developed and developing countries reached $25.7 trillion and $19.1 trillion, respectively, accounting for 57.4% and 42.6% of the global total, respectively, with their gap further narrowed[1]. In contrast, the proportion of the developing countries in global services trade is only 28.6%, which is significantly smaller than that of the developed countries, which is 71.4%; it means there is still a large room for the developing countries for them to catch up with the developed countries[2].

b. Brewing changes in the international investment environment

Since the beginning of the new century, the world has ushered in a peaceful and stable period of rapid development. Against the backdrop of globalization, international business exchanges have become increasingly close, and capital flows have become more frequent; the developing countries have vigorously ushered in foreign capital, more and more multinational companies have engaged in cross-border investment, and investment ties between countries have been continuously strengthened. The international investment has entered a fast track of development. Since 2020, the world economy has fluctuated drastically, and the uncertainties and risks of the global investment environment have increased remarkably. It is urgent to explore more new development opportunities.

In terms of investment scale, the scale of international investment has gradually increased and grown amid fluctuations. In the wake of the Cold War, international direct investment started to grow strongly. From 1990 to 2007, its average annual growth rate was as high as 8%. After the eruption of the global financial crisis in 2008, global FDI showed a weakening trend amid fluctuations. Since the outbreak of the COVID-19 pandemic, the global FDI flow has slumped to $963.14 billion, down 35% a year-on-year (see Fig. 4.2). The latest report released by the United Nations Conference on Trade and Development shows that in 2021, global FDI has returned to the pre-pandemic level, reaching $1.58 trillion, a year-on-year increase of 64.3%. However, due to the Ukraine crisis, the international business environment has been

---

①   UNCTAD STAT: accessed on July 2, 2022, https://unctadstat.unctad.org/wds/ReportFolders/reportFolders.aspx

②   WTO STATS: accessed on July 2, 2022, https://stats.wto.org/.

affected, and economic sanctions may lead some major economies to "decouple" based on geopolitical considerations and pursue greater self-sufficiency of production and trade. It is expected that in 2022, global FDI flow will not be able to maintain the previous growth momentum, and it will remain flat at most or even fall into a downward channel.

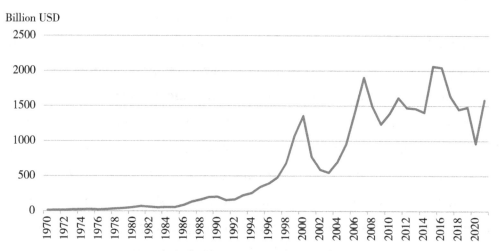

Fig. 4.2   Global FDI flow, 1970-2020

Source: Wind database, accessed on July 2, 2022.

In terms of capital flow direction, the focus of international investment has gradually shifted from the developed countries to the developing countries, and cross-regional flow has become more balanced. In terms of global FDI outflow, the proportion of the developed economies in the wake of World War II dropped from more than 90% to the current average of about 70%. In 2020, affected by the COVID-19 pandemic, the FDI flow of the developed economies fell sharply to $312.17 billion, a decrease of 58.3% from $749 billion in 2019; in other words, it shrank by more than 50%. The ability of the emerging economies to attract investment has been relatively stable, with FDI in those countries still standing at $662.56 billion in 2020, accounting for 66.3% of the total global FDI flow. In 2021, three-quarters of global investment was in advanced economies, a rise of 134%; investment flowing into the developing economies increased by 30% to hit an all-time high, mainly due to strong growth in Asia, the partial recovery in Latin America and the Caribbean, and growth in Africa.

In terms of investment structure, the direction of investment has gradually

shifted from labor-intensive industries to technology-intensive industries and services sectors, and the investment structure has undergone fundamental adjustments. Currently, the proportion of FDI stock in services has increased from about 25% in the early 1970s to more than 60% now. The FDI stock in the primary sector only accounts for about 6% of the total FDI, and the manufacturing sector accounts for about 26%[1].

II. Impact of COVID-19 Pandemic on Global Openness

Compared with other public health incidents and natural disasters, the impact of the COVID-19 pandemic is more globalized and has greater uncertainties. The outbreak and spread of the pandemic on a global scale not only threatens the lives of people around the world, but also has a serious impact on the world economy. It has severely damaged international trade and investment, widened the gap between the rich and the poor, intensified the anti-globalization sentiment, and slowed growth of the world economy and increased its systemic risks; it has brought shocks to the global value chains, and the adjustment of the international economic structure has accelerated; the world is facing a severe test in improving openness.

1. The pandemic hampers sustained global trade

The outbreak of the COVID-19 pandemic on a global scale has significantly inhibited cross-border trade activities, including both export and import activities. With new variants of the virus emerging, the situation has gradually become more complicated and begun to serve as the main risk factor to affect international trade growth. How to alleviate the impact of the pandemic and push international trade back on track of recovery is a major issue that the international community currently urgently needs to deal with.

a. The most important risk factor for international trade

The emergence of new variants of the virus has brought more uncertainties to the prevention and control of the pandemic, leading to increased vulnerability of

---

[1]   UNCTAD (2020). *UNCTAD Handbook of Statistics 2021 - Economic Trends.* December. https://unctad.org/system/files/official-document/tdstat46_FS09_en.pdf.

international trade partnerships.

It damages the confidence of traders and related entities. The results of the Global Economic Confidence Index 2022 survey show that although many respondents believe that the global pandemic will further ease, 53% of the respondents are still worried that it will recur; such worry may be related to the concurring spread of the Delta and Omicron variants and the fact that there have been no signs of them disappearing any time soon. Compared with the 2021 survey, the respondents this time have been significantly more worried about the continuation of the global supply chain disruption[①] (See Fig. 4.3). Such public panic is likely to disrupt the normal economic and social order and impact the psychological expectations of economic participants, thereby increasing the vulnerability of cross-border trade links.

It leads to countries strengthening trade protection. WTO members and observers have implemented a number of trade measures related to the COVID-19 pandemic, and almost all countries have formulated entry management measures in response to the pandemic, which has raised trade access barriers and led to a sharp increase in trade costs. The Global Trade Alert database shows that the number of global trade protectionist measures has been continually on the rise, with a sharp increase from 2019 to 2021; among them, trade restrictive measures have been on the rise accordingly. As of April 2022, there had been 515 global trade protection measures implemented, up 35% compared with the whole-year number of 2019[②] (See Fig. 4.4). It is clear that the pandemic is gradually leading to "safety" replacing "efficiency" to become the dominant factor in globalization. The global spread of the pandemic and its impact on life, society and economy are becoming an excuse for some countries to implement trade protection measures, leading to higher possibility of intensifying global trade frictions.

[①] Thinktank for Finance and Economy (2022). *Report on Confidence in Global Economy 2022*. March 18. http://www.china-cer.com.cn/guwen/2022031817338.html.

[②] Global Trade Alert Database, Estimates for harmful interventions, 2021-2022，https://www.globaltradealert.org/data_extraction.

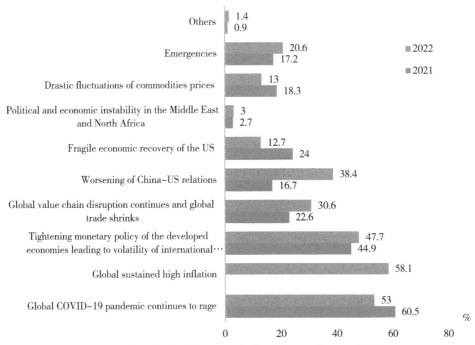

Fig. 4.3   Global Economic Confidence Survey 2022

Source: Financial Minds, Global Economic Confidence Index Report 2022, March 18, 2022, http://www. china-cer.com.cn/guwen/2022031817338.html.

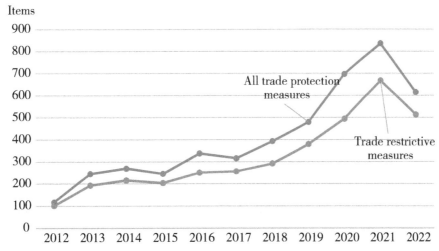

Fig. 4.4   Number of implemented trade protection measures, 2012-2022

Source: Global Trade Alert database, Estimates for harmful interventions, 2021-2022, https://www. globaltradealert.org/data_extraction.

b. Diversified prevention and control measures lead to varying levels of recovery

The diverging trend of economic recovery among different countries is deepening due to differences in vaccine supply and governance, which has had a direct impact on global trade recovery.

Infections have continued to increase and the movement of people has been restricted, slowing the pace of global trade recovery. The World Economic Outlook report, released by the IMF in January 2022, pointed out that "as the new Omicron COVID-19 variant spreads" and infections increase, "countries have re-imposed mobility restrictions"[1]. Meanwhile, the emergence of new variants may make the pandemic last longer, once again disrupting the economy, and, as a result, the economic conditions of countries may continue to be weaker than expected.

Unbalanced vaccination and slow recovery in some regions have combined to restrict the progress of global economic recovery. From early 2021, the research and development and promotion of the COVID-19 vaccine have greatly pushed forward the prevention and control of the pandemic and injected impetus into the recovery of the world economy. The widespread use of the COVID-19 vaccine has reduced measures that impose strict restrictions on economic activities, and economic activities are gradually returning to normal. However, affected by various factors, such as values and economic conditions, it will take a long time for vaccines to be accepted and administered globally. Moreover, the emergence of new variants of the virus, the rise of vaccine nationalism, and the continual spread of the virus around the world have continued to affect the global economy. In 2021, the IMF released a report stating that as of October 2021, the vaccination rate of the sub-Saharan African population barely reached 2.5%[2], while the region's GDP growth rate was only 4.5% that year, far lower than that of emerging markets and developing economies, which was 6.8% on average[3]. It is fair to say that the slow economic recovery in Africa is mainly attributable to the low vaccination rate. The COVID-19 virus continues to sweep the world, and even countries with a very small number of infections cannot guarantee a smooth economic and trade recovery. The vaccination rate continues to have a bearing on the global economy.

---

[1] IMF (2022). *World Economic Outlook*. January. https://www.imf.org/zh/Publications/WEO/Issues/2022/01/25/world-economic-outlook-update-january-2022.

[2] IMF (2021). *A Fraught Recovery. Despite Some Encourage Sign, Another Difficult Year.* October.https://www.imf.org/zh/Publications/REO/SSA/Issues/2021/10/21/regional-economic-outlook-for-sub-saharan-africa-october-2021.

[3] IMF (2022). *World Economic Outlook*. April. https://www.imf.org/zh/Publications/WEO/Issues/2022/04/19/world-economic-outlook-april-2022 accessed on April 2022.

2. The pandemic restricts free flow of international investment

The spread of the pandemic has disrupted the global supply chain, prompting countries to take protection of the integrity and upgrading of domestic supply chains as part of their national security strategy. In particular, the developed economies have continually reduced overseas investment and pushed reshoring of overseas capital and manufacturing. Meanwhile, investment disputes caused by the pandemic have also attracted widespread attention from the international community, and may lead to reform of international investment rules.

a. It intensifies the rise of international investment protectionism

The raging pandemic has prompted governments of relevant countries to give more priority to national security while pursuing economic growth. However, countries have very different understanding of pandemic prevention and control; as a result, policy restrictions and conflicting ways of thinking have adversely influenced international investment.

Increased government intervention in international direct investment. Some countries have introduced policies to encourage domestic enterprises operating overseas to return and invest in the domestic market and improve the domestic investment environment. Meanwhile, due to national security considerations, since 2016, many countries have increased restrictions and reviews on foreign investment in specific industrial sectors, and the proportion of restrictive and regulatory policies has risen to 33% in 2020[1]. Such restrictions and reviews mainly involve industrial sectors such as defense industry, critical infrastructure, and strategic industries, increasing the difficulty for international capital to enter.

It magnifies the conflict of values, intensifies mistrust among major countries, and dampens the confidence of international investors. A country's attitude towards pandemic prevention and control is influenced by values, and as the contradictions and conflicts among countries have increased, it has had a negative impact on the investment environment. In March 2020, the United Nations Conference on Trade and Development made a gloomy forecast of global FDI growth, expecting it to decline by 30%-40%[2]. It turned out that the forecast was very close to the actual growth of global

---

[1]   UNCTAD, https://unctad.org/.

[2]   UNCTAD (2020). *Global Investmetn Trend Monitor*. March 27. https://unctad.org/system/files/official-document/diaeiainf2020d3_en.pdf.

FDI, which was a negative 42%, even 30 percentage points lower than the lowest level recorded in the wake of the 2009 global financial crisis. The gloomy expectations brought by the pandemic have affected investor confidence, tilting them towards holding cash and monitoring the market instead of transactions, thereby dampening outbound investment and economic activities.

b. It triggers international investment disputes and accelerates rule adjustment

The pandemic has led to countries taking a large number of extensive prevention and control measures in health, travel, trade, investment, among others, which have inevitably affected free flow of investment. At the later stage of the pandemic, the possibility cannot be ruled out that a large number of foreign investors may file arbitration claims based on investment treaties, accusing the host country of violating investment protection obligations and requiring the host country to assume state responsibility.

It may increase investment-related disputes between foreign investors and host countries. Since the outbreak of the pandemic, global economic and trade frictions have continued to heat up. In 2021, India recorded the highest average monthly reading of the Global Economic and Trade Measures Index, and the US' index reading was at a high level for 10 of the 12 months in 2021[1]. Considering pandemic prevention and control and national security, a significant number of economies have tightened their foreign investment review measures, which has created some obstacles to the normal development of international trade and cross-border investment activities. The resulting investment arbitration cases, therefore, have gradually increased. Moreover, some countries' negative attitude towards pandemic prevention and control has prolonged efforts to contain the pandemic and increased risks. The resulting adverse effects, such as disrupted logistics and blocked economic activities, will aggravate the losses of foreign investors and are likely to trigger more investment-related disputes.

It may have an impact on international investment rules. The increase in litigation has also prompted the international community to reconsider the substantive and procedural rules of international investment agreements. The international law

---

[1] China Council for the Promotion of International Trade (2022). *Global Economic and Trade Measures Index 2021.* March 31. https://www.ccpit.org/image/1273893138053726209/9863c2f5973743 cca0c73ef341184d57.pdf.

community generally supports multilateral and bilateral investment treaties and international conventions, and the host country's various investment protection obligations to foreign investors can become a strong legal basis for claims of investors. Although international investment agreements that have been signed in recent years have paid more attention to the safeguarding of regulatory rights of host countries while protecting the rights and interests of investors, in reality, the effect of safeguarding the regulatory rights is not obvious. Therefore, the international community is considering and discussing systemic and institutional reform of investment dispute settlement mechanism to better resolve disputes between investors and host countries.

3. The pandemic undermines growth momentum of global value chains

The rapid development of globalization in the past decades, which is attributable to the market division of labor and scientific and technological progress, ensures a relatively stable environment for the continual extension of global supply chains. The outbreak of the COVID-19 pandemic has greatly increased the importance of the dimension of security in the supply chain system, which not only restricts the global allocation of means of production, but also affects the effective operation of global value chains.

a. It deals a blow to economic and trade activities on both the supply and demand side of value chains

To effectively prevent and control the pandemic, almost all countries have implemented social distancing measures of varying levels, such as isolation and quarantine, working from home, reducing social activities, restricting border entry, and reducing the flow of people, disrupting many sectors of the global supply chain system.

It seriously dampens production and export from the supply side. The strict logistics control policies of countries around the world have led to suspension of some logistics services, increased complexity of the inspection and quarantine process for transportation of goods, and in turn caused congestion of the international logistics network. According to a report on global air cargo, released by the International Air Transport Association (IATA)[1], global air cargo demand growth had slowed

---

[1]   IATA (2021). *Air Cargo Market Analysis*. November. https://www.iata.org/en/iata-repository/publications/economic-reports/air-freight-monthly-analysis---november-2021/.

in November 2021 due to factors such as supply chain disruptions and capacity constraints. Meanwhile, the resumption of work and production of enterprises had suffered setbacks, the supply of raw materials from upstream enterprises in the supply chain, such as steel, mining, and energy, had been reduced, and downstream enterprises are caught in the predicament of raw material shortage, blocked transportation, and shortage of labor. It is precisely because of the dual restraints of logistics and production that the global industrial chain faces the risk of rupture.

From the demand side, the pandemic has led to weak global demand. According to the statistics of the United Nations Conference on Trade and Development (UNCTAD), the pandemic may lead to the loss of 114 million jobs worldwide, and about 120 million people may fall into extreme poverty[1]. The unemployment risk, combined with a decline in income levels, have forced consumers to take emergency money-saving measures, thus showing a negative trend of suppressed individual consumption demand. An Ernst & Young survey shows that due to the economic uncertainties and rising inflation brought about by the recurrences of COVID-19 virus variants, 60% of the respondents - from across the world - want to save more money for the future; among them, 39% have made money-saving as a long-term goal. 52% of the respondents said their purchasing power has declined moderately, which in turn had influenced their spending decisions[2]. Meanwhile, pandemic prevention and control measures, such as home isolation, have also affected the normal production of enterprises, which, coupled with insufficient investment caused by uncertain corporate prospects, has led to weak corporate demand across the world.

b. It disrupts the optimal allocation of resources within the global value chain

The pandemic not only magnifies the vulnerability of the global supply chains, but may also cause major adjustments and restructuring of the global supply chains.

Industries across the world suffer from shocks. The economic disruption caused by the pandemic has reduced the volume of global trade in goods and services by about 10 percent[3], according to data released by the United Nations. The policy restricting

---

①   UN DESA (2021). *Financing for Sustainable Development Report 2021.* March.https://desapublications.un.org/publications/financing-sustainable-development-report-2021.

②   Ernst & Yong (2022). *EY Future Consumer Index.* April. 2022, Issue IX, P5.

③   UNCTAD (2022). *Key Statistics and Trend in International Trade 2021.* March 10. https://unctad.org/system/files/official-document/ditctab2022d3_en.pdf.

free flow of people, as part of the pandemic prevention and control measures, has directly led to a significant reduction in the supply and consumption of labor factors, thus bringing negative shocks to labor-intensive agriculture and manufacturing industries. Meanwhile, the pandemic has restricted the free movement of people, which, coupled with declining capital investment, has resulted in a decline in both the demand and output of the services industry.

The global value chain system faces the risk of fragmentation. The pandemic has raised concerns about material shortages. Governments of relevant countries have adopted export control policies on food, energy, and medical supplies in disregard of WTO free trade rules. In addition, air and shipping controls for the purpose of pandemic prevention and control have had an impact on the normal global economic and trade order and the global value chain system. Meanwhile, non-market factors, such as the fierce gaming among major powers triggered by the pandemic, have also caused otherwise avoidable damage to the global value chains, and the prevailing unilateralism has increased the risk of rupture of the global industrial and supply chains.

It exposes the fragility of the global industrial chains. Under the division of labor framework of the global value chains, the quality of the legal system and environment have a bearing not only on a country's export, but also on the positioning of specific industries in the global value chains. The pandemic has led to the global value chain system facing restructuring, and had higher requirements for optimizing relevant systematic arrangements to protect implementation of contracts.

III. Promoting the Positive Evolution of Globalization and Common Opening of the World

At present, the world is at a critical crossroad of historical development, security challenges are emerging one after another, and the global economic recovery is struggling. How to prevent pandemic risk, cope with the food and energy crisis, defuse downward pressure on the economy, maintain world peace and stability, and promote global sustainable development, are important issues of the current era. All major economies should work together, with global cooperation as the cornerstone, solidarity and innovation as the core, inclusiveness and inclusiveness as the criterion, to promote world openness and globalization, and build a community with a shared future for mankind.

1. Taking global cooperation as the cornerstone to jointly resolve risks

The world is facing profound and broad changes of the times. Coping with development risks and stabilizing economic recovery are major issues of common concern to the world. It is necessary for the world to pool strong forces to overcome difficulties and challenges and jointly resolve world economic risks.

a. Working together to resolve uncertainty risks

The *World Economic Outlook* report released by the IMF in July this year pointed out that the world economic situation will be gloomy in 2022, and related risks will begin to emerge, with increased uncertainty. In the face of uncertainties in the development of world economy, the international community should continue to address risks and challenges together on the basis of cooperation. We will work together to overcome the pandemic of the century. The pandemic is a tenacious war of resistance faced by the international community. Although the global fight against the pandemic has made breakthrough progress, the repeated delays of the pandemic and the multiple mutations of the virus still hinder the development of world economy. Strengthening confidence and jointly overcoming the pandemic is the right way to restore world economy. In the face of this global crisis, all countries should strengthen international cooperations in anti pandemic, drug research and development, accelerate the pace of vaccination and bridge the international "immunization gap" while ensuring the equitable distribution of vaccines. We will work together to resolve the negative impact of the Ukrainian crisis, which has brought about intertwined risks such as the disorder of global industrial chains and supply chains, continuous rise of commodity prices, and the shortage of energy supply. Only by abandoning unilateralism and hegemonism, strengthening solidarity and cooperation, enhancing coordination and communication, striving to maintain world peace and avoiding turbulence and division can we defuse and overcome the risks of uncertainty.

b. Jointly promote the stable recovery of world economy

The world economy has suffered many shocks, the development of many countries has frequently experienced crises, global inflation expectation has been raised, the financing environment has been tightened, trade growth has slowed down, and the risk of economic downturn has increased. All economies should adhere to cooperative development, jointly cope with inflation and other pressures, and promote stable recovery of the world economy.

Cooperate to resolve the inflation crisis. Under the combined impact of various risk factors, the economic recession and inflation wave swept the world. Many countries faced the pressure of currency devaluation. The rising prices squeezed the living standards of people around the world. The labor market in some economies was tense, and compound inflation risks were emerging. If the monetary policies of major economies "brake sharply" or "turn sharply", there will be serious negative spillover effects, bringing challenges to the world economy and finance. Therefore, all economies must establish a sense of community, strengthen macro policy coordination, promote transparency and sharing of policy information, and jointly prevent economic systemic risks.

Restructure the new pattern of world economic recovery. At present, the process of globalization is suffering a serious impact, and many development problems such as the North-South gap, recovery differentiation, development fault and technological gap are more prominent. In order to reduce domestic economic risks, some economies have stepped up their efforts to promote "manufacturing industry reflow", leading to a decline in international openness and cooperation, which has a negative impact on the long-term and stable development of world economy. Based on this, all major economies must adhere to openness without isolation, integration without decoupling, build an open world economy, and work together to reconstruct a new pattern of world economic recovery.

2. Focus on solidarity and innovation to promote development

At a time when the global development process is seriously impacted, it is the common goal of all economies to bridge the development gap and revitalize the global development cause. To achieve this goal, we must abandon the cold war mentality, embrace development with an open attitude, stimulate the potential and vitality of cooperation, and achieve mutual benefit and win-win results.

a. Building a global development community

Development is the key to solving problems. In the face of the first decline in the human development index in recent 30 years, promoting the recovery and development of less developed countries is a top priority. To promote balanced global development, we need not only to promote the synergy of existing development cooperation mechanisms, but also to implement the *United Nations 2030 Agenda for Sustainable Development* and create the necessary conditions for countries around the world to achieve sustainable development. Cooperation is a necessary condition for development. No single tree can make a forest. The common development of the world is the real development, and sustainable development can achieve long-term development. We should build an international consensus to promote development, create an international environment conducive to development, avoid politicizing, instrumentalizing and weaponizing the world economy, let the North and the South meet each other through deepening cooperation, build a global partnership for development that is united, equal, balanced and inclusive, and form a global joint force to achieve common development.

b. Cultivate new impetus of global development

With the rapid development of science and technology and the rapid change of industrial iteration, only by grasping the pulse of the times can we seize the opportunities of economic development, and only by pooling collective wisdom can we activate the driving force of global development. Exploring and cultivating new impetus of global development is the key to common development. In the process of going out of the downturn, the world economy is faced with many constraints. Pandemics, wars and other factors also increase the uncertainty of the economic recovery process. Therefore, all major economies must jointly explore and cultivate new drivers of economic growth under the conditions of normalized pandemic prevention and control, promote the integrated development and safe development of the international industrial chains and supply chains, turn crisis into opportunity, and promote the steady and solid process of world economic recovery.

Adhering to innovation is an important aspect of the new driving force of economic growth. Innovation is the first driving force for development. Whoever can give priority to new economic development opportunities such as big data and artificial intelligence will be able to keep pace with the times. The international community must work together to promote technological and institutional innovation, accelerate technology transfer and knowledge sharing, promote the development and upgrading of modern industries through innovation, constantly stimulate cooperation potential and market vitality, and promote more robust, green and healthy global development.

3. Expand openness and integration based on inclusiveness and inclusiveness

Although there have been many countercurrents and dangerous shoals on the road of development, the general direction of economic globalization has never changed and will not change. To seek further development, we must take fairness and justice as the concept, tolerance and inclusiveness as the criterion, promote the reform of the global governance system and economic globalization towards a more open, inclusive, inclusive, balanced and win-win direction.

a. Work together to improve global economic governance

In the face of the growing development gap, some economies are willing to beggar their neighbors for short-term economic benefits and undermine mutual trust, which makes global economic governance entering into a period of turbulence and change. Trade frictions in 2018 made the trend of anti-globalization increasingly popular. The pandemic situation in 2020 accelerated the further fermentation of this trend. The geopolitical conflict brought about by the Ukrainian crisis in 2022 further broke the original economic order and interest pattern, and global economic governance faced severe challenges. There is turbulence, there is change, and we must seek to eliminate or reduce turbulence in the process of change. The reform of global economic governance should conform to the trend of economic multi-polarization. To reduce conflicts around the world and actively reshape the new order of global economic governance with benign changes, we must adhere to multilateralism, abandon the old rules, rationally seek the greatest common denominator of the interests of all countries, run in with each other, constantly reduce the intensity and duration of the game in the anti-globalization stage, and accelerate to enter a new era of more stable, balanced and orderly global economic governance at the lowest cost.

b. Cooperation and inclusiveness to achieve mutual benefit and win-win results

There is inevitably competition and differences between countries, but history has repeatedly proved that zero sum game is not the right choice, and win-win cooperation is the right path in the world. Economic globalization is an objective requirement for the development of productive forces and an irresistible historical trend. With the continuous progress of globalization, the flow of goods and capital in the world is becoming increasingly frequent, the progress of science, technology and civilization is advancing rapidly, and the links between economies are becoming closer." Decoupling and breaking the chain" and building a high wall will only lead to the division of the world economy and even stagnation of growth.

In order to achieve the stability and long-term development of world economy, we must abandon the idea of "each closing the door to development", remove barriers that hinder the development of productive forces, and follow the trend of globalization. Inclusion, mutual benefit and win-win results are the only way to promote global common development. "Mount Tai is big because it does not allow soil; rivers and seas are deep because they do not choose small streams." In the face of the current complex and severe development environment, only by adhering to openness and inclusiveness, allowing capital and technology to flow freely internationally, and allowing innovation and wisdom to emerge and fully collide, can we pool the combined forces of world economic growth, thus guiding and promoting the healthy development of globalization, can we bring broader development space to all countries, and can we achieve mutual benefit and win-win results and create a more prosperous future.

Looking ahead, the new situation brings new challenges, and the new situation breeds new opportunities. Driven by the concept of openness and inclusiveness, collective wisdom and strength, the world economy will certainly glow with more brilliant light, and the destiny of mankind will certainly blossom into a brilliant flower of win-win cooperation.

Chapter 5　WTO Reform and Global Economic Governance

As an important part of global economic governance, the global trade governance system represented by the multilateral trading system is currently facing a complex and volatile international environment. The WTO has encountered multiple challenges as it carries out reforms, but members are still actively promoting negotiations to implement its reform agenda. At the 12th WTO Ministerial Conference held in June 2022, participants discussed WTO reform, including COVID-19 pandemic response, food security, fisheries subsidies, e-commerce, and other issues. They reached fruitful agreements and made achievements on the above-mentioned issues.

I. The Multilateral Trading System Faces Profound Restructuring

The world economic structure has undergone profound adjustments. Unilateralism and protectionism have been on the rise, economic globalization has encountered setbacks, and the authority and effectiveness of the multilateral trading system have been seriously challenged. Some countries advocate the inclusion of "values" in economic and trade rules, abuse security exceptions and unilateral measures, and even ignore existing international rules. Regional governance brings both opportunities and challenges to multilateral mechanisms. The crisscrossing bilateral and regional trade and investment agreements highlight the phenomenon of "spaghetti bowl", and the trend of global trade governance fragmentation has become more apparent. The WTO has failed to show the core leadership, and it lacks internal driving force. The operation of the WTO faces many contradictions and obstacles:

1. The dispute between North and South members over the right to formulate rules and speak is becoming increasingly fierce.

On the one hand, some developed members hope to keep the old rules that are beneficial to themselves, and on the other hand, they have continued to dominate the designing of new rules, in an attempt to occupy the commanding heights of the global economic governance system. They even tend to make use of the "elite club" model of bilateral or regional trade agreements, such as the previous TPP, to replace the multilateral trade rules system. Calls of the emerging economies to reform the global economic governance have failed to receive effective response for a long time. The developing members, therefore, are generally reluctant to continue to be "passive recipients" of rules and hope to participate more actively and substantially in rule-making to correct the inequality of existing rules. Meanwhile, the developed members have limited space to further open up their domestic markets, while some developing members have attached increasing importance to protection of their domestic policy space. As a result, the room for exchange of interests between the developed and developing members has narrowed.

2. Inefficiency of the consensus-based decision-making mechanism affects the progress of negotiations.

The WTO adopts a consensus-based decision-making method, and any member has the right to veto. While ensuring equal participation of all economies in decision-making, regardless of their size, this mechanism also hampers many major and complex negotiation processes that involve complicated interests. The Doha Round of negotiations has been more than 20 years, trapped in stalemate and achieved very limited progress on such issues as agriculture, development, and rules, resulting in a long-term stalemate. The mechanism has also failed to promptly respond to such new issues as digital economy, investment facilitation, green development, trade and the environment, and small, medium-sized enterprises. The operating efficiency of the negotiation mechanism urgently needs to be improved.

3. The dispute settlement mechanism and the shutdown of the Appellate Body.

Since 2017, the United States has abused its power of veto to repeatedly obstruct the selection process of new judges and paralyze the dispute settlement mechanism, citing the Appellate Body's "judicial overreach" and its "excessive term lengths", driving the mechanism towards "uncharted waters" and may even fall into a dangerous situation governed by the "law of the jungle". As an interim mechanism, the Multi-Party Interim Appeal Arbitration Arrangement (MPIA) is not a plurilateral agreement and does not belong to the category of international treaty. WTO members such as the United States, Japan, South Korea, and India have not joined the mechanism, whose operational space is limited.

4. Shortcomings in the review and notification mechanism.

In terms of deliberation and surveillance functions, the building of the surveillance mechanism for implementation of transparency and notification commitments should be strengthened. Given their differing transparency interests, the WTO members have been divided into two groups that advocate two types of governance philosophy, i.e., discipline restraint and capacity enhancement. The developed members, which advocate discipline restraint, have failed to take into consideration the differences in the notification capabilities of the WTO members; they have put the focus on increasing the cost of rule violation and advocated adoption of workable punitive clauses to spur member countries to fulfill their notification obligation. The developing members advocate capacity enhancement, emphasizing the provision of necessary capacity support for fulfilling notification commitments.

II. Fruitful outcomes of the 12th WTO Ministerial Conference

In June 2022, the 12th WTO Ministerial Conference (MC12) was held in Geneva, Switzerland. It achieved more-than-expected success, released one outcome document, and reached four agreements on COVID-19 pandemic response, fisheries subsidies, food security, and e-commerce. The conference not only enabled the WTO to "survive a desperate situation", but also boosted the confidence of the international community in the multilateral trading system and multilateralism.

1. Safeguarding the multilateral trading system and advancing the reform of the WTO

The MC12 reached agreement on the outcome document of the conference, it was the second time when all members reached consensus — 7 years after the 10th Ministerial Conference in Nairobi, Kenya in 2015. In the outcome document of the conference, all parties reaffirmed the strengthening of the multilateral trading system with the WTO at the core, emphasized the important role of international trade and the WTO in promoting global economic recovery, enhancing people's well-being, and achieving sustainable development, and reiterated that special and differential treatment is an integral part of the WTO agreement. All parties expressed their support for the necessary reform of the WTO to ensure that the reform process is member-driven, open, transparent, and inclusive, and address the concerns of all members; they also agreed to authorize the General Council and its subordinate bodies to carry out relevant work, so that the next ministerial conference can review advancement in relevant areas. The parties pledged to secure a fully functioning dispute settlement mechanism accessible to all members by 2024. Moreover, members also made political commitments on WTO accession work, service trade, and issues related to the least developed countries.

2. COVID-19 pandemic response

The MC12 reached the Ministerial Decision on the Agreement on Trade-Related Aspects of Intellectual Property Rights, allowing developing members to exempt from the protection obligations of the COVID-19 vaccine patents, and developing members can authorize production and export vaccines to other eligible developing members without the consent of the patentee. The developing members enjoy greater flexibility in the way of implementing authorization, notification obligations, and providing appropriate remuneration to patentee. For example, they can authorize production through legislative acts as well as other acts, such as executive orders and emergency decrees, and they can notify the WTO after the authorization; they can also take account of the humanitarian and not-for-profit purpose in determining adequate remuneration for the patentee. The MC12 decision also has it that members will decide, no later than six months from the date of the MC12 decision, on the extension of the patent right obligation exemption to cover the production and supply of COVID-19 diagnostics and therapeutics. The decision encourages developing members with COVID-19 vaccine production capacity to waive the exemption. Before the MC12, China had voluntarily announced it would not seek the treatment provided by the exemption decision so that agreement could be reached at an earlier time regarding the negotiations on intellectual property right exemption of COVID-19 vaccines.

MC12 also reached the Ministerial Declaration on the WTO Response to the COVID-19 Pandemic and Preparedness for Future Pandemics, which covers comprehensive measures to respond to and actively cope with the pandemic and get well-prepared for any future pandemic; they include improving policy transparency, eliminating as many export restraints as possible, promoting trade facilitation, supporting the role of service trade, supporting an inclusive recovery, strengthening cooperation with international organizations, and implementing future action plans.

3. Fisheries subsidies

The WTO fisheries subsidy negotiation is part of the Doha Round of negotiations and have been underway for 21 years. The negotiations aim to promote the sustainable development of marine fishery resources by formulating new subsidy rules to restrain harmful fishery subsidies. After intensive negotiations and hard work among the WTO members, the MC12 finally reached the agreement on the fisheries subsidies, the first WTO agreement aimed at achieving sustainable environmental development goals.

The agreement contains two core disciplines. One is to prohibit illegal, unreported and unregulated (IUU) fisheries subsidies; the other is fishing, and the other is to prohibit subsidies for overcapacity and overfishing. To implement the negotiated authorization, the agreement provides special and differential treatment for developing members, stipulating that within two years after the agreement comes into force, relevant subsidies provided by developing members will not be subject to the WTO dispute settlement procedures, and a fisheries fund will be established to provide developing members with technical assistance and capacity building. The fund is financed voluntarily by members and will engage in cooperation with the Food and Agriculture Organization of the United Nations and the International Fund for Agricultural Development.

4. Agriculture and food security

The MC12 adopted the Ministerial Declaration on the Emergency Response to Food Insecurity to actively cope with the current global food insecurity problem.

The ministers of member countries expressed concerns about the disruption of trade in food and agricultural products, excessive fluctuations in international food prices, and relevant trade restrictions; they emphasized that trade, like domestic production, plays an important role in improving global food security; ministers of member countries committed to taking steps to facilitate trade in agricultural products, improve the functioning of global food and agricultural markets, to increase their long-term resilience; they reaffirmed not to impose export bans or restrictions that are inconsistent with WTO rules; they committed to minimizing the trade-distorting effects of any emergency measures taken to ensure food security and making them abide by WTO rules; food aid is encouraged to poor and weak countries to help least developed countries and net food-importing developing countries increase agricultural production capacity; it is emphasized that sufficient grain reserves are helpful for members to achieve domestic food security objectives, and it is important for information on policies that may affect agricultural trade to be rapidly shared.

Moreover, the MC12 also reached the Ministerial Decision on World Food Programme (WFP) Food Purchases Exemptions from Export Prohibitions or Restrictions, pledging not to impose export bans or restrictions on WFP's humanitarian food purchases.

5. E-commerce

The WTO started to clarify temporary exemption of customs duties on electronic transmission from 1998 through the Ministerial Declaration on Global Electronic Commerce and other forms of decision, but this practice can only be maintained after consensus at the ministerial conference. The MC12 passed the Ministerial Decision on the Work Programme on Electronic Commerce. It claimed to reinvigorate the work under the Work Programme on Electronic Commerce, emphasize the development dimension, intensify the discussions on the temporary exemption of customs duties on electronic transmissions, regularly review relevant research reports, and agreed to maintain the current practice of not imposing customs duties on electronic transmissions until next ministerial conference.

Previously, in December 2021, 86 WTO members announced that they had made substantial progress in the negotiation of eight articles on e-commerce, including open Internet access, electronic signature and verification, and paperless transactions, and they will strive to complete the negotiations by the end of 2022.

In addition, the MC12 also adopted outcome document on issues such as supporting the development of small economies, sanitary and phytosanitary.

At a difficult time when the multilateral trading system is facing severe challenges, the success of MC12 marks a crucial and important victory for multilateralism, fully demonstrates the solidarity and cooperation of WTO members and their determination to overcome the difficulties together, further boosts the international community's confidence in the multilateral trading system, and injects a strong shot in the arm of the international community as it copes with global challenges and recovery of the world economy.

III. Progress in Negotiations on WTO-related Issues

Apart from a package of agreements the MC12 has reached, the WTO members have also made positive progress in promoting negotiations on investment facilitation and services domestic regulation in recent years.

1. Investment facilitation

In December 2021, 112 WTO members, including China, the European Union, Russia, and Japan, co-sponsored a Joint Statement on Investment Facilitation for Development, which aims to establish international rules, improve the transparency of investment policies worldwide, and simplify and speed up investment approval procedures, so that international investment cooperation can be further promoted. The joint statement is a transformation of the outcomes of the G20 Hangzhou Summit 2016 on G20 Guiding Principles for Global Investment Policymaking. Negotiations on that topic were co-sponsored at the WTO in 2017, and Chile is the current coordinator of the negotiations. The participants have reached a preliminary consensus on the agreement framework and main rules. They stressed in a statement that they will continue to adhere to the development orientation and advance the negotiations based on the existing negotiation text. The text-based negotiation is expected to conclude before the end of 2022, and ultimately the multilateral investment facilitation agreement will be inked.

The expected multilateral investment facilitation agreement will create a more transparent, stable and predictable environment for global investment, promote global investment and trade development, and provide useful references for negotiations and reforms regarding WTO in other fields.

2. Domestic regulation of service trade

In December 2021, 67 WTO members, including China and the United States, jointly released the Declaration on the Conclusion of Negotiations on Services Domestic Regulations, announcing that they reached agreement on the Reference Paper on Services Domestic Regulations and that all participants will complete their respective formal approval work within one year. The agreement is the first plurilateral negotiation outcome based on the relevant joint statements and initiatives of the Buenos Aires Ministerial Conference in December 2017. It is a key outcome of the development and innovation of international service trade regulatory rules, covering 90% of the world's total volume of service trade. The document will help businesses around the world save around $150 billion in annual costs, and the agreement is expected to attract more economies to join it, increasing its representation and multilateralism.

3. Trade and Environmental sustainability

The WTO members actively integrate environmental sustainability into the multilateral trade agenda. In December 2021, co-sponsors of the Trade and Environmental Sustainability Structured Discussion Initiative (TESSD), the Informal Dialogue on Plastics Pollution and Environmentally Sustainable Plastics Trade (IDP), and the Fossil Fuel Subsidy Reform (FFSR) initiatives issued three ministerial statements simultaneously, marking achievements in pushing international trade to help address global environmental challenges.

4. Transparency

Disclosure and notification of trade-related information by WTO members in accordance with the rules of transparency is an important benchmark for monitoring whether they fulfil their obligations and keep disciplines, and it is also necessary factual evidence for the WTO to adjudicate trade disputes.

As normative procedural proposals, the joint statement released by the US, EU, and Japan after their trilateral meeting of trade ministers in 2020 may become the text of basic rules for the discussion of the issue of transparency, and may be elevated to multilateral rules if approved by other WTO members. The proposal by India and South Africa in 2019 is a position paper representing the views of developing countries, which clearly demonstrates interests and demands of those countries regarding WTO transparency rules. China's Proposal on WTO Reform, submitted in 2019, provides a useful reference for solving the problem of insufficient capacity of developing members, and seeks a balance between safeguarding the interests of developing members and promoting the necessary reform of transparency rules.

IV. Priorities for Future Global Economic Governance Reform

Currently, the great changes "unseen in a century" and the COVID-19 pandemic, have been intertwined, posing serious challenges to the recovery of the world economy, and global development has encountered serious setbacks. All parties should hold high the banner of multilateralism, firmly safeguard the multilateral trading system with the WTO at its core, and actively build a more just and reasonable global economic governance system and institutional environment to jointly cope with global economic challenges.

1. Leading the interaction and integration of regional and global governance to shape a mutually reinforcing positive relationship

In an international environment where economic globalization has encountered "adverse currents" and the global economic governance mechanism has stagnated, regional economic governance is an important starting point for enabling the high-quality development of global economic governance. Efforts should be made to further amplify the effect of regional trade and investment to make use of regional economic governance to promote global economic governance. First, the strength of regional economic and trade partners should be united, and the idea of mutual opening-up should be promoted to disintegrate the "clique multilateralism". Second, the core values of the non-discrimination and openness of the multilateral trading system should be effectively safeguarded, and it should be ensured that the new regional governance mechanism is consistent with the WTO rules in terms of macro development direction.

On the basis of integrating existing regional economic governance mechanisms, a model of "integration before expansion" should be adopted, so that regional experience can be drawn to facilitate global practice; in this way, the antagonism in various governance rules can be resolved and regional economic governance can become a beneficial supplement to, and vital component of, global economic governance. Third, the guiding role of Asia-Pacific regional cooperation should be brought out to promote the building of an open world economy. With the implementation of the RCEP, a favorable environment for economic and trade cooperation should be promoted, groundwork should be laid for the creation of rules and regulations, and an "Asia-Pacific solution" based on common regional interests should be explored, so that a strong impetus can be injected into world economic recovery and global economic governance reform.

2. Promoting South-South and North-South cooperation and Properly Handling Relationship between Developed and Developing economies

Properly dealing with the disputes of the traditional major powers and emerging powers that arise from conflicting interests are important parts of promoting the reform of the global economic governance system. The developed economies should work together with the emerging and developing economies to address global economic issues. On the one hand, the emerging and developing economies have been catching up with the developed economies and even surpass them in terms of their status in the global economic governance; therefore, they should bring out their respective strengths to actively participate in bridging the global economic governance deficit and make greater contributions in new industries, renewable energy, and ecological protection, among others. On the other hand, the North and the South should gradually converge in their targets of international trade and investment cooperation and bridge their distance. Through taking advantage of the inclusiveness of the new governance rules, they should gradually eliminate their differences arising from conflicting interests, take into account the economic development levels of countries at different stages of development, reach a basic consensus on important issues, and actively bridge their differences and reach a consensus, so that a new impetus can be injected into North-South cooperation.

3. Giving full play to the role of G20 and other multilateral platforms to improve the global economic governance system and rules

The major economies are still the main providers of global and regional public goods, and their willingness and ability to provide global public goods have the most profound impact on global governance. Therefore, it is urgent to use the core multilateral economic governance platforms to mediate the relationship between the major economies in the system. First, the role of the G20 as a core platform for global economic governance should be fully brought out and efforts should be ensuring the G20 summits, ministerial conferences and other supporting meetings achieve more results. Second, the cooperation benefits of multilateral mechanisms involving emerging economies, such as BRICS, should be brought out; the BRICS spirit of openness, inclusiveness, and win-win cooperation should be promoted; the BRICS+ mechanism and other mechanism innovations should be fully utilized, so that mutual understanding and trust among different parties can be promoted and progressive forces can join hands to form a stronger force to expand the cooperation and solve the fundamental problem of peace, development, governance and trust deficits.

4. Firmly upholding the core values of the multilateral trading system and actively promoting WTO reform

All parties should consistently and firmly uphold the multilateral trading system and maintain its status as the main channel in the process of global trade liberalization and facilitation. They should support the development of WTO reform in the right direction, the inclusive development of the multilateral trading system, and the legitimate rights and interests of developing members. They should uphold the core values of the multilateral trading system, such as non-discrimination and openness, follow a consensus-based decision-making mechanism, and jointly determine the specific issues, work agenda, and final outcomes of reforms on the basis of mutual respect, equal-footed dialogue and participation by all parties. Priority should be given to key issues that threaten the survival of the WTO, the problem of fairness of trade rules should be resolved in response to the needs of the times, special and differential treatment for developing members should be ensured, and the respective development models of WTO members should be respected.

Chapter 6   New trends of RCEP, CPTPP and other RTAs

Despite economic globalization encountering headwinds, regional trade agreements have still been advancing in recent years. At present, the development of regional economic and trade cooperation is faced with both new opportunities and new challenges, and promoting the realization of a comprehensive, open and high-level free trade area in the Asia-Pacific region which remains an important part of safeguarding and promoting an inclusive and open global trade order.

I. World Openness Being Led by Regional Economic and Trade Cooperation

1. Accelerated regional economic and trade cooperation against the backdrop of globalization encountering headwinds

In recent years, economic and trade frictions between China and the United States, the COVID-19 pandemic and the Ukraine crisis have put economic globalization under a more severe test. The instability of global industrial and supply chains has increased, and the global supply chain has flown back to Europe, North America, East Asia, Southeast Asia and other regions, promoting the booming development of regional trade and investment cooperation. From 2018 to June 2022, the number of trade agreements in goods, trade agreements in services and newly established trade agreements notified to the WTO was 62, 41 and 5, respectively, and a total of 63 newly established regional trade agreements under implementation were notified to the WTO. North America, the European Union and Asia have all launched trade agreements with regional influence, such as the US-Mexico-

Canada Agreement (USMCA), the UK-EU Trade and Cooperation Agreement, the Regional Comprehensive Economic Partnership (RCEP) and the Comprehensive and Progressive Trans-Pacific Partnership (CPTPP).

Table 6.1   New FTAs involving China, the US, the EU and Japan that have taken into force in the past five years

China	US	EU	Japan
• RCEP(Jan. 2022) • China-Cambodia (Jan. 2022) • China-Mauritius (Jan. 2021) • China-Georgia(Jan. 2018)	• USMCA(Jan. 2020	• EU-UK(Jan. 2021) • EU-Vietnam(Aug. 2020) • EU-Singapore (Nov. 2019) • EU-Japan(Feb. 2019) • EU-Canada(Sept. 2017)	• RCEP(Jan. 2022) • UK-Japan(Jan. 2021) • EU-Japan(Feb. 2019) • CPTPP(Dec. 2018)

Source: WTO RTA Database.

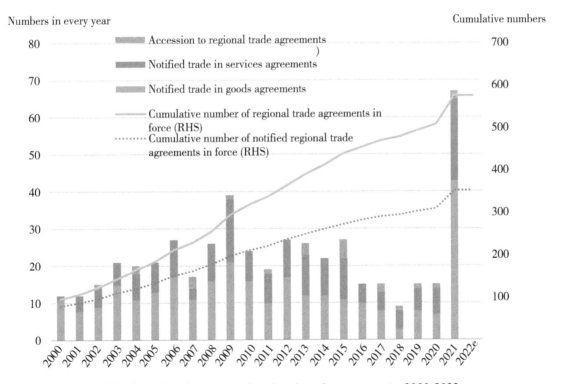

Fig. 6.1   Developments of regional trade agreements, 2000-2022

Source: based on relevant WTO data

2. Ever-strengthening of RTAs in depth

The new generation of regional trade agreements (RTAs) has been increasingly strengthened in depth. The Deep Trade Agreements (DTAs) cover not only trade but also other policy areas, such as investment and labor mobility, and the protection of intellectual property rights and the environment. These agreements are still called trade agreements, but their goal goes beyond traditional trade agreements and aims to promote freer movement of goods, services, capital and people across borders. DTAs are of crucial significance to economic development, in that trade and investment regimes determine the degree of economic integration, competition rules affect the efficiency of economic operations, intellectual property rules play an important role in promoting innovation, the environmental and labor rules help promote environmental and social development, and digital economic rules promote new technologies. In the process of deep integration, some rules involve the distribution of interests between economies, such as limiting the speed at which competitors can catch up by setting excessive intellectual property protection requirements. In the process of pursuing deep integration, regional trade agreements need to build an open, inclusive and balanced system of rules.

II. RCEP Promotes Economic Openness and Integration in Asia-Pacific

The Regional Comprehensive Economic Partnership (RCEP) is a comprehensive, modern, high-quality and mutually beneficial free trade agreement reached by 15 countries in the Asia-Pacific region. The RCEP has established a new regional governance mechanism model for global openness and inclusiveness, and all RCEP members have been actively promoting its implementation, demonstrating the goodwill of all countries to deepen economic cooperation in the region in the context of a complex and volatile world economy. The implementation of the agreement will help all parties boost confidence in fighting the pandemic and recovering the economy, promote the steady development of industrial and supply chains in the Asia-Pacific region, and inject new impetus into the building of an open world economy.

1. RCEP helps promote economic and trade growth in Asia-Pacific and beyond

At a time when the global economy is facing several destabilizing factors such as the impact of the pandemic and power games among major countries, the implementation of the RCEP will help stabilize global economic cooperation, raise market expectations and lead the process of global recovery. The RCEP covers about one-third of the world's total economy, population and trade, making it the largest regional trade agreement in the world. According to the basic forecast data of the IMF, the RCEP, the USMCA, the EU and the CPTPP, the four major global regional economic cooperation mechanisms, accounted for 30.5%, 27.6%, 18% and 12.6% of global GDP in 2021, respectively. The RCEP will leverage the effects of scale, competition, value chain integration and institutional coordination brought about by deep regional integration.

Since the implementation of the RCEP on Jan 1, 2022, policy dividends have become increasingly evident. According to the data of the China Council for the Promotion of International Trade (CCPIT), in the first seven months of 2022, the value of certificates of origin within the CCPIT system totalled $233.31 billion, up 23.7% year-on-year, among which the issuance of the RCEP certificates of origin has become a new growth point. In the first seven months, 70,200 RCEP certificates of origin were issued, with the value of visas amounting to $3.432 billion and the number of certified enterprises exceeding 15,000, and it is estimated that China's export products have been exempted from customs duties in RCEP member countries by about $52 million. From January to June 2022, China's import and export with RCEP members totalled 6.04 trillion yuan, up 5.6% year-on-year, accounting for 30.5% of China's total import and export value. From January to July 2022, China's trade with ASEAN countries reached $544.9 billion, up 13.1% year-on-year, accounting for 15% of China's total foreign trade. Of the total value, China's exports to ASEAN countries reached $316.4 billion, up 19.1% year-on-year, and the imports reached $228.5 billion, up 6% year-on-year, with a trade surplus accounting for $87.9 billion on China's part, an increase of 76.4%. The top three ASEAN countries in terms of total trade with China are Vietnam, Malaysia and Indonesia. From January to July 2022, South Korea was China's fourth largest trading partner, with a total trade volume reaching $214.5 billion, up 8.9% year-on-year, while China's trade with New Zealand reached $15.2 billion, up 7.7% year-on-year.

The implementation of the RCEP has benefited all member states. Thailand's trade with RCEP partners totalled more than $169.04 billion in January-June 2022, up 13%

from the same period last year. Of the total value, Thailand's exports reached $78.17 billion, up by 9% year-on-year, with the main export markets being the ASEAN, China, Japan and South Korea, and Thailand's imports rose 14% year-on-year. In the first quarter of 2022, Vietnam's trade with China, Japan, South Korea and other ASEAN countries grew by more than 10%, while Japan's trade with RCEP partners totalled nearly $200 billion, accounting for 47.6% of Japan's total foreign trade, up 11.5%. Since the RCEP became effective on Feb 1, 2022, South Korea's exports rose 18.2% year-on-year to $63.48 billion in March, the biggest increase since the country began collecting trade statistics in 1956.

2. RCEP helps promote industrial integration and upgrading in the Asia-Pacific

The RCEP will promote industrial integration and upgrading in the Asia-Pacific region and enhance the stability and security of the region's industrial chain. The economic structures of RCEP member countries are highly complementary, and the region has complete production factors including labor, capital, land, knowledge, technology, management and data. The RCEP's more facilitated trade and investment arrangements will help promote the flow of all kinds of factors of production and people within the region, improve the efficiency of enterprise production, promote deep industrial chain integration between member countries, form a network of production, consumption and supply chains with complementary advantages and inclusive development with Asia at the core, and promote the coordinated development of regional economies.

Box 6-1   Rules of Origin: Cumulation

The RCEP adopts the cumulation provision in rules of origin, under which all the materials of other member countries used by enterprises of RCEP member countries in the production process can be regarded as the materials of origin. This rule can increase the proportion of the components of origin value cumulatively, and make it easier for export commodities of member countries to obtain the RCEP's qualification of origin and reach the threshold of enjoying tariff preferences. The products that eventually enjoy zero tariffs in overall goods trade will exceed 90%.

From January to June 2022, many enterprises in major foreign trade provinces have fully benefited from the RCEP's entry into force, including the regional rules of origin accumulation. In Zhejiang, 5,190 preferential certificates of origin were issued in the first month after the RCEP came into effect on January 1, 2022, with a value of more than $240 million and a tariff reduction of more than RMB 13 million yuan for related enterprises. From January to April, the RCEP brought an import and export tax preference of more than RMB 40 million yuan for Zhejiang's enterprises, and Zhejiang's import and export to other RCEP member countries increased by 10.5% year-on-year.

3. RCEP helps promote the coordination of economic and trade rules and institutions in the Asia-Pacific

By setting clear and transparent rules and procedures, the RCEP provides an institutional system for economic and trade cooperation among members to improve supply chain efficiency. It has promoted greater openness in such areas as tariff cuts and service liberalization and introduced a negative list model in the investment sector. The RCEP has expanded many areas of the existing 10+1 FTA rules, and, about high-standard international trade and economic rules, formulated provisions that are in line with regional characteristics on such issues as intellectual property rights, e-commerce, trade remedies, competition and government procurement. These rules apply to all member countries in a unified manner, which will help increase confidence and policy certainty in conducting business activities in the region, enhance the region's overall competitiveness, make the region a more attractive destination for international trade and investment, and provide long-term institutional guarantees for the economic development of all member countries.

Box 6-2   The Chinese Government promotes the high-quality implementation of RCEP rules

In January 2022, the Ministry of Commerce and five other government departments jointly issued the Guidelines on High-quality Implementation of the RCEP, aiming to promote deeper reform through high-quality implementation of the RCEP and a higher level of opening-up.

Under the Guidelines, China will closely align RCEP development opportunities with local development strategies to promote high-quality economic development; guide and encourage enterprises to take the RCEP's implementation as an opportunity to further upgrade trade and investment, expand international cooperation, raise quality standards, promote industrial upgrading, and enhance their competitiveness in the international market. As a highland of institutional opening-up, various pilot free trade zones in China can play a leading role in the high-quality implementation of the RCEP.

4. RCEP helps shape a new mechanism for open and inclusive regional governance

The RCEP has been built as a platform for regional economic and trade cooperation that reflects the aspiration and development level of Asia-Pacific economies. RCEP members have relatively large differences in economic development stages, which include both high-income countries, middle-income countries and low- and middle-income countries. To serve the interests of member states to the greatest extent, the RCEP fully takes into account the development stage and level of domestic reform of each economy and emphasizes the "development" orientation in the design of rules, which has provided a template for building an international economic and trade cooperation mechanism reflecting development diversity and will help promote the innovative development of the multilateral trading system, enhance the effectiveness of multilateral cooperation and advance open and inclusive multilateralism. The RCEP also has two special chapters on small and medium-sized enterprises (Chapter 14) and economic and technical cooperation (Chapter 15), respectively, proposing to promote information sharing and cooperation and enhance the ability of SMEs to take advantage of and benefit from the RCEP and share its fruits.

III. CPTPP Promotes A New Round of Trade Liberalization

The Comprehensive and Progressive Trans-Pacific Partnership Agreement (CPTPP), a high-standard free trade agreements reached by 11 countries in Asia-Pacific, is currently in force for eight members: Australia, Canada, Japan, Mexico, New Zealand, Singapore, Vietnam and Peru. The full implementation of the CPTPP will significantly improve the well-being of all CPTPP members, promote regional economic integration in the Asia-Pacific region, and facilitate a higher level of trade and investment liberalization on a global scale.

1.Pursing high standards of economic and trade rules

Based on the text of the Trans-Pacific Partnership (TPP), the CPTPP retains most of TPP's provisions. The final agreement, which includes 30 Chapters, not only covers traditional requirements such as tariff reduction and trade facilitation measures but also sets higher standards on government procurement, state-owned enterprises and designated monopolies, intellectual property rights, labor and the environment. Its core Chapters can be divided into four categories: management of trade in goods, the openness of services and investment, horizontal issues, and capacity building.

Table 6.2 CPTPP text terms: Classification and main features

Categories	Chapters	New features
Trade in goods liberalization and facilitation measures	National treatment and market access for goods Rules of origin and origin procedure Textile and apparel goods Customs Procedures and Facilitation of Trade Trade remedies Sanitary and phytosanitary measures Technical barriers to trade	Rapid and substantial reduction of tariff barriers, immediate elimination of most tariffs among existing members, and eventual elimination of tariffs on about 99% of tariff items. Improving trade facilitation and reducing export costs; promoting the integration of value chains and supply chains within the region.
Market access for investment and services	Investment Cross-border trade in services Financial services Temporary entry for business persons Telecommunications Electronic commerce Government procurement	The negative list model, the inclusion of new provisions for investor-host dispute settlement (ISDS), new rules on the cross-border flow of telecommunications, finance, source code, and business information. In the area of digital trade, the CPTPP has not shelved any digital trade commitments.
Horizontal issues (Behind-the-Border Measures)	Competition policy State-owned enterprises and designated monopolies Intellectual property Labor Environment	Creating a transparent and level playing field; strengthening intellectual property protection in areas such as Internet services and pharmaceuticals; strict labor protection standards and enforceable environmental protection commitment mechanisms.
Capacity building and development	Cooperation and capacity building Competitiveness and business facilitation Development Small and medium-sized enterprises Regulatory coherence Transparency and anti-corruption	Promoting educational, cultural, and gender equity, encouraging members to adopt good regulatory practices and improve policy consistency and transparency among members; establishing anti-corruption and anti-bribery standards.

Source: based on CPTPP text terms.

2. Promoting high-quality economic growth

According to the theory of regional economic integration, the implementation of regional trade agreements can bring static and dynamic benefits to members, such as trade creation, increasing returns to scale, strengthening market competition, stimulating investment, and driving economic growth. The 11 CPTPP member countries have pledged to implement zero tariffs on more than 80% of their products on average. Among them, Canada, Australia, New Zealand, Singapore, Brunei, and Chile have committed to zero tariffs on more than 90% of their products. The full implementation of the CPTPP will greatly improve the well-being of all CPTPP members, promote high-quality economic development in Asia-Pacific, and further consolidate the region's position as the engine of global economic growth.

3. Leading high-level openness and development

The high-standard rules represented by the CPTPP will help further enhance trade and investment liberalization and facilitation in Asia-Pacific and beyond, vigorously promote high-level market openness in the region and even the world as a whole, and promote structural reform and sustainable and inclusive development. For example, in the field of intellectual property, the CPTPP provides "comprehensive and ultra-high standard" intellectual property rules, and strengthens the protection and law enforcement of drugs, computers, patents, and copyrights, which is conducive to further protecting innovation subjects, stimulating innovation vitality and promoting innovation development. In the field of the digital economy, the CPTPP sets high standards in open networks, network access and use, source code, personal information protection, and localization of computing facilities, which will play a guiding and promoting role in the development of global digital trade, digital technology, and the digital economy.

IV. Regional Economic and Trade Cooperation should Be Inclusive and Open

The development of regional economic and trade cooperation faces both new opportunities and new challenges. As an important carrier of international economic cooperation besides multilateral agreements, regional trade agreements are conducive to promoting regional economic integration and maintaining an inclusive and open global economic and trade order.

1. Regional economic cooperation should be free from the interference of non-economic factors

The nature, principles, and content of regional economic and trade cooperation are being systematically adjusted. With the in-depth development of global value chains, cooperation among economies has entered the stage of intra-product cooperation, and policy coordination has change from border policies, such as tariff and non-tariff barriers, to domestic policy coordination among economies. With the intensification of competition among major powers, "maintain national security" has been used by some countries as a strategic tool for their foreign economic policies and their reconstruction of international economic order. Some economies also emphasize the so-called differences in values in an attempt to build a geopolitical and economic alliance based on values.

Regional trade agreements are an important part of international trade rules. According to Article 24 of the General Agreement on Tariffs and Trade (GATT) and relevant provisions of the WTO, WTO members need to reach regional trade agreements under certain conditions. At present, it is necessary to strengthen the role of regional trade agreements in promoting the multilateral trading system, building an open and inclusive trading system, and avoiding excessive interference of political factors in the world economy.

2. Regional economic cooperation should be more open and inclusive

Regional trade agreements include two dimensions: member countries and rule systems. From the perspective of member countries, the overlapping of different FTAs in the same region, as well as artificial exclusionary design, will increase the complexity of the regional economy. From the perspective of the rule system, the "spaghetti bowl" phenomenon of multiple free trade agreements in a region causes the overlapping of economic and trade rules, which makes it difficult to promote their integration and coordination.

Regional cooperation needs to be more inclusive and accommodate the interests of all parties. All parties need to enhance consensus and mutual trust in regional economic cooperation. Facing such new issues as digital economy and trade, supply chain flexibility, export controls, labor standards, decarbonization and clean energy, taxation and anti-corruption, and infrastructure, all countries should strengthen communication and coordination, promote the formation of accommodative market operation rules, improve economic efficiency, and at the same time balance the interests of all parties and reduce exclusionary mechanisms or rule systems.

3. Regional trade agreements should be an important vehicle for promoting global openness and cooperation

Against the backdrop of rising anti-globalization and trade protectionism, promoting the construction of regional trade agreements is an important way to reform the international trading system. As a major platform for regional opening-up, regional trade agreements have been highly valued by major economies as important carriers of international economic cooperation. All parties should make active use of free trade agreements and other platform mechanisms to promote diversified development of the international economic and trade governance system and uphold and advance an inclusive and open global economic and trade order.

Chapter 7   Global Manufacturing Landscape and Industy and Supply Chain Resilience

The development of the manufacturing industry has an important bearing on the world economy. Since World War II, the global manufacturing industry has undergone many transfers of locations to form a landscape where the global industry and supply chains center around the "three major manufacturing hubs" of China, Germany, and the United States. At present, the industry and supply chains of the global manufacturing industry are increasingly regionalized, localized, diversified, and digitized, due to factors, such as reverse globalization, intensified trade protectionism, the COVID-19 pandemic, and the Ukrainian crisis.

I. The Three Major Manufacturing Hubs

Since the Industrial Revolution in the 19th century, the center of the global manufacturing industry has been transferred from the United Kingdom and the United States to Japan and Germany, then to the "Four Little Dragons" in Asia, and then to China. Thus three major supply chain networks have taken shape, i.e. the North American supply chain with the United States at the core, the European supply chain with Germany at the core, and the Asian supply chain with China, Japan, and South Korea at the core.

1. The "three manufacturing hubs" have given way to Asian dominance in manufacturing

The most significant change in the global manufacturing industry in recent years is that the power and role of developing countries have grown enormously, while the comparative advantage of developed countries has begun to diminish. This is embodied in the rising proportion of manufacturing value added (MVA) of East Asia and the Pacific region in the world's total, from 31.9% in 2007 to 46.5% in 2021, up 14.6 percentage points, while that of Europe and Central Asia dropped from 33.6% to 21.8%. The number for North America dropped from 21.4% in 2007 to 17.5% in 2014, and then rose to 18.4% in 2020 (See Fig. 7.1).

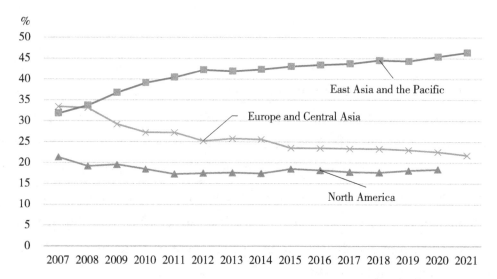

Fig. 7.1   MVA of major regions in the world's total, 2007-2021
Source: World Bank.

2. The "three manufacturing hubs" have their distinctive characteristics and advantages

The global manufacturing industry revolves around the United States, Germany, China, Japan, and South Korea, which have formed three hubs of industry and supply chains through cooperation with their neighboring countries (see Fig. 7.2).

One is the North American manufacturing hub, with the United States at the core, and Canada and Mexico at the perimeters. The United States, as one of the most developed industrial countries in the world, registered an MVA of $2.56 trillion, accounting for 11.1% of its GDP and 15.7% of the world's total MVA, ranking second in the world. Regional manufacturing clusters of steel, automobile, aviation, petroleum, computer, and chip, among other fields, have taken shape in the northeast, south, and Pacific coast of the United States. Besides, the United States has built close

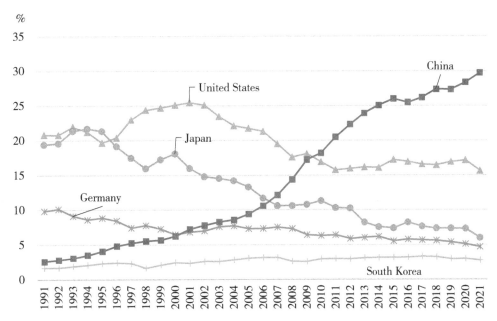

Fig. 7.2   MVA of the United States, Germany, China, Japan, and South Korea in the world's total, 1991-2021

Source: World Bank.

partnerships with Canada and Mexico in industry and supply chains. Statistics from the US Bureau of Economic Analysis show that the United States' imports of goods from Canada and Mexico account for about 1/4 of its total imports, and its exports to Canada and Mexico account for 1/3 of its total exports (see Fig. 7.3).

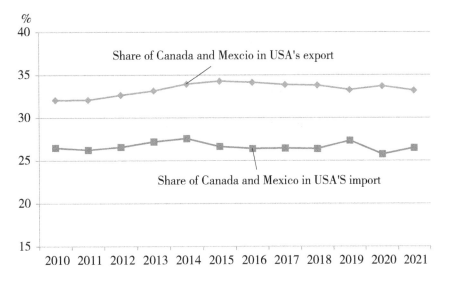

Fig. 7.3   Share of Canada and Mexico in USA's total trade, 2010-2021

Source: US Bureau of Economic Analysis.

The second is the European manufacturing hub, with Germany at the core, and France and the UK at the perimeter. The European manufacturing hub is where the modern industrial revolutions took place. With a long manufacturing history, it also has a large number of small and medium-sized enterprises (SMEs), which have injected vitality into the development of European manufacturing. In 2021, Germany's MVA accounted for 4.7% of the world's total, ranking fourth in the world. The share of France and the UK was 1.5% and 1.7%, respectively. Meanwhile, the MVA of the EU accounted for 15.6% of the world's total, roughly the same as that of the United States.

The third is the Asian manufacturing hub, with China, Japan, and South Korea at the core, and Southeast Asia, South Asia, and other countries at the perimeter. Thanks to the demographic dividend, a rapidly growing consumer market, and economic vitality, the Asian manufacturing hub has built the most complete industry chains in the world and is developing toward mid-to-high-end manufacturing. As for certain manufacturing technologies, it has even gained a competitive advantage over Europe and the United States. Since China joined the WTO in 2001, the proportion of China's MVA in the world's total has been growing steadily to surpass Germany in 2001, Japan in 2007, and the United States in 2010. By far, China has been the world's largest manufacturer for 12 consecutive years. In 2021, China's MVA reached 31.4 trillion yuan, accounting for 29.8% of the world's total, up from 18.2% in 2010. The MVA of Japan and South Korea accounted for about 7.8% and 3.0% of the world's total, respectively, making the two countries an important presence in the industry and supply chains of Asian manufacturing. Meanwhile, in Southeast Asia, Vietnam leverages its labor-cost advantage to actively undertake industrial transfers. As a result, its MVA grew from $15.01 billion in 2010 to $48.16 billion in 2021, though accounting for merely 0.3 % of the world's total. In South Asia, the MVA of India also grew from $285.35 billion in 2010 to $446.5 billion in 2021, accounting for roughly 2.7% of the world's total (see Fig. 7.4).

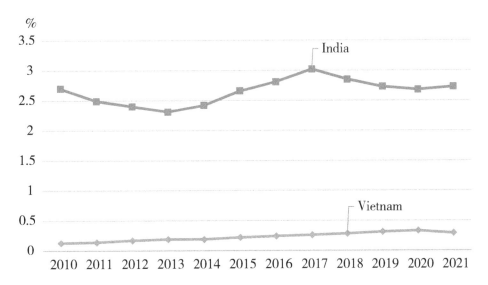

Fig. 7.4   MVA of Vietnam and India in the world's total, 2010-2021

Source: World Bank.

3. Global manufacturing has highly interdependent industry and supply chains

In the age of economic globalization, the manufacturing industry, which has a direct bearing on the world economy, has inseparable and highly interdependent industry and supply chains. This is mainly manifested in two aspects.

Firstly, more than 60% of the global trade in manufactured goods is done in Europe and Asia. From 2010 to 2021, the manufactured goods exports of East Asia and the Pacific, Europe and Central Asia, and North America accounted for a decreasing proportion of the world's total, down from 28.8%, 43.2%, and 12.7% in 2010 to 26.9%, 39.5%, and 11.8%, respectively, in 2021. However, the combined proportions of East Asia and the Pacific and Europe and Central Asia remained above 60% (see Fig. 7.5).

Secondly, the global trade in intermediate goods develops robustly. Trade in intermediates is one of the key indicators of the robustness of the global supply chain of manufacturing. McKinsey's report shows that in 1993, the global trade in intermediates accounted for about 1/4 of the global trade, yet now this proportion has exceeded 2/3. The total trade in intermediates of the top five countries accounts for more than 1/3 of the world's total. The WTO's quarterly report on global intermediate exports shows that global intermediate product exports maintained a 20%+ growth in each quarter of 2021, and the trade in intermediates of major exporting countries exceeded the levels before the COVID-19 outbreak.[①]

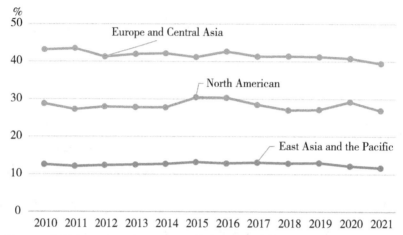

Fig. 7.5   Shares of three regions in the world's total manufactured goods exports, 2010-2021
Source: World Bank.

II. The Global Industry and Supply Chains Reshaped

The global manufacturing industry is facing a growing tendency of de-globalization and protectionism, the reformulation of international economic and trade rules, the efforts of developed countries to relocate industry chains back to their homelands, a new round of technological revolution, and the pursuit of a balance between efficiency and security by multinationals. As a result, the industry and supply chains tend to be more regional, local, diversified, and digitized.

1. Reformulation of international economic and trade rules to drive the regionalization and nearshoring of supply chains

Since the 2008 global financial crisis, economic globalization has entered a period of slowdown, divergence, and reformulation. As regional free trade agreements (FTAs), such as the Regional Comprehensive Economic Partnership (RCEP), the Comprehensive and Progressive Trans-Pacific Partnership (CPTPP), and the United States-Mexico-Canada Agreement (USMCA), were signed and implemented, intra-regional economic and trade cooperation is strengthening. These FTAs not only

---

① WTO (2022). Export of intermediate goods see continued growth in the fourth quarter of 2021. May 22. https://www.wto.org/english/news_e/news22_e/stat_25may22_e.htm.

promote the development of intra-regional trade and investment by reducing tariffs down to the point of zero tariffs but also include a series of high-standard and exclusive measures as barriers to trade and investment, thus forming exclusive supply chain alliances. For example, regarding the rules of origin, USMCA and CPTPP have set the "yarn forward" principle for textile and apparel products. CPTPP requires that the weight of non-originating fibers and yarns must not exceed 10% of that of the raw material components, rather than 10% of the total weight of the goods as stipulated in general trade agreements. The USMCA increased the regional value content for zero-tariff automobiles and their parts from 62.5% to 75%.[①] This regulation will urge key production links to relocate to the major production bases in North America, Europe, and Asia, thus making each of the three major networks more tightly knitted within.

2. The intensified game between China and the United States affects the supply chain landscape

The COVID-19 pandemic has intensified the game between China and the United States, leading the market logic, global governance, and trade rules to be replaced by long-arm jurisdiction and state interventionism, as containing China has become a key strategy of the United States. The United States has not only initiated challenges in the fields of economy, trade, high-tech, and manufacturing but also built de-Sinicized industry and supply chains by urging the American companies in China to return to their homeland and exerting ideological pressures. The game between China and the United States will lead to the reshaping of the global economic and political landscape, which in turn will promote the reconfiguration of the global manufacturing industry and supply chains.

a. The United States continues to upgrade its supply chain security strategy by moving US manufacturers back to their homeland

Manufacturing has always been a key area in the strategic game between China and the United States. In this context, the industry and supply chains have become the focal point that attracts the attention of both countries. The United States has always emphasized that manufacturing supply chain security has a bearing on national

---

①   *China Economic Times*, China should speed up its adaptation to the new international economic and trade rules, July 27, 2020, https://jjsb.cet.com.cn/show_514954.html.

strategic security. To safeguard the economy, people's livelihood, and national security, the United States must ensure sufficient supply and flexibility of key products that cannot be produced domestically. In 2018, the United States began to issue a series of administrative decrees and policies which comprehensively assess its industry and supply chain security, dependence on foreign countries, and specific responses in manufacturing and defense industries, as part of an effort to cope with the fierce international competition. Since the COVID-19 outbreak in 2020, the US's supply chain security strategy has been upgraded continuously to cope with China's growing influence.

Box 7-1　United States initiatives related to global supply chains in recent years

In May 2018, the US Department of Defense Office of Industrial Policy joined hands with multiple departments to issue the report "Assessing and Strengthening the Manufacturing and Defense Industrial Base and Supply Chain Resiliency of the United States". Key findings of the report include: the United States currently has a high degree of dependence on competitor countries; many United States sectors are still moving critical capabilities overseas to seek competitive prices and to penetrate foreign markets.

In June 2019, the US Department of Commerce released a report titled "A Federal Strategy to Ensure Secure and Reliable Supplies of Critical Minerals", which finds that the United States is heavily dependent on foreign sources of critical minerals and foreign supply chains. Specifically, the United States is import-reliant (imports are greater than 50 percent of annual consumption) for 31 of the 35 minerals designated as critical by the Department of the Interior. The United States does not have any domestic production and relies completely on imports to supply its demand for 14 critical minerals.

In January 2021, the US Department of Commerce issued the Executive Order: Securing the Information and Communications Technology and Services Supply Chain, which proposes the establishment and improvement of processes and procedures "for identifying, assessing, and processing information and communications technologies or services designed, developed, manufactured, or supplied by persons owned by, controlled by, or subject to the jurisdiction or direction of a foreign adversary".

In February 2021, US President Biden signed the "US Supply Chain Executive Order", which includes a supply chain risk review and industry and supply chain assessment, intending to strengthen the flexibility, diversity, and security of the US supply chains, and recover and revitalize the country's manufacturing capabilities.

In June 2021, the US Senate passed the "United States Innovation and Competition Act of 2021", which specifies that the United States will promote the development of US semiconductors, microchips, telecommunications equipment, artificial intelligence, and other fields, in an effort to tackle the increasingly fierce international competition, especially China's growing influence, and to reduce dependence on Chinese companies for production.

In June 2021, the US government released a new report titled "Building Resilient Supply Chains, Revitalizing American Manufacturing", which proposes that for the supply chain of critical products, the United States should not only invest in domestic R&D and production, and cultivate high-skilled workers, but establish a US Trade Representative-led trade strike force to identify unfair foreign trade practices that have eroded US critical supply chains and make amends through tariff and other trade-related measures.

In June 2022, the US Congressional Research Service submitted to Congress the "Summary of Selected Biden Administration Actions on Supply Chains", which presents a series of executive orders aimed at addressing supply chain problems and other measures taken to reduce supply chain disruptions.

b. Excluding China from the industry and supply chains of key industries by establishing alliances

To prevent the rise of key Chinese manufacturing industries, such as chips, and to maintain its advantages in the high-tech industry chains, the United States and other countries intend to exclude China by establishing key industrial alliances. In May 2021, the United States proposed to forge the Semiconductors in America Coalition (SIAC) by incorporating a total of 64 semiconductor companies from Europe, Japan, South Korea, Chinese Taipei, and other regions. Mainland Chinese companies were excluded. In February 2022, the US House of Representatives passed the America COMPETES Act of 2022, which pledges to provide substantive support for chip manufacturing, and semiconductor production. Specific measures include the creation of a chip fund, the allocation of $52 billion to encourage companies to invest in the semiconductor industry, and the authorization of $45 billion for improving US supply chains and strengthening manufacturing. In April 2022, the United States proposed to form the Chip4 Alliance with Japan, South Korea, and Chinese Taipei, to establish a new semiconductor supply chain to curb the development of the semiconductor industry in mainland China. It is foreseeable that the United States will launch more measures in an attempt to exclude mainland China from high-end chip manufacturing and supply. On August 9, 2022, Biden signed the Chip and Science Act, which pledges to provide a subsidy of $52.7 billion for US semiconductor R&D, manufacturing, and workforce development, but requires that any company receiving the subsidy must make chips on US soil. The United States has continued to set blockades on China's advanced technologies by calling on Western countries to form export control alliances in high-tech fields.

c. The United States attempts to reconstruct a global supply chain system with itself at the core, and promote the de-Sinicization in the manufacturing sector

Since the Biden administration came to power, it has made continued efforts to strengthen cooperation with its allies, such as Japan and South Korea, in the name of multilateralism. For example, in May 2022, the Indo-Pacific Economic Framework for Prosperity (IPEF) was launched, which was joined by the United States, Japan, Australia, South Korea, India, and other countries and regions. In terms of supply chain cooperation, the framework plans to establish an early warning system to enhance the traceability of key supply chain links, such as raw materials, semiconductors, key minerals, and clean energy technologies. It also pledges to cooperate with participating countries to promote a diversified production layout. Diversification is, in essence, "limited globalization", that is, avoiding excessive dependence on specific countries for manufacturing. Each participating country had its strategic considerations for joining the framework, but there is also the possibility that the United States and its allies promote the de-Sinification of global supply chains through non-market-oriented means, such as political and economic bundling and direct subsidies. Besides, the complex and volatile world nowadays makes it increasingly difficult to separate economic and trade from broader national interest considerations, including national security. Therefore, the United States is trying to promote trade integration to reshape free trade values so that it can trade only with "countries it can count on". Therefore, the values and supply chain vulnerability may become considerations for developed countries to reconstruct the international trade landscape, which in turn will fundamentally impact the multilateral trading system and aggravate risks in global supply chains.

3. Developed and developing countries promote the localization and friend-shoring of supply chains

After the 2008 financial crisis, the global economy started to fall back to the real economy; developed countries started to implement the reindustrialization strategy; and major emerging economies vied to adopt preferential policies to improve the investment environment, thus triggering a new round of competition among countries in manufacturing.

On the one hand, developed economies, such as the US, the EU, and Japan have tried to revive their manufacturing industries in recent years by encouraging their manufacturers overseas to return to their homeland. The COVID-19 pandemic has shed light on the importance of supply chain security. Out of emergency security, basic security, economic development, and social stability considerations, developed countries have adopted legal regulations, economic subsidies, and political means to encourage domestic enterprises to increase investment in their home countries. For example, in the Strategic Competition Act of 2021, the United States explicitly proposed to appropriate $15,000,000 for each fiscal year from 2022 through 2027 to support supply chains to exit from China market and identify alternative markets for production or sourcing outside of China. The Japanese government allocated 220 billion yen in 2020 to encourage Japanese companies to return to Japan or transfer to other countries. In the Basic Policy on Economic and Fiscal Management and Reform issued in June 2021, the Japanese government proposed to focus on investing in strategic products, such as semiconductors, to rebuild the country's production system, and encourage enterprises to diversify and decentralize their production bases. These measures will, to a degree, change the regional layout of value chains and make them more local.

On the other hand, Southeast Asian and South Asian countries represented by Vietnam and India leveraged their cheap labor and investment policies to vigorously attract foreign investment and undertake international industrial transfers. These moves have led some foreign-funded enterprises in China to relocate to Vietnam, India, and other countries. Lately, Vietnam has become one of the major destinations for investment from multinationals thanks to its open market environment, superior geographical location, abundant and cheap labor resources, and multilateral and bilateral FTAs signed with other countries and regions. From 2012 to 2021, the amount of foreign capital utilized by Vietnam's manufacturing industry rose, albeit fluctuations, from $5.46 billion to $18.1 billion (see Fig. 7.6).

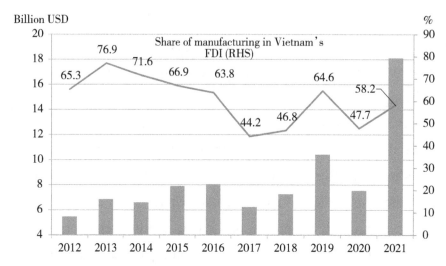

Fig. 7.6   FDI in Vietnam's manufacturing, 2012-2021

Source: Foreign Investment Agency, Ministry of Planning and Investment, Vietnam.

Moreover, Vietnam has a massive labor market -- people aged 15-64 account for about 70% of its population, and the labor costs are relatively low. In 2020, the average hourly wage in Vietnam was $2.99, while that in China was $6.50 (see Fig. 7.7). In addition, Vietnam introduced a series of tax exemptions and cuts to attract investment. These preferential policies did attract some multinationals to relocate from China to Vietnam.

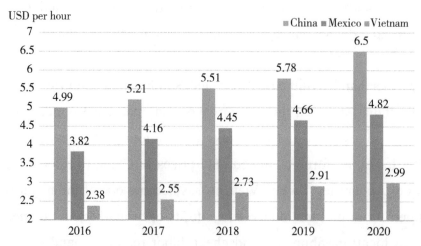

Fig. 7.7   Hourly labor costs in the manufacturing of China, Mexico and Vietnam, 2016-2020

Source: Statista.

Another example is India, which launched a series of policies such as "Made in India", "National Manufacturing Policy" and "Indian Skills" in the past five years, aiming to promote India as a global manufacturing hub. For example, India lowered the basic tax rate for newly established and operating manufacturers from October 1, 2019, to March 31, 2023, from 25% to 15%, to further attract international investment. Meanwhile, the import tariffs of mobile phones and their components were raised, so that their manufacturers had to build factories in India. These policies have urged some multinationals to transfer their supply chains from China to India, thus enabling the rapid rise of India's manufacturing industry. In the automobile industry, eight of the top ten Indian auto companies in the 2021-2022 fiscal year were foreign-owned companies, with Japan's Suzuki (43.65%) and South Korea's Hyundai (15.78%) accounting for nearly 60%. In the mobile phone industry, the top five mobile phone manufacturers in India in 2021 were all foreign-funded companies, of which 67% were Chinese ones.

4. Multinationals make strategic adjustments to diversify the global supply chain layout

As economic globalization proceeds, multinationals lead the internationalization of production through international investment. They play as organizers of the world's production to build global value, industry, and supply chains. Multinationals invest on a global scale, mainly in pursuit of maximized profits, lower costs, and higher efficiency. Recent years have seen the rise of trade protectionism, the impact of the COVID-19 pandemic, intensified geopolitical conflicts, and growing global supply chain risks. These factors, coupled with the pressure from the government of their home country, have forced multinationals to change the way they plan and obtain supply chains.

In the short term, the global layout of multinationals will not undergo substantial changes but may scale down their operations. Over the past few years, cross-border investment has not been as robust as it used to be. According to UNCTAD statistics, the size of global manufacturing FDI absorption is going downward, from $775.20 billion in 2018 to $535.48 billion in 2021, a decline of 30.9%. Its proportion in the world's total also dropped from 48.5% in 2017 to 38.6% in 2021 (see Fig. 7.8). The pandemic has seriously impacted the operations of most multinationals, whose profitability has plummeted. The COVID-19 pandemic has put the world economy in distress. As companies become more cautious in their global investment, cross-border investment activities will be subject to heightened pressures. Most multinationals choose to wait and see as they slow their pace of global investment, especially in large projects. Meanwhile, the headquarters of multinationals will pay more attention to cash and profitability. Some multinationals may suspend overseas businesses with uncertain prospects and speed up the divestiture of non-performing assets. Multinationals may, to a degree, shorten their global supply chains.

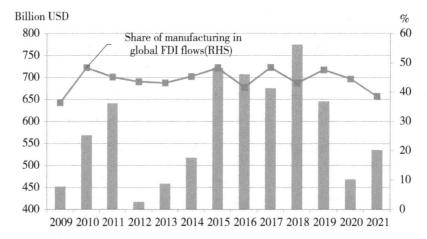

Fig. 7.8   FDI in global manufacturing, 2009-2021

Source: UNCTAD.

In the long run, multinationals will take the initiative to adjust the layout of industry and supply chains out of safety and efficiency considerations. Global supply chain disruptions caused by the pandemic have brought huge pressures on the production and operations of multinationals, making them feel the urgency of dispersing supply chain risks. Therefore, they start to exert stricter control over costs and efficiency and take the initiative to adjust the supply chain layout, in order to strike a balance between safety and efficiency. As such, the way in which the global supply chains are organized will undergo significant changes, while the global supply chain layout relying on the global free trade system and intra-product specialization will be deconstructed. Besides, in recent years, multinationals have been adjusting the layout of their supply chains, either actively or passively. In the context of economic globalization, multinationals take profit maximization as their utmost goal. That is why their interests are not always in line with those of their home country. When multinationals expand their overseas markets, there is also a need to cater to the demand of the home country's government in urging them to return. However, to maximize their interests, some multinationals may use alternative methods to achieve a balance between the two. As the international political landscape changes in the post-pandemic era and developed countries led by the United States reconstruct an independent and complete industrial system, multinationals may choose to diversify their supply chains. But to pursue maximized profits, they will not relocate the entire industry chains they invested in countries of high growth and high returns back to their home country or other countries.

5. The new round of technological revolution promotes the digitization and intelligence of supply chains

Along with the new technological revolution and industrial transformation, big data, the Internet of Things, artificial intelligence, and 3D printing are gradually penetrating into all aspects of the industry and supply chains, thus fundamentally changing the ways in which R&D and manufacturing and trade are done and industries are organized.

a. The technological revolution promotes the change in the mode of production and makes the industry and supply chains shorter and more intelligent

On the one hand, the combination of internet technology and manufacturing has made the R&D design, production, and sales management more segmented, the production more decentralized, the factories smaller, and the lead time significantly shorter, thereby shortening the industry and supply chains. For example, 3D printing technology will make local production possible. On the other hand, 4D printing technology, which is a combination of intelligent manufacturing, intelligent materials, and 3D printing, drives the transformation of the manufacturing industry from a mass-standardized production approach to an intelligent mass-customized one supported by the internet. As raw material procurement, product processing, and market sales will all be completed locally, dramatic changes will take place in the supply chain systems of companies.

b. The technological revolution makes it faster for machines to replace human labor, which may consolidate the division of labor in the global industry and supply chains

According to the International Federation of Robotics (IFR), the global robot sales in 2021 reached 486,800 units, a significant increase of 27% year-on-year, of which Asia and Australia registered the largest growth rate of 33%, totaling 354,500 units. The electronics industry (132,000 units) and the automotive industry (109,000 units) are the two industries with the greatest demand for industrial robots, followed by the metal and machinery industry (57,000 units), the plastics and chemical industry (22,500 units), and the food and beverage industry (15,300 units)[①]. The pandemic has made countries more willing to replace human labor with machines, as they hope to produce faster and more efficiently at lower costs. Compared with developing countries that lag behind economically, developed countries and emerging markets, such as China, have obvious advantages in technology and digital economy. The use of machines to replace human labor may change the past practice in which manufacturers tended to move to countries with lower labor costs. Meanwhile, data will become an important factor of production that lead to substantial changes in the factor endowments between different economies. Such changes will fundamentally affect the investment decisions of multinationals and prompt the industry and supply chains to tilt towards developed economies or developing countries with advantages in digital technology.

c. New products and services brought about by advanced technologies may affect the layout of the global industry and supply chains

The use of digital technology may change the products and services of certain sectors, generate new business forms or new products and services, and even affect the content and quantity of trade flows. For example, thanks to digital technology, new energy technology, and government subsidies, pure electric vehicles registered a sales amount of approximately 4.6 million units in 2021, a YoY increase of 220%, while the number for hybrid electric vehicles was approximately 3.1 million, a YoY increase of 33% only[②]. Going forward, the growing sales of electric vehicles may partially replace the trade volume of auto parts, and also inhibit the import of oil. This will have a greater impact on the imports, exports, and supply chains of related industries and countries or regions.

[①] Xinhua Finance, Global robot sales grew robustly in 2021, June 23, 2022, https://baijiahao. baidu.com/s?id=1736378027211376076&wfr=spider&for=pc.

[②] Changjiang Daily, Global sales of pure electric vehicles surpass that of hybrid vehicles for the first time in 2021, April 21, 2022, https://baijiahao.baidu.com/s?id=1730685652324221408&wfr=spider &for=pc.

III. Challenges and Opportunities Facing China's Manufacturing Industry

China's manufacturing industry has maintained steady growth and has been one of the centers of the global manufacturing industry chains and supply chains. With the accelerated adjustment of these chains, China's manufacturing will inevitably face great challenges. However, we can see that under the pandemic, global prices have risen, the trade structure has undergone major changes, and industrial chains and supply chains of many countries have shrunk. Only China's industrial chains and supply chains are relatively stable. At the same time, new competitive advantages of China's manufacturing are being fostered to be more deeply integrated into the global supply chain system. It is difficult to cut the global supply chain artificially.

1. Current situation of China's manufacturing industry

China's manufacturing is rather sound as a system. Its scale ranks first in the world, its status of export competitiveness and international division of labor are constantly improving, and its impact on the world's manufacturing chains is gradually increasing. China is moving from a big manufacturing country to a strong manufacturing power.

First, the structure of China's manufacturing is sound and its scale continues to grow steadily. China's manufacturing has 41 major categories, 207 medium categories and 666 small categories. It is the only country in the world that has all the industrial categories in the International Standard of Industrial Classification released by the United Nations. It has set up many industrial clusters with centralized product production, professional cooperation, and mature industrial chains. These industrial chains and supply chains have strong resilience. Most of China's industrial categories account for more than 30 percent of the world's production, including 90 percent of the world's personal computers, 80 percent of air conditioners, 75 percent of solar panels, 70 percent of mobile phones and 63 percent of shoes. More than 40 percent of the world's 500 major industrial products are contributed by China, which ranks first in the world. In the 21st century, added value of China's manufacturing has grown rapidly, gradually surpassing developed countries such as Japan, Germany and the United State. From 2004 to 2021, China's manufacturing added value grew 12.8 percent annually. In the past three years, China has withstood the test of the COVID-19 and the drastic changes in international environment by its strong capacity in manufacturing.

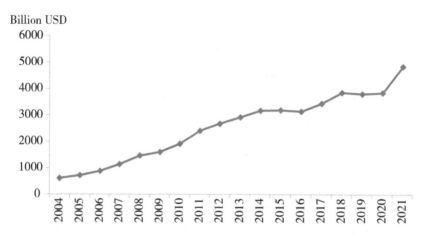

Fig. 7.9   Value added of China's manufacturing industry, 2004-2021

Source: World Bank.

Secondly, China is deeply integrated into global industrial chains and supply chains and highly dependent on each other. Along this process, China's economy is playing an increasingly important role in the global trade and production system. From 2003 to 2021, China's imports increased from $0.41 trillion to $2.69 trillion, accounting 11.9 percent to global imports from 4.4 percent; China's exports increased from $0.45 trillion to $3.36 trillion, accounting 15.1 percent to global exports from 4.7 percent. At the same time, China has become the largest country with a contribution of 20 percent to global trade in intermediate goods. According to the WTO, China exported $1.458 trillion intermediate goods to others in 2021, 1.8 times and 2 times that of the United States (second) and Germany (third), respectively; and imported $1.676 trillion intermediate goods, 65 percent and 176 percent higher than that of the United States (second) and Germany (third).

Third, China's manufacturing industry is moving toward the middle and high-end, which constantly increases its international competitiveness. By firmly grasping the trend of scientific and technological revolution as well as promoting the intelligent upgrading of the manufacturing industry, *made in China* is moving towards *creation in China*. China's export of technology intensive electromechanical products and high-tech products has basically doubled from RMB 7.4 trillion yuan and 3.8 trillion yuan in 2012 to 12.8 trillion yuan and 6.3 trillion yuan in 2021. From the perspective of innovation investment, the R&D intensity of China's manufacturing industry has increased from 0.85 percent to 1.54 percent during the same period. The average R&D intensity of *small giants* specializing in special new products has reached 10.3 percent, and more than 570 industrial enterprises have been shortlisted among the top 2500 global R&D investment enterprises. According to United Nations Industrial Development Organization, China's competitiveness in manufacturing ranks second in the world, only lower to Germany. In the list of the world's top 500 enterprises released in August 2022, 78 Chinese industrial enterprises were shortlisted with an increase of 33 over 2012.

2. The stability and security of China's manufacturing chains are facing challenges

In recent years, some labor-intensive industries and low value-added technology intensive industries in China have tended to transferring to Southeast Asian countries due to the weakening of the demographic dividend, the rise of factor costs and Sino-US economic and trade friction. In the long run, with the adjustment of the global manufacturing chains in the direction of regionalization, diversification, nearshore and localization, China's manufacturing industry will also face the pressure of competition in international investment and optimization and upgrading of industrial structure.

First, the intensified competition in foreign investment will have a certain impact on China's manufacturing industry. On the one hand, many countries have begun to emphasize the autonomy and controllability of industrial chains, gradually attached importance to the development of their own manufacturing, guided the return of key industries and reduced their investment abroad. On the other hand, more emerging developing countries are also actively attracting foreign investment in manufacturing, and the new investment around the world shows a decentralized trend. These objective factors have intensified the competition in global manufacturing industry, may making foreign investment in China's manufacturing downward in the future.

Second, the superposition of multiple internal and external factors has accelerated the transfer of some manufacturing from China. In recent years, some labor-intensive industries or low value-added processing and manufacturing have shown a trend of shifting to Southeast Asia and other countries. For example, Adidas, Nike, Nintendo, Samsung, etc. have gradually moved their factories from China to Vietnam. Thus, Vietnam has become Samsung's largest mobile phone production base in the world, and more than 50% of Samsung's mobile phone are exported by Vietnam. In the future, with the transformation and upgrading of China's industry and the intensification of competition for investment from Vietnam, India and other economies, such transfer of Chinese industry may be further accelerated.

Third, the disturbed global supply chain system has affected the upgrading of China's manufacturing. The interruption in the supply of high-end parts and technologies has a great impact on Chinese enterprises and their downstream that are highly embedded in the global supply chains. The supply of key technologies and products in the Chinese manufacturing supply chains has been restricted in recent years, which was harmful to the upgrading of China's industrial structure.

3. New competitive advantages of China's manufacturing chains are being fostered

Influenced by the objective laws of economic development, coupled with the superimposed impact of the anti-globalization trend, Sino-US economic and trade friction and the COVID-19 pandemic in recent years, the competitive advantage of China's manufacturing industry is changing.

a. The Low-cost advantage is being transformed to comprehensive-cost performance advantage

A key factor for China to become a *world factory* and a center for global supply chains is its significant advantage of low-cost manufacturing. However, this advantage weakened in recent years. For example, in terms of monthly wages in the manufacturing, China grew 9.84 percent by average from 2016 to 2020, significantly higher than those of developed countries such as the United States (3.77 percent), Japan (0.75 percent), South Korea (1.60 percent), and also higher than those of other developing countries such as Vietnam (4.54 percent), India (1.47 percent). In terms of level, China's labor cost lies between developed countries and other developing countries. In 2020, the United States, South Korea and Japan were 4.8, 3.8 and 2.6 times that of China, respectively. The average monthly wage of manufacturing in Vietnam and India was 1 / 3 and 1 / 5 of that of China (see Fig. 7.10). In addition, the energy cost and the total tax rate of China's manufacturing industry are also relatively high.

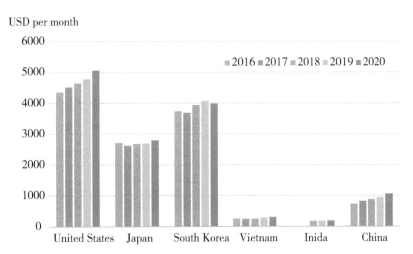

Fig. 7.10   Monthly wage rate in manufacturing: United States, Japan, South Korea, Vietnam, India and China, 2016-2020

Source: ILO, National Bureau of Statistics of China.

However, China's cost-effective advantages in labor productivity, supply-chain efficiency and business environment are increasingly prominent. From 2010 to 2021, China's annual average growth rate of labor productivity was 6.7 percent, 5.1 percentage higher than the global average (1.6 percent), also significantly higher than Vietnam (5 percent), India (5.5 percent), Thailand (2.1 percent), Indonesia (2.5 percent) and the Philippines (3 percent) and other Southeast Asian countries. Thus, China has become one of the countries with the fastest growth rate of global labor productivity. It has reached $16,512 per labor in 2021, which is also at a high level in the world (see Fig. 7.11). At the same time, the ranking of China's business environment has also been improved in recent years. In 2021, China's business environment score was

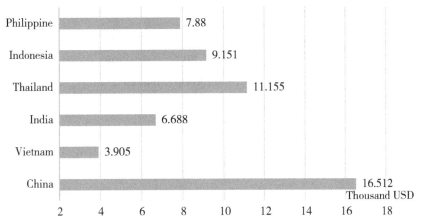

Fig. 7.11   Labor productivity: China, India, Indonesia, Philippine, Thailand, and Vietnam, 2021

Source: ILO.

4.38, an increase of 0.03 points year-on-year. More than 50 percent of foreign-funded enterprises regard China as the world's top investment destination. Judging from this, China still has a strong attraction to global manufacturing enterprises.

b. Transform the advantage of scale into the advantage of innovation

At present, China's advantages in the global supply chains are mainly concentrated in the field of large-scale production and manufacturing. However, in recent years, the innovation of digital technologies such as the internet, big data, cloud computing, artificial intelligence, and blockchain have accelerated, and are becoming a key force in reorganizing global manufacturing factor resources and changing the layout of global supply chains. China's advantages of large space for development, multiple scenarios for application and strong innovation will gradually become prominent, which help China to become an important region for the market application and industrial transformation of advanced technologies in the world. China's advantages in scientific and technological innovation have been continuously strengthened. Its R&D intensity has increased from 1.9% to 2.4 percent, basically reaching the average level of 2.5 percent of OECD countries (before the pandemic) (see Fig. 7.12).

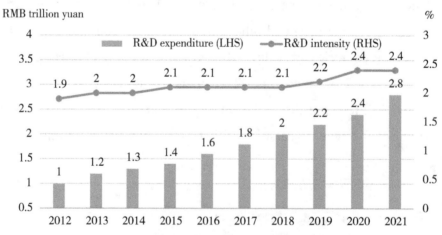

Fig. 7.12   R&D expenditure: China, 2012-2021

Source: National Bureau of Statistics of China.

New generation of information technology is accelerating its penetration into the manufacturing industry, which brings new advantages in promoting the digital transformation of the manufacturing industry. At present, the share of digital controlled parts among key processes of industrial enterprises above designated size in China has reached 55.3 percent, and the penetration rate of digital R&D tools has reached 74.7

percent. The share of enterprises carrying out networked collaboration and service-oriented manufacturing reached 38.8 percent and 29.6 percent respectively (see Fig. 7.13). China is also the country with the largest number of '*Lighthouse' factories* in the world. Among the 44 members of *Global Lighthouse Network* announced by the World Economic Forum (WEF), 12 are located in China, which is significantly higher than Germany (4), the United States (3), Japan (2) and other countries. China leads the world in terms of digital infrastructure and governance environment, providing the best fundamental market environment for the next stage of development in intelligent supply chains. This will attract global innovative enterprises to accelerate the agglomeration in Chin, which promotes China's transformation to a highland for innovation and application in global supply chains.

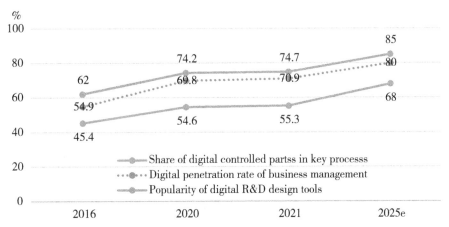

Fig. 7.13   Digitalization in manufacturing: China, 2016-2025

Source: National Bureau of Statistics of China; Ministry of Industry and Information of China.

c. Transform the advantage of extensity expansion into the advantage of intensity dominance

With the adjustment of the global supply chains to regionalization, the scale of interregional trade is gradually shrinking, which will limit the extensity of China's radiation to the global market as a *world factory*. However, relying on China's vibrant domestic market and Asian regional market, the status of *China factory* and *regional factory* will become more prominent, and China's expansion in intensity dominance in regional markets are expected to be strengthened. Along with the trend of more regionalization and localization, global supply chains will be further arranged around the main global markets.

On the one hand, the great demand of China's huge market for final consumer goods and intermediate goods has a strong magnetic attraction on the investment of multinational enterprises. It is estimated that by 2027, 1.2 billion people in China will be in the middle class, accounting for one fourth of the world's total. According to Purchasing Power Parity (PPP), about one quarter of global consumption growth in the next decade may happen in China. By 2030, the number of middle and high-income families in China may increase to about 400 million, close to the sum of Europe and the United States. On the other hand, the Asian market is active. In 2021, it also took the lead in achieving recovery under the impact of the pandemic: calculated by PPP, the Asia's share in world's real GDP rose to 47.4 percent (see Fig. 7.14) [1], which was only 32 percent in 2000. It is expected that this share will continue to increase to 52 percent by 2040.[2] 。

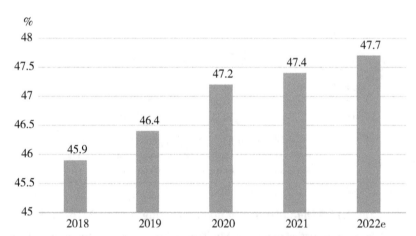

Fig. 7.14   Share of Asia in world real GDP, 2018-2022

Source: the Boao Forum for Asia.

Asia has become an important force to revitalize global trade and develop industrial and supply chains. China has also fostered a pattern of supply chains that cooperates with neighboring economies. In line with the general trend of decentralized distribution of global supply chains, China will establish a closer supply chain network

---

① The Boao Forum for Asia (2022). Asian Economic Outlook and Integration Progress Annual Report 2022. https://english.boaoforum.org/newsDetial.html?navId=6&itemId=2&permissionId=519&detialId=15121.

② McKinsey Global Institute (September 2019). Asia's future is now. www.mckinsey.com/featured-insights/future-of-asia.

with other Asian economies so as to consolidate the advantage of dominating regional markets by strong capacity of supply and huge demand market. While continuing to expand the scope of global cooperation, China will strive to be a global center by enabling Asia and Asian supply chain networks.

d. Transform the advantage of "domestic manufacturing base" into the advantage of "global manufacturing network"

Compared with developed countries such as the United States, Europe and Japan, China's dominant position in global supply chains is mainly based on *local* advantages. However, with the acceleration of internationalization of Chinese enterprises and preliminary improvement of their overseas supply chains, the new competitive advantage of "internal and external coordination" of China's supply chains is being shaped. In 2021, China's overseas direct investment was 145.2 billion US dollars with an YoY growth of 9.2 percent. Among them, China's domestic investors have made non-financial direct investment in 6,349 overseas enterprises across 166 economies, with a cumulative investment of 113.6 billion US dollars and a YoY growth of 3.2 percent. China has become a major international investor in the world, and ranks as one of the top investors in the world by overseas investment stock. Specially, China's overseas investment in the economies along the "the Belt and Road" Initiative has increased rapidly, and the number of big foreign contracted projects has increased, mainly in infrastructure and related manufacturing. China's overseas investment covers 70 percent of the world's economies and builds links with main categories of China's domestic manufacturing. During the pandemic, these overseas enterprises performed well in ensuring China's domestic markets. This means that China's advantage in supply chains will be further enhanced as China's manufacturing extends overseas, and transform to be based rather on "China's global manufacturing network" rather than on "China's domestic manufacturing capacity".

IV. Supply Chain Resilience in the Process of Globalization

In response to the changes in the global manufacturing industry and the risk of global supply chain disruptions caused by emergencies such as the pandemic, all countries should join hands to further strengthen infrastructure construction, accelerate the digital transformation of industries, and promote trade and investment liberalization and facilitation, strengthen global macro policy coordination, so as to improve international governance capabilities and establish a safe, reliable, and flexible industry and supply chain system.

1. Strengthening infrastructure construction and improving the level of industrial cooperation

Since 2021, black swan events have kept emerging, e.g. the Suez Canal obstruction, the cold wave hitting the North American continent, and the big supply chain congestion in the United States. These events reveal that there are still loopholes in global transportation and logistics infrastructure, which are not easy to overcome. Coupled with the impact of the pandemic, supply chain disruptions have occurred frequently as factories around the world have difficulties starting operations, and suffer from insufficient production capacity, decreased transportation capacity, and inventory shortages due to insufficient supply. Therefore, in the context of economic globalization, strengthening infrastructure construction and improving the level of industrial cooperation is of great importance to ensure the stability of industry and supply chains.

The first is to ensure quality when building the "Belt and Road" and vigorously promote the interconnection of traditional infrastructure, e.g. transportation and logistics. Countries along the Belt and Road should invest more in highways, railways, shipping, aviation, and other fields, strengthen the mutual recognition of standards and rules, and break traffic and logistics congestion points, in an effort to build stable transportation channels for energy, resources, and products, and realize the coordinated development of supply chains through cooperation.

The second is to strengthen the construction of new infrastructure and improve the intelligence level of transportation and logistics. Efforts should be stepped up to achieve integrated development of traditional transportation and logistics with 5G, big data, cloud computing, and other digital technologies, to enhance the level of automation and intelligence of ports, airports, and railway transportation, to improve transportation efficiency, and to reduce dependence on human factors.

The third is to deepen industrial cooperation among countries, leverage international production capacity cooperation to promote the orderly transfer of capital-intensive, technology-intensive, and labor-intensive industries among countries, and give play to the comparative advantages of each country to build a robust system of division of labor.

2. Stepping up the digital transformation of the manufacturing industry and optimizing the global layout of supply chains

The pandemic has hindered the flow of people, logistics, and transportation, thus leading to the low operational efficiency of supply chains. Nevertheless, it is easier for highly-digitized enterprises to break through the boundaries of space to enable more extensive multi-party collaboration and communication in more fields and industries. According to UNCTAD statistics, in 2021, the net income of the top 100 digital multinationals in the world rose by 60%, while that of the top 100 traditional multinationals grew slowly.

The first is to actively develop new businesses, products, and models leveraging 5G, smart economy, and big data to build a new model organized by the government and led by the market that combines digital technologies with traditional manufacturers.

The second is to improve the digital level of large multinationals, especially manufacturers so that they can play a pivotal role to coordinate upstream and downstream enterprises, integrate and allocate production resources, and deepen strategic cooperation with SMEs. All these are aimed at building efficient, collaborative, agile, and flexible supply chains, strengthening control over industry chains, and optimizing the global layout of industry and supply chains.

The third is to improve the digital level of SMEs, use reasonable digital solutions to achieve information sharing and flexible adjustments, and encourage SMEs to increase their capacity to turn out products that are new, distinctive, specialized, and sophisticated to build their advantages. All these are aimed to improve their survivability so that they can better merge into the supply chain system of large enterprises.

3.Strengthening the coordination of industry and supply chain policies to improve international governance capabilities

Recent years have seen the global industry chains become regionalized, localized, and shortened, while the risks of chain disruptions and decoupling continue to rise. One of the reasons is the pandemic, of course, but the main reason is the decline in the international governance level due to insufficient policy coordination among countries. To improve the resilience of the global manufacturing industry and supply chains, countries must build a consensus on cooperation, continue to expand the scale of trade and investment, and strengthen cooperation in key industries and fields.

The first is to continue maintaining the multilateral trade system with the WTO at its core, strengthening the communication and coordination of various countries on macroeconomic policies, and protecting the rights and interests and development space of each country. Full play should be given to the role of international organizations, such as the International Customs Organization, the International Maritime Organization, and the Universal Postal Union to establish an effective and regular communication and coordination mechanism, and jointly build flexible cross-regional supply chains.

The second is to strengthen multilateral, bilateral, and regional cooperation, continue to promote trade and investment liberalization and facilitation, reduce unreasonable restrictions on the flow of goods and factors, and guide enterprises in the region to expand the scale of trade and investment, thus building a more open and inclusive regional industry and supply chain system.

The third is to establish a coordination mechanism for major industries and fields, e.g. medicines, automobiles, and chips, create a benign cooperation environment, strike a balance between safety and efficiency, and let the market play a leading role in resource allocation, to avoid the industry and supply chains being artificially severed.

Chapter 8   Status Quo and Prospects of Global Financial Openness

Recent years have seen a divide in the global financial openness landscape. While developed economies still maintain a high level of financial openness, some emerging and less developed economies have slowed down or even showed signs of retrogression. China remains determined to adhere to its financial openness policies and stepped up its implementation in many fields. Although global financial openness is faced with many challenges in the short term, promoting openness in the long term is still mainstream. In this context, countries should strengthen global financial supervision and coordination and negotiate crisis relief policies, as part of an effort to strike a balance between financial openness and security.

I. The Global Financial Openness Landscape

The 1980s marked the beginning of an era of widening financial openness. When the outbreak of the 2008 global financial crisis put a halt to the process, countries around the world began to reflect on the benefits and security issues brought by financial openness. While developed economies with mature financial markets maintained a relatively high level of financial openness, emerging and underdeveloped economies started to put more focus on security issues. Some chose to slow down their pace of opening up, while others even regressed a bit.

Due to data availability, this paper will mainly analyze global financial openness based on the degree of capital account openness. The Chinn-Ito index (KAOPEN) is an index measuring a country's degree of capital account openness. It is also an important indicator of financial openness incorporated by the World Openness Index. KAOPEN is based on the binary dummy variables that codify the tabulation of restrictions on cross-border financial transactions reported in the IMF's Annual Report on Exchange Arrangements and Exchange Restrictions (AREAER). The higher the KAOPEN value of a country, the higher the degree of capital openness.

1. Status Quo of Financial Openness in Developed Countries

Developed countries have maintained a high level of financial openness. The degree of financial openness in developed countries is significantly higher than that in underdeveloped countries. In 2019, the average KAOPEN of developed countries was 1.34, while that of emerging markets and developing countries were -0.16 and -0.23, respectively. The degree of financial openness also diverged within developed countries. In 2019, the median KAOPEN of developed countries was 2.32, with the highest value as 2.32, the lowest value as -1.92, and the standard deviation as 1.31. More than 30 countries, including the US, the UK Germany, and Japan, had a KAOPEN of 2.32, meaning they were economies with the highest degree of financial openness. The Bahamas was at the bottom of the developed world, with a KAOPEN of -1.92. The general trend was that the degree of financial openness in developed countries was still growing. Overall, the average KAOPEN of developed countries in 2018 was 1.33, which rose by 0.01 in 2019. In 2019, Greece's KAOPEN index rose sharply by 1.07, while those of Iceland and Lithuania rose by 0.25.

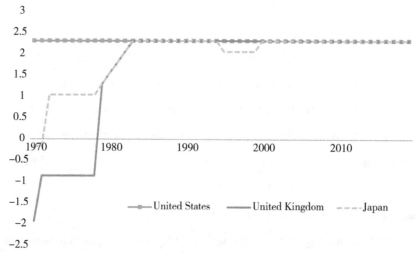

Fig. 8.1　KAOPEN Index for the United States, United Kingdom and Japan, 1970-2019[①]

---

2. Status Quo of Financial Openness in Developing Countries

Developing countries around the world can be divided into emerging markets and other developing countries.

Emerging markets are generally more open financially, but certain markets have regressed. The financial openness of emerging markets is generally higher than that of other developing countries. The average KAOPEN of emerging markets in 2019 was -0.16, higher than that of other developing countries (-0.23). There were also huge divergences in the degree of financial openness within emerging markets. In 2019, the median KAOPEN of emerging markets was -0.15, with the lowest value as -1.92, the highest value as 2.32, and the standard deviation as 1.44. The general trend was that some emerging markets had seen a significant regression in their financial openness. For example, Russia's KAOPEN index was 1.12 in 2013, which dropped to 0.1 in 2019. Brazil's KAOPEN index was 0.36 in 2009, which dropped to -1.23 in 2019.

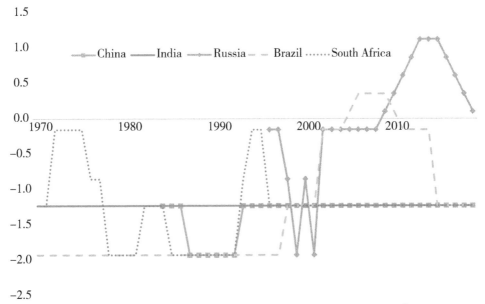

Fig. 8.2   KAOPEN Index for BRICS countries, 1970-2019[①]

---

①   Since 1996, China, India, and South Africa have had the same KAOPEN index of -1.23. So the lines of the three countries overlap.

Other developing countries maintain lower levels of financial openness. The financial openness of most developing countries was generally lower than that of developed countries and emerging markets. In 2019, the average KAOPEN of developing countries other than emerging markets was -0.23, which was lower than the world average. There were also huge divergences in the degree of financial openness within developing countries. In 2019, the median KAOPEN was -1.23, with the lowest value as -1.92, the highest value as 2.32, and the standard deviation as 1.31. The general trend was that the degree of financial openness in these developing countries had remained unchanged. Overall, the average KAOPEN for these developing countries in 2018 was -0.23, roughly the same as in 2019, while the median was -1.22, 0.01 higher than in 2019. By country, Tajikistan's KAOPEN index fell by 0.44 in 2019, and Bulgaria's dropped by 0.25.

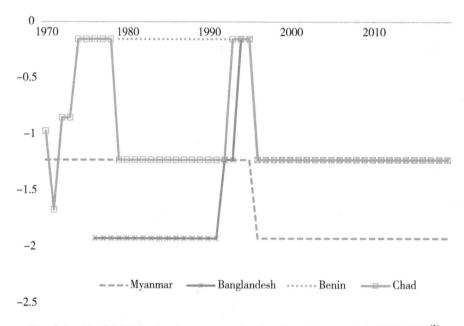

Fig. 8.3   KAOPEN Index for some underdeveloped countries, 1970-2019[1]

II. Status Quo of China's Financial Openness

China remains determined to promote financial openness and has taken implementation measures in many fields. In 2018, Chinese President Xi Jinping

---

[1]   Since 1996, Bangladesh, Benin, and Chad have had the same KAOPEN index of -1.23. So the lines of the three countries overlap.

emphasized at the Boao Forum for Asia that more efforts should be made to open up the services industry, especially the financial sector, and the implementation of the opening-up policy "should better be sooner than later, faster than slower". At the forum, Yi Gang, Governor of the People's Bank of China, announced the "three principles and twelve measures" for opening up China's financial sector. In July 2019, the Office of the Financial Stability and Development Committee under the State Council announced the introduction of 11 measures to open up the financial sector to the outside world.

Box 8-1   Three Principles and Twelve Measures for Opening up China's Financial Sector

In 2018, when he attended the Boao Forum for Asia, Yi Gang, Governor of the People's Bank of China, announced the following "three principles" for opening up China's financial sector:

The first is the principle of pre-entry national treatment and negative list.

The second is that the opening-up of the financial sector to the outside world shall be promoted in tandem with the reform of the exchange rate mechanism and the process of capital account convertibility.

The third principle is to prevent financial risks while opening up and to make sure the level of financial supervision is commensurate with that of financial openness.

In the meanwhile, he announced the launch of "twelve measures for opening up", and gave a detailed timeline for implementation.

1) Remove the foreign ownership cap for banks and asset management companies, treating domestic and foreign capital equally; allow foreign banks to set up branches and subsidiaries at the same time.

2) Lift the foreign ownership cap to 51% for securities companies, fund managers, futures companies, and life insurers, and remove the cap in three years.

3) No longer require joint-funded securities companies to have at least one local securities company as a shareholder.

4) To further improve the stock market connectivity of the Chinese mainland and Hong Kong, we will increase the daily quota by three times from May 1, after which the daily quota for Shanghai-bound and Shenzhen-bound investment will be increased from

RMB 13 billion to RMB 52 billion, while that for Hong Kong-bound investment from RMB 10.5 billion to RMB 42 billion.

5) Allow eligible foreign investors to provide insurance agent and loss adjuster services in China.

6) Lift restrictions on the business scope of foreign-invested insurance brokerage companies, treating them as equals of domestic companies.

7) Encourage foreign ownership in trust, financial leasing, auto finance, currency brokerage, and consumer finance.

8) Apply no cap to foreign ownership in financial asset investment companies and wealth management companies newly established by commercial banks.

9) Substantially expand the business scope of foreign banks.

10) Remove restrictions on the business scope of jointly-funded securities companies, treating domestic and foreign institutions equally.

11) Foreign insurance companies will no longer need to have a representative office in China for two consecutive years prior to establishing a fully-owned institution.

12) The preparatory work for Shanghai-London Stock Connect is proceeding as desired. We are aiming for launching the Shanghai-London Connect in 2018.

The results indicate that China is tapping deeper into financial openness through the following measures.

1. Significantly relaxing the access of foreign financial institutions

China has removed the restrictions on foreign ownership cap in banking, securities, fund management, futures, and life insurance institutions, and relaxed the limits on the business scope, asset scale, operating years, and shareholder qualifications of foreign financial institutions, which have been granted national treatment in corporate credit, credit rating, and payment clearing. According to the data made public by the People's Bank of China, since 2018, China has approved foreign organizations to establish more than 100 banks, insurance institutions, 12 foreign-controlled (including wholly-owned) securities, fund management, and futures companies, and 6 foreign-funded corporate credit, rating, payment, and clearing agencies.

Box 8-2   Further opening up the banking and insurance sectors by working on five key fronts

At a sub-forum of the Boao Forum for Asia Annual Conference 2022, the Vice-chairman of the China Banking and Insurance Regulatory Commission pointed out the five fronts the Commission will work on to open the banking and insurance sectors wider.

Firstly, institutional openness. The "pre-entry national treatment plus a negative list" system for managing foreign capital will be put in place to encourage more foreign-funded institutions to enter the Chinese market. Coordination and cooperation in international financial supervision will be strengthened to better implement the RCEP. These efforts serve as the preparatory work for China to apply to join the CPTPP and DEPA.

Secondly, the quality and efficiency of opening up. Quantitative access restrictions on foreign capital will be reduced. The requirement that foreign financial institutions acting as initiators or strategic investors of Chinese-funded commercial banks shall have a total asset of no less than $10 billion will be canceled. Accordingly, administrative licensing regulations will be revised as soon as possible to remove the foreign ownership cap in Chinese-funded commercial banks.

Thirdly, fairness and transparency. Non-discriminatory national treatment shall be implemented for domestic and foreign institutions alike. In line with this principle, the time limit for processing the applications of foreign-funded corporate banks to establish branches in China shall be shortened to 4 months, and approval will not be needed for foreign-funded banks to issue general financial bonds. These measures are aimed to support the quality development of foreign-funded institutions in China.

Fourthly, the philosophy of openness. The philosophy of green development shall be put in place as part of an effort to achieve carbon peaking and carbon neutrality. The financial sector will be encouraged to channel capital into energy consumption, transformation, and upgrading.

Fifthly, the rhythm and safety of opening up. Continued efforts will be made to improve China's supervision capabilities, by strengthening the monitoring of traditional risks, such as global monetary policy adjustments, imported risks, and inflation, doing more research on new risks, such as the pandemic, climate, and technological risks, and getting prepared for overseas emergencies. The bottom line is no systemic risk happens.

2. Steadily promoting the opening-up of the financial market

China will lift investment quota restrictions on Qualified Foreign Institutional Investors (QFII) and Renminbi Qualified Foreign Institutional Investors (RQFII) across the board. The restrictions on the proportion of foreign institutional investors' remittances in domestic and foreign currencies will be relaxed. On top of the Shanghai-Hong Kong Stock Connect, Shenzhen-Hong Kong Stock Connect, and Shanghai-London Stock Connect, among other mechanisms, the Southbound Bond Connect and the Cross-boundary Wealth Management Connect Scheme in the Guangdong-Hong Kong-Macao Greater Bay Area have been launched. As China's achievements in opening up its financial market have been recognized by the international market, foreign capital has flooded into China. MSCI Emerging Markets Index, FTSE Russell Index, S&P Dow Jones Indices, and other internationally famous indexes have incorporated China A shares successively, while Bloomberg Global Aggregate Bond Index, JPMorgan Government Bond Index-Emerging Markets Global Diversified Index, FTSE World Government Bond Index have successively incorporated Chinese bonds. According to the People's Bank of China, as of the end of May 2022, foreign investors held RMB 3.25 trillion of domestically listed stocks, accounting for 5.0% of the total circulating value of A-shares. They also held RMB 3.78 trillion of Chinese bonds, accounting for 2.8% of China's bond market.

Box 8-3　Eleven Measures of the Financial Stability and Development Committee for the Opening-up of the Financial Sector

To implement the decisions and arrangements of the CPC Central Committee and the State Council on opening China wider to the outside world, in July 2019, the Office of the Financial Stability and Development Committee under the State Council announced the launch of the following 11 measures to open up the financial sector to the outside world, under the principle of "better faster than slower, better sooner than later" and based on in-depth research and evaluation.

1) Foreign-invested rating agencies can give ratings to all kinds of bonds that are traded on China's interbank market and exchanges.

2) Foreign financial institutions are encouraged to participate in the establishment of or investment in the asset management subsidiaries of commercial banks.

3) Foreign asset managers are allowed to partner with the subsidiaries of Chinese banks or insurers to set up asset management companies that are controlled by a foreign party (parties).

4) Foreign financial institutions are allowed to set up or invest in pension fund management companies.

5) Foreign investors will be given support to establish or invest in currency brokers.

6) The transition period for relaxing restrictions on foreign ownership in life insurance companies from 51% to 100% will end in 2020, instead of 2021 as previously stated.

7) The restriction that domestic insurers must hold in aggregate not less than a 75% equity interest in an insurance asset management company will be removed and foreign investors can hold more than 25% in insurance asset management companies.

8) The qualification for a foreign insurer that is eligible to invest in China will be further relaxed, with the abolishment of the requirement that the foreign insurer should have been in business for no less than 30 years.

9) Foreign ownership restrictions in securities companies, fund management, and futures firms will end in 2020, one year earlier than originally planned.

10) Foreign-invested financial institutions are allowed to obtain type-A underwriting licenses in the interbank bond market.

11). Additional measures will be implemented to further facilitate foreign institutional investors' investment in the interbank bond market.

3. Making consistent efforts to internationalize RMB

Over the years, the People's Bank of China has continued to improve the infrastructure for RMB internationalization, deepened bilateral currency cooperation with relevant countries, and further enhanced the role of RMB as a currency for international payment and reserve. By the end of 2021, the People's Bank of China had authorized 27 RMB clearing banks in 25 countries and regions and had signed bilateral local currency swap agreements with central banks or monetary authorities from 40 countries and regions. In December 2021, RMB accounted for 2.70% of international payments, ranking the 4th most active currency for global payments. In May 2022, the IMF announced that it would raise the RMB's weighting in the Special Drawing Rights (SDR) basket of currencies from 10.92% to 12.28%. The percentage of RMB in global foreign exchange reserves rose from 2.79% in the fourth quarter of 2021 to 2.88% in the first quarter of 2022, ranking fifth among all currencies.

III. Major Events Affecting Global Financial Openness

The Fed has started a new round of interest rate hikes, which have significant spillover effects. Under capital outflow pressures, certain countries may strengthen capital flow management and slow down their pace of financial openness. Distributed financial systems based on digital currency and blockchain are taking shape. They have the potential to change the international financial structure and domestic financial ecosystem as major forces that may both promote financial openness and affect financial security.

1. The Fed's interest rate-hiking cycle

The new round of Fed interest rate hikes is stronger and its spillover effect more obvious than ever. Since March 2022, the Fed has raised interest rates four times in a row, up to 225 basis points cumulatively. Compared with the rate-hiking cycle that started in December 2015, this new round of rate hikes is much faster and bigger. **As the Fed raises interest rates due to inflationary pressures, the spillover effect on other countries is even worse.** If the Fed's rate hikes were out of consideration of improving employment and stimulating all-around economic recovery, the US's economic growth would increase import demand from other countries, which can partially offset the impact of capital outflows from these countries due to the rate hikes. Unfortunately, that's not the case. As the rate hikes were due to inflationary pressures, they will further dampen the US's import demand, while impacting other countries in terms of capital outflow. **This rate-hiking cycle may lead to greater capital outflows from emerging markets and underdeveloped countries.** The economies of most emerging markets and underdeveloped countries have suffered a major blow from the pandemic. As their fiscal stimulus is far less than that of developed countries, their economic recovery is relatively slower. Due to inflation pressures, some countries have followed the Fed to raise their interest rates, yet their economic fundamentals don't allow them to continuously do so. Countries with low-interest rates and high inflation will thus face greater risks of capital outflows.

Owing to the pressure of exchange rate depreciation and the risk of capital flight, emerging markets and underdeveloped countries are likely to slow down their pace of financial opening-up, if not strengthen capital controls. According to the Impossible Trinity theory, if a country is to maintain monetary policy independence and free capital movement, it will have to sacrifice exchange rate stability. During the Fed's rate-hiking cycle, emerging markets and underdeveloped countries generally face greater capital outflow pressures and exchange rate depreciation risks, which may cause heavier debt pressures for countries already overwhelmed by external debts. Taking into account the pressure of capital outflows and foreign debt risks, these countries will tend to slow down the pace of financial opening-up and pay more attention to financial security.

2. Distributed digital financial systems gradually take shape

Distributed digital financial systems based on blockchain and digital currency will change the international financial structure and domestic financial ecosystems. Not only will they drive the diversification of the international monetary and financial systems, but they will facilitate financial and economic openness.

a.Distributed digital financial systems have a major influence on the international monetary system.

Distributed finance refers to a new digital financial system based on blockchain and digital currency, which is essentially about achieving a certain degree of decentralization. In real life, be it a central bank digital currency or a stable currency issued by a single institution, it is highly centralized when issued, i.e. there is only one issuing organ, yet its circulation is decentralized and featured by peer-to-peer transactions. Therefore, the future distributed financial system will be a combination of single-center, multi-center, and no-center. A diversified governance structure like this will serve to promote the diversification of cross-border payment systems and currency forms. As a result, traditional fiat money, digital stablecoins, central bank digital currencies, and unanchored digital currencies will be both competitive and cooperative, thus forming a truly diversified landscape of the international monetary system in the long run.

Box 8-4　New Approach to Cross-border Payment

Distributed payment systems based on blockchain and digital currency will become a new approach to cross-border payments that competes with traditional payment platforms.

The existing cross-border payment systems are centralized in terms of both technology platforms and business operations. Traditional cross-border payment platforms typically adopt a centralized underlying technology architecture, where the information flow and the capital flow are separated. This architecture relies heavily on batch processing and runs short of real-time processing control capabilities. So it is often plagued by low efficiency in data exchange, transmission, and processing. Meanwhile, to enhance system security, payment institutions have to develop a new security platform on the underlying platform, thus making the system more complex and the operations and maintenance more costly.

Global cross-border payments are primarily made through correspondent banking. In this mode, at least four bank intermediaries are required to complete a cross-border payment. The procedure is complicated and the costs are high, yet the efficiency is low.

In contrast, cross-border payment platforms based on blockchain and digital currency are emerging with a new distributed technology architecture and governance model. The combination of peer-to-peer transactions enabled by blockchain and the merge of information and capital flows serve not only to improve cross-border payment efficiency and reduce costs, but enhance trust mechanisms, protect user privacy, and prevent insider manipulation. Therefore, with the technology, it is possible to establish a more just, inclusive, secure, and efficient cross-border payment system on a global scale.

b.Distributed digital financial systems serve to promote financial openness

Distributed digital financial systems promote financial openness by reducing cross-border transaction costs and improving transaction efficiency. Correspondent banking in traditional cross-border transactions has the following problems: an excessive number of intermediaries, backward infrastructure, and low level of automation, which result in a long time span (usually takes 3-5 days), high costs, and complicated operations for processing a cross-border payment. The peer-to-peer transaction model of distributed financial systems based on blockchain and digital currency eliminates correspondent banking that relies on multiple intermediaries, thus making cross-border payments receivable within a day or even seconds. The average cost for a bank to execute a cross-border payment via correspondent banking network remains in the range of $25 to $35, more than 10 times of an average domestic ACH payment. (McKinsey, 2016).[1] If digital currency is used for cross-border payment, the cost can be reduced to close to domestic payment levels. Therefore, distributed financial systems can significantly facilitate cross-border financial services and expedite cross-border capital flows, thereby promoting financial openness.

Distributed digital financial systems drive financial openness by enhancing trust mechanisms and ensuring transaction security. Firstly, the trust mechanisms of distributed financial systems are based on algorithms and computer networks, rather than on the morality of centralized entities or individuals. So it is characterized by disintermediation and strong trust. Secondly, the payment network based on blockchain and digital currency naturally allows transaction traceability and tamper resistance, which provides an effective guarantee for payment security. By effectively maintaining the data and financial security of individuals, institutions, and countries, distributed financial systems elevate the "Internet of Information" into the "Internet of Value", which serves to promote financial openness through expanded cross-border trade and financial services based on the Internet.

Box 8-5   Distributed cross-border payment systems are emerging globally

So far, certain private companies, international organizations, and national central banks have begun their attempts to build distributed cross-border payment networks.

In April 2021, JPMorgan Chase, the largest bank in the US, joined hands with Singapore's DBS Bank and Temasek Group to establish Partior, a global payment company based on blockchain and digital currency. The company enables cross-border payments in a variety of digital currencies, including JPM Coin, and provides services, such as trade finance, foreign exchange transactions, and securities settlement. JPM Coin is 1:1 anchored to the US dollar and aims to use blockchain technology to reduce customers' cross-border counterparty settlement risks and reduce capital requirements for

---

[1]   McKinsey & Company (2016). "Global Payments 2016: Strong Fundamentals Despite Uncertain Times", from https://www.mckinsey.com/~/media/McKinsey/Industries/Financial%20 Services/Our%20Insights/A%20mixed%202015%20for%20the%20global %20payments%20industry/ Global-Payments-2016.ashx

instant value transfer. Cross-border payment settlement with JPM Coin can be completed instantly at any time of the day, and such use can reduce the cost of checking by 70%-80%. "The establishment of Partior is a global watershed for digital currencies, marking the shift from experimentation and pilot to commercialization and real-time application," said the Chief Financial Technology Officer of the Monetary Authority of Singapore.

SWIFT (Society for Worldwide Interbank Financial Telecommunication), a global cross-border payment message provider established based on the traditional centralized model, also takes distributed technology as its prioritized strategy and has begun to create a new blockchain-based messaging system to simplify the cross-border payment process. It is SWIFT's hope to apply blockchain technology to reduce the cost of reconciliation between independent databases for maintaining members, thereby reducing operating costs. For that reason, SWIFT is integrating open-source blockchain technology into its system to create Proofs of Concept to replace account verification in a distributed ledger system.

In addition, many countries and regions have established partnerships on distributed cross-border payment arrangements, such as with the Bank of Canada and the Monetary Authority of Singapore, the Bank of Japan and the European Central Bank, the Bank of Thailand and the Monetary Authority of Hong Kong, China.

IV. Prospects for Global Financial Openness

In the short term, the pace of global financial openness may slow down, with certain countries going backward. But in the long run, advancing global financial openness remains the mainstream. The world is faced with the ongoing COVID pandemic, the cumulative risk of stagflation, and worsening debt distress. There is an urgent need to strengthen financial cooperation and exchanges around the world, align daily macro-prudential and micro-compliance supervision measures, and negotiate remediation policies in times of crisis. As digital currency and blockchain technologies continue to evolve, the distributed and intelligent digital model of financial openness will become a new trend. Meanwhile, it is also necessary to strengthen regulations by improving the technological level of supervision, carrying out international coordination, and establishing corresponding international rules for supervision.

1. Trends in global financial openness

In the short term, the current global financial openness landscape faces many challenges. Certain countries may experience a temporary slowdown or even a setback. **Facing greater capital outflow pressures and debt default risks, developing countries are now very cautious about expanding financial openness.** The World Bank estimates that 60% of low-income countries are already in, or are at high risk of, debt distress. The situation may deteriorate in 2022. The plans of major powers and international organizations to help heavily indebted developing countries to restructure their debts progress slowly, putting developing countries under heavier debt pressures. **In the post-pandemic era, the shrinking of the global industry chain may lead to a slowdown in the speed of financial globalization.** On the one hand, the pandemic has hindered the free flow of raw materials for production and skilled workers around the world and put the supply chains in a state of obstruction for years, thus objectively severing part of the global industry chains. On the other, the pandemic has exposed the vulnerability and instability of the current industry chain which is excessively long and thin. Countries have begun to make industry chains more local and regional, thus subjectively severing the global industry chains. The restructuring of the industry chain in the opposite direction of globalization will undermine cross-border investment, leading to curtailed demand for cross-border capital.

In the long run, the support for global financial openness remains robust, and advancing financial openness in various countries is still mainstream.

Firstly, multinationals, as an important champion of financial globalization, are still motivated to deploy and allocate resources globally. Since the 1980s, multinationals have become the main driver of economic globalization. As pursuing high profits is the main goal of multinationals in their global operations, they are likely to continue investing in regions with a benign business climax and low production costs, thereby promoting economic and financial globalization. In addition, as information technology develops, multinationals tend to be a hybrid of emerging and traditional enterprises that break through geographical limitations.

Secondly, emerging markets represented by China have become an important driver for financial globalization. These countries, as both beneficiaries and promoters of globalization, will continue expanding financial openness. On the one hand, they bring in long-term institutional investors and international leading institutions to provide sufficient liquidity for the market, improve the level of market services, pricing, and investment, and enhance the market's resilience and vitality. On the other, they allow domestic financial institutions to raise and allocate funds around the world and enhance their ability to gain profits and compete in the international financial market.

Thirdly, the distributed, intelligent, digital model of financial openness will become a new trend in advancing global financial openness. As digital currency and blockchain technologies develop, future international economic activities, including cross-border payments, trade, investment, and financial services, will increasingly count on distributed financial systems. Distributed financial systems establish algorithm-based rules and multi-center governance models at the international level through smart contracts and different decentralization mechanisms, thus enabling a more just, safe, and efficient model of global financial openness. As distributed cross-border payment networks continue to develop, it is possible to build multiple digital currency areas across geographical borders in the future, which will become the highlight of digital financial and economic openness.

Box 8-6　Digital Currency Area

A digital currency area refers to an area in which multiple countries use one or multiple digital currencies and conduct international economic and trade activities on the same distributed cross-border payment platform.

It will be an updated version of the traditional optimal currency area (OCA) in the digital economy era. Cross-border payment platforms based on blockchain and digital currency have a strong "network effect". As more institutions, businesses, and consumers join the network, the economic and social value generated by the network will grow as well. When it grows to a certain scale, the distributed cross-border payment platform will surpass the financial platform to become an international economic cooperation platform integrating trade, investment, and financial services that utilize digital currency. This is how a digital currency area takes shape.

In recent years, empirical research by the IMF has found that the circulation speed of digital currency is significantly higher than that of traditional currency (Manmohan Singh, Caitlin Long, 2020).[1] According to economic principles, when other conditions remain

---

① Manmohan Singh, Caitlin Long (2020). "How programmable digital assets may change monetary policy", from https://www.ft.com/content/773d0eac-8d75-43ea-b62e-ba8ef39e51f2

unchanged, the increase in the velocity of currency circulation will boost the growth of GDP. Therefore, the formation of digital currency areas will deepen regional economic cooperation and promote the economic growth of countries in them.

2. Challenges facing global financial regulation

The difficulty to supervise the rapid cross-border capital flow due to the varying policies and legal systems of different countries poses systemic and structural challenges to their financial systems. Some countries have even encountered financial crises brought about by financial openness. That said, although expanding financial openness remains a general trend of world economic development, opening up must be accompanied by effective supervision, because it is a necessary condition for the efficient operation of the financial market and the stability of the financial system, and a prerequisite for financial openness. To continue advancing financial openness, global financial regulatory authorities must address the following challenges.

Firstly, the costs of coordinated regulation are not commensurate with its benefits. That is why some countries are not willing to do so for political considerations. As financial markets in developing countries are generally immature and less competitive, the space for the financial development of developing countries may be restrained if the world adopts a unified supervision model. Such a model may also hinder the long-term development of financial institutions in developing countries. Moreover, the legal systems and regulatory standards vary by country, which puts a damper on global financial supervision.

Secondly, effective enforcement agencies are lacking in global financial regulation. The existing executive agencies mainly include the IMF, the Bank for International Settlements, the World Bank, and regional financial institutions. However, these agencies run short of resources and are not legally binding in terms of risk prevention, institutional supervision, and crisis relief, because their authority is not universally recognized. In the international community nowadays, there aren't any legally binding, and politically independent institutions that are both capable of mobilizing resources and are recognized for the legitimacy of law enforcement to assume the responsibility of global financial regulation.

Thirdly, it is not easy to coordinate prudential regulation on the macro level and compliance regulation on the micro level. After the 2008 global financial crisis, countries around the world started a round of financial regulatory reforms focusing on building macro-prudential mechanisms. However, as the objectives and responsible agencies of macro-prudential and micro-compliance policies are different, the two policy tools are different yet highly overlapping. Therefore, however the mechanism is designed, the two tools may complement and conflict with each other at the same time. Moreover, the significant differences in the macro-financial environment of different countries, the diverse development level of micro-financial institutions, and the individualized requirements of each country's supervision make it all the more difficult to coordinate macro-prudential and micro-compliance regulation on a global scale.

Fourthly, distributed digital financial systems make it more difficult to supervise money laundering and illegal financing behaviors. Existing regulatory rules and technologies cannot effectively supervise unanchored digital currencies and certain stablecoins. The non-anchored digital currencies represented by Bitcoin are characterized by distributed storage and issuance, transaction anonymity, high encryption level, and difficulty to crack. They can be used for capital flight, illegal money laundering, online gambling, and drug and gun trading, with little risk of being tracked and identified. There are even cases in which cryptocurrencies are issued entirely by the issuer for illegal fundraising, fraud, and other purposes. If digital stablecoins issued by market-oriented institutions are not subject to the strict supervision of the government, there will also be problems of insufficient guarantees and excessive currency issuance.

Box 8-7　Supervision of Distributed Digital Financial Systems

The future regulations of distributed financial systems are expected to develop in the following two directions.

The first is to use fin-tech to supervise fin-tech. The innovative development of distributed financial systems, in essence, benefits from the development of fin-tech. Therefore, it is also advisable to leverage fin-tech for the supervision of such systems. Compared with centralized networks, the Internet of Value, which is built based on blockchain, is a pro-supervision system in terms of the technical architecture, which allows for penetrative supervision. Blockchain is characterized by traceability, difficulty to tamper with, and high transparency. With adequate regulatory technology, distributed financial systems will be effectively regulated, thus becoming a safe and stable Internet of Value.

The second is to strengthen international coordination to establish international rules for supervising distributed financial systems. The use of digital currency and distributed financial systems will change the currency circulation model and improve financial efficiency. It may even redefine the role of central banks and commercial financial institutions, and reshape the domestic financial ecosystem and international financial architecture. Owing to the complex design of digital currencies, as well as the divergent legal frameworks of different countries, digital currencies are now in a fragmented and disorderly international regulatory environment, where regulation inconsistencies and loopholes abound. Therefore, it poses a challenge to improve the interoperability of digital currencies in different countries and distributed financial systems.

All these problems need to be solved by establishing new international rules. Under the G20 framework, countries around the world may discuss and build international rules for supervising distributed financial systems.

In this regard, China has a part to play in the formulation of technical standards and regulatory frameworks for digital currency and distributed financial systems, through extensive bilateral and multilateral exchanges and cooperation. China stands ready to participate in global financial infrastructure construction, and develop distributed financial systems and cross-border platform economy, as part of an effort to promote financial and economic openness.

Chapter 9   World Openness in Digital and Green Fields

In recent years, the world's fields of openness have been expanding, forming digital, green and other "new tracks", which become key forces in restructuring global factors and resources, reshaping global economic structure and changing global competition pattern. These "new tracks" are formed in the era of globalization and have innate attributes of openness. For example, the digital domain requires free flow of data across borders, which promotes and leads openness. Climate change, carbon emissions and other global issues require all countries to strengthen cooperation and jointly deal on the premise of openness. Therefore, digital and green are both closely related to openness, and the continuous promotion of digital and green openness will benefit more countries and people in the world.

I. Booming Development of Global Digital Openness

With the development and commercial application of big data, cloud computing, internet of things, artificial intelligence and other technologies in recent years, the empowering role of digital technology has been further intensified, and its penetration into all industries of the national economy has accelerated, which promote the transformation of the economy to the digital, networked and intelligent directions. The scale and scope of digital economy have greatly expanded, covering a wealth of products, services, business models and industrial forms supported by digital technology and with data as an important factor of production. This paper aims to analyze the current status of global digital openness from the four aspects of infrastructure, rules and standards, digital trade, and cross-border flow of data.

1. Infrastructure "hard connectivity": Rapid development, but the gap is clear

As a new concept, there is no unified definition of "digital infrastructure" so far, but it can be roughly divided into three parts: 1), the communication network infrastructure represented by 5G, Internet of things, industrial Internet and satellite Internet; 2),new technological infrastructure represented by artificial intelligence, cloud computing and blockchain; 3), computing infrastructure represented by general computing center, supercomputing center, intelligent computing center and edge data center.

From the perspective of global Internet transmission capacity, global Internet bandwidth, average Internet traffic and peak Internet traffic have all showed a rapid increasing trend from 2017 to 2021 (see Table 9.1). In terms of intra-continental transmission capacity, Europe, Asia and North America rank the top three in the world in intra-continental Internet bandwidth, with Latin America, the Middle East and Africa lagging far behind (see Table 9.2). In terms of transmission capacity between continents, a distribution structure has been formed with America, Europe and Asia as the first tier, Latin America and the Middle East as the second tier, and Africa and Oceania as the third tier (see Fig. 9.1). There are 7 core hub cities in Europe, 2 in Asia and 1 in North America.

Table 9.1 **Global Internet transmission capacity indicators in 2017-2021**

Unit: Tbps

	2017	2018	2019	2020	2021
Peak traffic	89	125	161	263	347
Average traffic	25	50	73	134	179
Bandwidth	285	362	453	609	786

Source: The author's compilation based on the materials published by TeleGeography[1].

Table 9.2 **Global Internet bandwidth and CAGR**

	bandwidth（Tbps）	CAGR in 2017-2021 (%)
Europe	503	27
Asia	192	37

---

[1] https://global-internet-map-2022.telegeography.com/

	bandwidth（Tbps）	CAGR in 2017-2021 (%)
North America	163	23
Latin America	91	26
Middle East	57	33
Africa	27	45

Source: The author's compilation based on the materials published by TeleGeography[①].

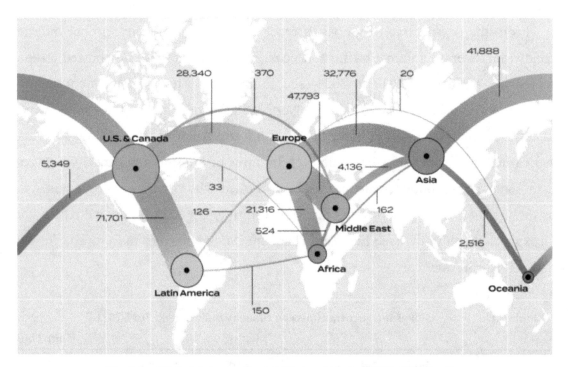

Fig. 9.1　Global intercontinental Internet bandwidth distribution

Source: The author's work based on the materials published by TeleGeography[②].

In the new technology infrastructure, the technical characteristics of artificial intelligence and blockchain are relatively prominent, while the open characteristics of cloud computing remain relatively prominent. In view of this, this section mainly analyzes the connectivity of global cloud computing infrastructure. In terms of global public cloud infrastructure, the number of cloud regions continues to increase, with an average of 15 new cloud regions launched every year[③]. As of 2021, Asia and Europe have the highest density of public cloud infrastructure, accounting for 66% of

---

① https://global-internet-map-2022.telegeography.com/.
② ibid.
③ ibid.

existing facilities globally, while North America accounts for approximately 23.5% of existing facilities, and South America, Oceania, and Africa together account for 10.3%.[1]

Table 9.3   Number of Public Cloud Regions in the Continents in 2021

	Number of cloud regions
Asia	42
Europe	28
North America	25
South America	5
Oceania	4
Africa	2
Total	106

Source: The author's compilation based on the materials published by TeleGeography[2].

Computing infrastructure includes general computing center, intelligent computing center, supercomputing center and edge data center, etc. At present, there is no statistical data covering above data centers in the world. Considering servers are the core infrastructure for building data centers, the increase of global servers can reflect the development trend of global data centers to a certain extent. In 2021, the total number of new servers in the world remained stable, and the growth of the total size of data centers slowed down. North America, Asia-Pacific, and Western Europe accounted for more than 90% of the new servers in 2021, and Asia-Pacific in particular, has become an important pole of global growth.

[1]   https://www.cloudinfrastructuremap.com/#/service/cloud-regions.
[2]   https://www.cloudinfrastructuremap.com/#/service/cloud-regions.

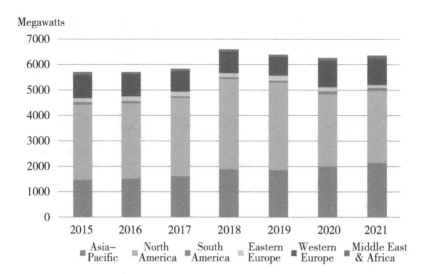

Fig. 9.2 Global annual server additions

Sources: White Paper on Data Center (2022), China Academy of Information and Communication Technology.[1]

Countries, especially data powers, have made positive progress in rapidly promoting the construction of their data infrastructure and data connectivity. However, after economic globalization encountered serious setbacks, infrastructure "hard connectivity" among various economies has been increasingly strictly regulated due to various factors.

At present, digital technology has become the core field of great power competition. Major economies have all formulated digital technology development strategies to promote the development of digital technologies mainly represented by 3D printing, blockchain and 5G technology. In the field of 3D printing, the United Nations Digital Economy Report 2019 shows that the US, China, Japan, Germany and the UK account for 70% of the total number of 3D printing enterprises in the world[2], while the rest of the economies only account for 30%. In the field of blockchain technology, the number of patent applications in China accounts for about 50% of the total number of global applications, and the US accounts for more than 25%. In the 5G domain, North America and China are expected to have a 5G penetration rate of more than 45% by 2025, while the Middle East, North Africa and sub-Saharan Africa are all expected

---

① http://www.caict.ac.cn/kxyj/qwfb/bps/202204/t20220422_400391.htm.

② The United Nations, Digital Economy Report 2019.https://unctad.org/webflyer/digital-economy-report-2019.

to have a 5G penetration rate of less than 10%; In the field of artificial intelligence, China, the US and Japan combined accounted for 78% of all patents applied for in 2019. It can be seen that digital technology has been advancing by leaps and bounds, but digital divide is deepening.

2. Rules and standards "soft connectivity": gradual improvement but with respective emphasis

The "soft connectivity" of digital openness is mainly manifested in the level of rules and standards, which is specifically reflected in digital economic and trade rules in the free trade agreements or digital trade agreements concluded between countries. Before 1994, there were almost no issues related to digital trade in the WTO framework. However, with the vigorous development of digital trade, digital technology and digital economy, the game between major economies around digital economic and trade rules have become increasingly fierce. After experiencing the four stages of absence, germination, formation and development, global digital economic and trade rules have formed a relatively complete rule system.

a. Four major characteristics of global digital economic and trade rules

Digital economic and trade rules have gradually formed their characteristics in the process of evolution. (1), ever-expanding scope of coverage. The regulatory targets started from producers, and gradually extended to consumers, governments and such emerging business forms as Internet platforms. The areas of rules adjustment started with digital trade facilitation and gradually expanded to areas such as data development and flow, and digital governance. The Digital Economy Partnership Agreement (DEPA), for example, extends from digital trade to digital economy and it also introduces digital governance arrangements such as the regulatory framework for digital economy and digital competition policy. (2), taking into account balance in the process of rules advancing toward a high level. The US-Mexico-Canada Agreement (USMCA) once pushed digital trade liberalization and cross-border information transfer liberalization to extremes, but very soon the subsequent US-Japan Digital Trade Agreement (UJDTA) negotiations retreated from aforementioned extreme trade liberalization provisions. (3), increasingly strengthened mandatory rules. The increase of mandatory clauses is the result of increased interest consensus of the parties, which is also helpful to improve the FTA utilization rate. (4), transforming from single substantive rules to integrated development of substantive rules and procedural rules. The continuous improvement of procedural rules has greatly improved the FTA utilization rate.

Box 9-1   Digital Economy Partnership Agreement (DEPA)

The Digital Economy Partnership Agreement (DEPA) is a digital trade agreement initiated by Singapore, Chile and New Zealand and signed online on June 12, 2020.

The pact consists of 16 thematic modules, involving initial terms and general definitions, business and trade facilitation, digital products treatment and related problems, data, the broad trust environment, business and consumer trust, digital identity, emerging trends and technology, innovation and digital economy, cooperation of small and medium-sized enterprises, digital convergence, transparency, joint committees and liaison, dispute settlement, exceptions and final terms, etc.

The features are as follows.

(1) The DEPA deeply draws on the essence of the Comprehensive and Progressive Trans-Pacific Partnership Agreement (CPTPP), the US-Mexico-Canada Agreement (USMCA) and the US-Japan Digital Trade Agreement (UJDTA).

(2) The DEPA is open and inclusive and has a considerable development prospect.

(3) The scope of the DEPA has been further expanded from digital trade to digital economy. Based on the focus of previous high-level agreements on digital trade, the DEPA takes into consideration digital technology arrangements, including artificial intelligence and fintech arrangements, proposes digital governance arrangements, such as digital economy regulatory framework, digital competition policy and digital convergence, and further strengthens extensive cooperation among the Parties in digital economy, making it the broadest digital trade agreement that has ever been signed in the world.

(4) It deletes some provisions on the protection of intellectual property rights in the digital sector and gives special attention to digital start-ups and small and medium-sized enterprises.

(5) Procedural rules have been further consolidated and the implementation of the agreement has been greatly enhanced.

b. Main contents of global digital economic and trade rules

Digital economic and trade rules currently form three main sections, mainly involving digital trade facilitation, data development and flow, and digital governance. The digital trade facilitation section aims to reduce tariff barriers and promote digital trade facilitation in order to promote the development of global digital trade. The data development and flow section aims to solve two problems: one is how to maximize the promoting effect of digital elements through data development and utilization, and the other is how to maximize free flow of data across borders without infringing on personal privacy, impairing data sovereignty and national security. The digital governance section focuses on how to solve various social problems arising in the process of the development and openness of digital economy through international coordination and regulatory consistency. It includes information governance, intellectual property protection, Internet platform governance, technology governance, industrial governance, security precaution and dispute settlement, etc. The main contents are shown in the following table.

Table 9.4　　　　　**Main contents of global digital economic and trade rules**

Main sections	Main contents	CPTPP	USMCA	UJDTA	EPA	RCEP	DEPA
Digital trade facilitation	Tariff-free for electronic transmissions	√	√	√	√	√	√
	Non-discrimination of digital products	√	√	√	×	×	√
	Domestic electronic transaction regulatory framework	√	√	√	√	√	√
	Electronic authentication and electronic signature	√	√	√	√	√	√
	Paperless trading	√	√	×	×	√	√
	Logistics, electronic invoices, express delivery	×	×	×	×	×	√
Digital development and flow	Data development	×	×	×	×	×	√
	Government data openness	×	√	√	×	×	√
	Network openness, access and use	√	√	√	√	×	√
	Electronic transfer of information across borders	√	√	√	√	√	√
	Location of computing facilities (non-localization of data storage)	√	√	√	×	√	√

(Continued)

Main sections	Main contents		CPTPP	USMCA	UJDTA	EPA	RCEP	DEPA
Digital governance	Information governance	Online consumer protection	√	√	√	√	√	√
		Personal information protection	√	√	√	√	√	√
		Unsolicited commercial electronic information	√	√	√	√	√	√
		Digital identity	×	×	×	×	×	√
	Intellectual property protection	Source code (algorithm) protection	√	√	√	√	×	×
		Protection of information and communication technology products with encryption technology	×	×	√	×	×	√
	Internet platform governance	Internet platform intellectual property exemption	×	√	√	×	×	×
		Internet interconnectivity cost sharing	√	×	×	×	×	×
	Technology governance	Innovation and digital economy	×	×	×	×	×	√
		Emerging trends and technologies	×	×	×	×	×	√
		Digital inclusion	×	×	×	×	×	√
	Industry governance	Regulatory framework for digital economy	×	×	×	×	×	√
		Digital competition policy coordination	×	×	×	×	×	√
	Security precaution	Network security	√	√	√	×	√	√
		Exception clauses	×	×	√	×	×	√
	Cooperation and dispute settlement	SMEs cooperation	×	×	×	×	√	√
		Joint committees and liaisons	×	×	×	×	√	√
		Transparency	×	×	×	×	√	√
		Disputes settlement	√	×	×	×	√	√

Source: The author's conclusions based on the texts of free trade agreements and digital trade agreements.

c. Comparison of global digital economic and trade rules

Different countries have different emphasis on digital economic and trade rules, but there is still a basis for cooperation in many aspects. At present, a diversified digital trade rules pattern represented by the United States, Europe and Asia-Pacific has been formed, with the driving force in Asia-Pacific being mainly led by Singapore and China. The similarities and differences of different regions are as follows:

Difference remains relatively little in digital trade liberalization and facilitation In terms of rules and positions, there is little difference, and the emphases in the future can be put on trade facilitation to promote the development of digital trade. For example, some of China's domestic trade facilitation measures have been very successful, but most of them have not yet been elevated to the international level, and there is great room for such kind of development in the future.

Differences remain relatively large in data sharing and flow Domestic data sharing is a policy area that all countries are pushing forward, but the stances on free flow of data across borders remain quite divergent. The US and Singapore advocate full development and free flow of data, with the US focusing on free flow, while Singapore focusing on full development. The EU and China remain more aligned and relatively cautious, believing regulatory and security challenges posed by free flow of data should be taken into full consideration.

Digital governance is a key area for future advancement The US attaches great importance to intellectual property rights protection and the development of Internet platforms, reflecting a development-oriented nature. Europe has high requirements in the area of information governance mainly represented by personal information protection, but its rules and concepts in applying digital technology such as digital identity to promote development lag behind, with the emphasis placed on regulating the development of Internet platforms and digital monopoly industry. Singapore and other DEPA parties has a perfect digital governance rule system and plays a leading role especially in industrial governance and technological governance. China attaches greater importance to the balance between development and governance, and there will be more room for cooperation with the US in information governance, Internet platform governance and industrial governance. In the area of intellectual property rights, the economic and trade propositions of China, Europe and Singapore are more similar. Meanwhile, China and Singapore have been relatively active in cooperation and dispute settlement.

3. Digital trade: Coverage is expanding, but varies widely from country to country

As a new thing, the definition and measurement of digital trade are dynamically adjusted as its scope continues to expand. At present, some representative institutions like the UNCTAD, OECD, WTO, IMF, CAICT, and USITC have different interpretations and statistics on it, but the analysis of cross-border e-commerce and digital service trade as two most important variables can better outline the map of global digital trade openness.

With the strong support of digital technology, cross-border e-commerce platforms have risen rapidly and cross-border e-commerce has entered a period of rapid growth. Global retail e-commerce sales exceeded $4.9 trillion in 2021, up 14% from 2020. From 2015 to 2021, global retail e-commerce sales grew at an average annual rate of 17%.

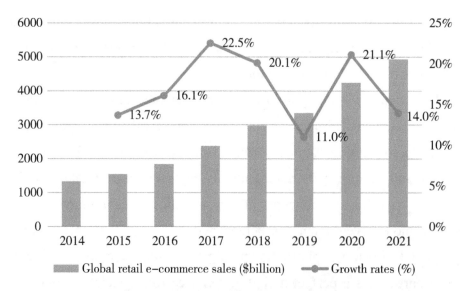

Fig. 9.3 Global retail e-commerce sales and growth rates in 2014-2021
Source: Statista. https://www.statista.com/statistics/379046/worldwide-retail-e-commerce-sales/

In terms of country, data from China's Bureau of Statistics shows that China's online retail sales reached 13.1 trillion yuan (RMB) in 2021, the largest in the world and far ahead of other countries. China's customs data showed that the import and export volume of China's cross-border e-commerce in 2021 was 1.92 trillion yuan.

From 2010 to 2020, global trade in digital services increased from $1.87 trillion to $3.16 trillion, accounting for 63.6% of total global service exports.

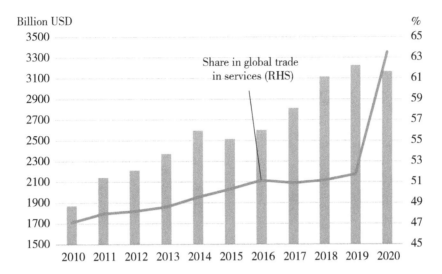

Fig. 9.4   Global trade in digital services and its proportion in global total trade in services, 2010-2020

Source: UNCTAD Database[①].

From the perspective of growth rate, global digital service trade generally maintained a rapid growth trend, with an average growth rate of 5.6% from 2010 to 2020, compared with 1.04% and 2.16% average growth rate of trade in goods and trade in services during the same period. The COVID-19 pandemic had a big impact on global trade in 2020, but the growth rate of digital services trade only decreased by 1.78% year-on-year, which was far lower than that of services trade (down 21.7% year-on-year) and goods trade (down 7.7% year-on-year).

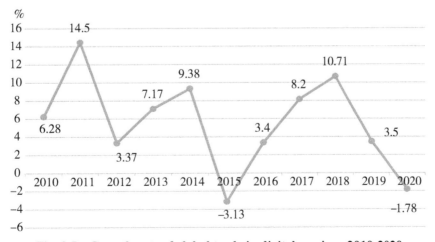

Fig. 9.5   Growth rate of global trade in digital services, 2010-2020

Source: UNCTAD Database.

---

① https://unctadstat.unctad.org/wds/TableViewer/tableView.aspx?ReportId=158358

From a specific country perspective, the top 10 countries in terms of import and export of digital services trade are concentrated in North America, Western Europe and Asia-Pacific. Differences vary greatly in size from country to country, but the US, with its huge advantage in digital trade, has long remained the leader.

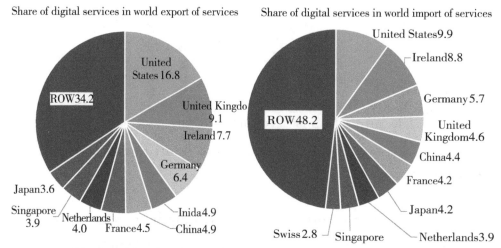

Fig. 9.6 Top 10 economies by share of digital services trade, 2020

Source: UNCTAD Database[1].

4. Free flow of data across borders: important factor of production, but not to a high degree of value

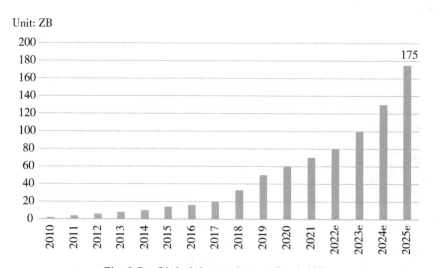

Fig. 9.7 Global data volumes, 2010-2025

Source: Data Age 2025[2], IDC.

---

① https://unctad.org/system/files/official-document/tn_unctad_ict4d19_en.pdf.

② https://www.sgpjbg.com/baogao/62098.html.

Global data volume has shown exponential growth, and according to the IDC[①] forecast, it will reach 175ZB by 2025. Data has jumped to become the most promising production factor. Fig. 9.7 gives a comprehensive picture of the scale of global data. The world big data centers are concentrated in the US, China and Japan, with the US accounting for 39%, China 10% and Japan 6% in 2021[②]. The revenue of the global data center market has been steadily growing, reaching $67.93 billion in 2021 and is projected to reach $74.65 billion in 2022 (see Fig. 9.8).

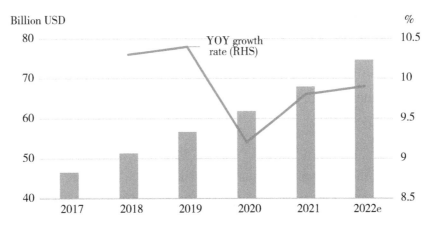

Fig. 9.8   Market revenues and growth rates of Global data center, 2017-2022
Source: White Paper on Data Center 2022[③], CAICT.

There seems to be a positive correlation between the rapid growth of global data volume and the steady rise of data center market revenues, but the growth rate of data center market revenues is far lower than that of global data volume, which actually reflects a problem that cannot be ignored, that is, data value is not high. As a factor of production, data has not acquired a value commensurate with its volume and growth trend. There are two main reasons for this. First, in most countries, there is no mature experience to follow in the relevant practices of valuing data. Rules for data empowerment and trading are still being explored in most economies and consensus

---

① IDC, whose full name is International Data Corporation, is a wholly-owned subsidiary of International Data Group, which is headquartered in the US. The company is a professional provider of marketing consulting, consultancy and event services for information technology, telecommunication and consumer technology sectors. Its website often publishes market information, forecasts and opinion articles by senior analysts on hot topics in the industries.

② http://dc.infosws.cn/20210901/50596.html.

③ http://www.caict.ac.cn/kxyj/qwfb/bps/202204/t20220422_400391.htm.

is yet to be reached at the international level. Second, based on personal privacy, data sovereignty, national security and other considerations, many countries have carried out supervision to varying degrees on cross-border data transmission, which restricts the play of data value.

II. Broad Prospects of Global green Openness

Green economy is a new model that pursues efficiency, harmony and sustainability and supports sustainable economic and social development with less and cleaner energy consumption. It is the redefinition and shaping of the whole economic development paradigm, which not only enjoys broad prospects and extensive cooperation opportunities, but also faces numerous challenges.

1. Global consensus on green economic transformation

In the wake of the 2008 global financial crisis, "green stimulus" packages became a policy choice for many countries to improve economic resilience. At the United Nations Conference on Sustainable Development (Rio+20) in June 2012, participating countries agreed to make green economy a priority area for achieving sustainable development. Subsequently, most developed and developing countries put green development high on government agenda when designing and implementing national sustainable development strategies. Especially with the global signing of the Paris Agreement on Climate Change in 2015, achieving carbon neutrality has become an important part of green economic strategies of all countries.

EU

Green transition features prominently in a range of EU medium- and long-term programs and strategies, including *Europe 2020 Strategy, 7th Environment Action Programme, EU Framework Programme and Sectoral Policies*. At the end of 2019, the EU adopted the *European Green Deal*, which aims to set the EU on the path to green transition that will eventually lead to its carbon neutrality by 2050 (Table 9.5). In 2022, the EU further proposed the *REPowerEU* plan, emphasizing the need to accelerate the pace of green transition, rapidly reduce dependence on Russia for oil and gas, and improve the resilience of the EU energy system.

Table 9.5   Strategic deployment of green economy in the EU

Main programs	Main contents
The European Green Deal	A package of policies includes: Achieving climate neutrality by 2050; The "fit for 55" package to translate Green Deal ambitions into law; The Climate Change Adaptation Strategy to help restore Europe's biodiversity; EU Biodiversity Strategy 2030; A Farm to Fork Strategy to promote sustainable development of the EU food system; A European industrial strategy to lead the transition of European industry to climate neutrality; The Circular Economy Action Plan to decouple economic growth from resource use; A clean, affordable, and secure energy plan; The sustainable and intelligent transport initiatives to accelerate the deployment of clean energy and technologies; The sustainable finance initiative to mobilize private capital to invest in green industries and develop financial standards for green bonds and others; The Just Transition Mechanism to provide financial and technical support to regions most affected by the low-carbon transition with a total budget of 17.5 billion euros.

Source: EU official website documents.

US

During the Donald Trump administration, the budget was considerably slashed in the field of environmental protection, resulting in relatively weak development of green economy in the US, but a lot of investments have been made in renewable energy, electric vehicles, energy efficiency, hydrogen energy and other fields at the state level. After taking office in 2021, Joe Biden led the US to re-join the Paris Agreement and signed a number of executive orders to deal with the climate crisis at home and abroad, making climate change once again the strategic focus of green transformation for the US (Table 9.6).

Table 9.6   Green Economy Initiatives in the US

Green stimulus programs during the pandemic	The Coronavirus Aid, Relief, and Economic Security Act (CARES) in March 2020 provides more than $250 million in payroll relief funds to clean energy businesses; The American Rescue Plan in January 2021 plans to earmark $30 billion for mass transit system; The Infrastructure Investment and Jobs Act signed into a law on November 2021 plans to increase renewable energy grids, electric vehicle charging stations, public transport, clean energy research and development support, and other green infrastructure over the next four years; In June 2021, the Hydrogen Shot program was launched, with $8 billion allocated to support the construction of regional Hydrogen energy centers and $1.5 billion to support the research and development demonstration of the Hydrogen energy industry chain.

(Continued)

"The Long-term Strategy of the United States - Pathways to Net Zero Greenhouse Gas Emissions by 2050" submitted to the UNFCCC in 2021	Power sector targets: achieving 100% clean electricity by 2035; Transportation sector: improving fuel efficiency and emissions standards; supporting the construction of zero-emission vehicles and charging piles; promoting the use of renewable fuels; Construction sector: applying new technology, new materials and new building standards, etc.; Heavy industry sector: supporting low-carbon industrial technology and equipment, and using government procurement to support zero-carbon industrial early stage markets; Other targets include agriculture, forestry and marine protection.

Source: Compiled according to IEA and United Nations Framework Convention on Climate Change (UNFCCC) official website documents.

Japan

Japan is one of the countries that has vigorously implemented the *Green New Deal*. After the 2008-2009 financial crisis, Japan adopted documents such as *Japan's Vision and Actions toward Low-Carbon Growth and a Climate-Resilient World* to support green and low-carbon transition. In December 2020, Japan released *Green Growth Strategy Through Achieving Carbon Neutrality in 2050*, which took carbon emission reduction and digital economy as two important engines for economic development in the post-pandemic era, and formulated five policy tools to accelerate the construction of Japan's green economic policy ecosystem (Table 9.7).

Table 9.7   Five policy tools of Japan's 2050 Carbon Neutrality and Green Growth Strategy

Policy tools	Main contents
Financial supports	Green Innovation Fund: 2 trillion yen (about 122.7 billion yuan) over 10 years; PPP stimulates private R&D and investment worth 15 trillion yen; Increasing government procurement.
Tax incentives	Enterprises that invest in research and development of new fuel cells, wind power generation, semiconductor and other projects will be exempted from corporate tax by 5% to 10%; Tax incentives to stimulate private investment worth 1.7 trillion yen over 10 years; Encouraging the export of advanced technologies such as offshore wind power generation and hydrogen energy, and increasing the amount of export insurance coverage from 90% to 100%.
Financial policies	Formulating guidelines for transformation financing and establishing a long-term fund discount plan (1 trillion yen in 3 years based on business scale); Attracting global ESG investment.
Regulatory reform	Considering regulatory changes in areas such as hydrogen, offshore wind power, and mobile battery; Discussing carbon boundary adjustment and related policies to ensure a level playing field globally.

(Continued)

Policy tools	Main contents
International cooperation	Carrying out cooperation on innovation policies with developed and emerging countries, including projects in third countries; Carrying out standardization and rules-making; Providing a variety of decarbonization solutions; A global promotion campaign.

Source: the website of the Ministry of Economy, Trade and Industry Japan.
https://www.meti.go.jp/english/policy/energy_environment/global_warming/ggs2050/index.html.

China

Green and low-carbon are also key words in China's 12ᵗʰ Five-Year Plan (2011-2015) and 13ᵗʰ Five-Year Plan (2016-2020).

During this period, China issued a series of policy documents on controlling greenhouse gas emissions, promoting energy conservation and emissions reduction, and building a green financial system to promote green transformation. After announcing the goal of achieving carbon dioxide peaking before 2030 and achieving carbon neutrality by 2060 in September 2020, China issued the *Guiding Opinions on Accelerating the Establishment and Improvement of the Green and Low-carbon Circular Development Economic System*, the *14ᵗʰ Five-Year Plan (2021-2025)*, *Guidance for Carbon Dioxide Peaking and Carbon Neutrality*, and *Action Plan for Carbon Dioxide Peaking before 2030*, to ensure that carbon emissions peaking and carbon neutrality are achieved (Table 9.8).

Table 9.8   China's work deployment for carbon dioxide peaking and carbon neutrality

Phased goals	Forming an economic system for green, low-carbon and circular development by 2025; Achieving significant progress in comprehensive green transformation and peaking carbon emissions by 2030, and promoting steady decline of carbon emissions; Realizing carbon neutrality by 2060;
Strategic visions	Strengthening the "dual control" of energy consumption intensity and total energy consumption, and build a clean, low-carbon, safe and efficient energy system; Promoting industrial green and low-carbon transformation, vigorously developing green and low-carbon industry; Comprehensively promoting green and low-carbon development of urban and rural construction; Promoting the construction of low-carbon transportation system; Promoting nature-based solutions at a faster pace to maximize the role of agriculture, forestry and marine ecosystems; Promoting comprehensive green transformation of economic and social development and optimizing regional distribution.

(Continued)

Technological paths	Promoting the progress of energy-saving technology; Upgrading the electrification of the terminal energy sector; Developing technologies for renewable energy and nuclear energy, new energy plus energy storage, hydrogen, natural gas, biofuels, and carbon capture, utilization and absorption; Enhancing carbon sequestration capacity and ecological restoration of the ecosystem.
Capacity building	Raising the level of green and low-carbon development in opening up to the outside world; Improving laws, regulations, standards and statistical monitoring systems; Improving investment, green finance, fiscal and tax pricing policies; Promoting the building of market-based mechanisms.

Source: UNFCCC website, *China's Mid-Century Long-Term Low Greenhouse Gas Emission Development Strategy*, https://unfccc.int/documents/307765.

Other countries

Singapore announced its *Green Plan 2030* in February 2021, and South Korea unveiled its $37 billion *Green New Deal* stimulus plan, and also submitted its *2050 Carbon Neutral Strategy* to UNFCCC Secretariat. India also announced at COP26 that it would become carbon neutral by around 2070. According to the UNFCCC website on May 31, 2022, 194 Parties to the Paris Agreement have submitted their information on Nationally Determined Contributions (NDCs), covering 91.3% of global emissions, of which more than 140 countries have announced or are considering net zero emission targets (Table 9.9).

Table 9.9   INDC targets and carbon neutrality commitments of major economies
（till May 31, 2022）

Main economies	Summary of latest commitments and goals	Long-term emission strategic commitments
EU	Reducing emissions by at least 55% from the 1990 level by 2030 (the original target was 40%); Raising the share of renewable energy to 45% (the original target was 32%).	Achieving carbon neutrality by 2050
US	Achieving a 26-28% emission reduction from 2005 levels by 2025; Reducing net greenhouse gas emissions by 50-52% from 2005 levels by 2030; Realizing 100% carbon pollution-free electricity by 2035.	Achieving carbon neutrality by 2050
Canada	Reducing carbon emissions by at least 40-45% from 2005 levels by 2030.	Achieving carbon neutrality by 2050
Singapore	Achieving carbon emissions peaking around 2030 and halved from the level by 2050; Realizing clean energy for all vehicles by 2040.	Achieving carbon neutrality as soon as possible after the middle of the century
New Zealand	Reducing greenhouse gas emissions by about 50% by 2030 (the original target was 30%).	Achieving carbon neutrality by 2050

(Continued)

Main economies	Summary of latest commitments and goals	Long-term emission strategic commitments
Japan	Lowering emissions reduction by 46% by 2030 from 2013 levels (the original target was 26%); Raising the share of renewable energy to 36-38% by 2030 (the original target was 22-24%).	Achieving carbon neutrality by 2050
South Korea	Reducing emissions reduction in 2030 by 40% from the 2018 level (the original target was 26.3%).	Achieving carbon neutrality by 2050
China	Peaking carbon emissions by 2030; Increasing the share of non-fossil energy to 25% by 2030 (the original target was 20%); Cutting carbon intensity by more than 65% by 2030 from the 2005 level (the original target was 60-65%).	Achieving carbon neutrality by around 2060
Australia	Reducing emissions by 30-35% by 2030 (the original reduction target was 26-28%).	Achieving carbon neutrality by 2050
India	Lowering carbon intensity by 45% by 2030 from the 2005 level (the original target was 33% to 35% lower); Raising the share of electricity generated from non-fossil sources to 50% (the original target was 40%).	Achieving carbon neutrality by 2070
South Africa	Reducing carbon emissions by 28% by 2030, with a cap of 510 million tonnes of carbon dioxide equivalent in 2025 and 398-440 million tonnes in 2030 (the original cap was 614 million tonnes).	Achieving carbon neutrality by 2050

Source: based on NDCs reports at the UNFCCC official websites submitted by member countries.

Stakeholders

Since 2008, the United Nations Environment Programme, the United Nations Department of Economic and Social Affairs, the United Nations Conference on Trade and Development, and the International Labour Organization have successively launched Green Economy or Green Growth Initiatives. International institutions and organizations such as the World Bank, the OECD, the Partnership for Action on Green Economy, Green Growth Knowledge Platform, Green Economy Alliance, and the Stakeholder Forum are also working to promote green transition on a global scale. The G20 Task Force on Climate-Related Financial Disclosure (TCFD) has issued a series of regulatory guidelines, action plans and regulatory statements related to climate risk governance, among which the TCFD recommendations on climate-related financial disclosures is the most influential climate information disclosure standard in the world.

Banks and asset manager companies representing 40% of global financial assets have pledged to meet the targets of the Paris Agreement. In 2020, the climate finance by Multilateral Development Banks (MDBs)[1] reached $66 billion, with climate finance accounting for 29% of their total business operations, compared with 19.2% in 2015. As of November 2021, the Glasgow Financial Alliance for Net Zero (GFANZ), convened by the United Nations, had been signed by more than 450 financial firms which together own $130 trillion in assets. The Principles for Responsible Banking, led by the UNEP Finance Initiative (UNEP FI), has been signed by more than 240 banks representing more than a third of the global banking sector. More and more banks and insurance institutions in the financial market have announced that they will stop providing financing and insurance services for coal power projects.

More and more companies are joining the carbon-neutral campaign. According to the World Bank, as of December 2020, 127 countries, 823 cities, 101 regions and 1,541 companies had committed to decarbonization by mid-century. As the first step towards achieving "Breakthrough 2030", more than 6,200 members from 110 countries/regions have joined the UN-backed Race to Zero campaign, including major multinational corporations, educational and medical institutions, and others.

2. Positive progress made in green industries and green investment

Backed by ever-growing ambitions and policy actions, investors, businesses and governments are more committed than ever to green and low-carbon transition.

Energy transition has accelerated. Global investment in energy transition totaled a record $755 billion in 2021, up 6.5% from the previous year[2]. Clean energy and electrification accounted for the vast majority of the investment, at $731 billion. From an individual country perspective, China is the largest energy transition investor, with $266 billion invested in 2021, followed by the US ($114 billion). The EU as a whole made an investment of $154 billion. On top of the $755 billion, investment in climate technology reached $165 billion in 2021.

Renewable energy industry has been growing rapidly. The new installed capacity of global renewable energy continued to grow during the pandemic, reaching a record

---

[1] Group of Multilateral Development Banks (2021). *Joint Report on Multilateral Development Banks' Climate Finance*. June 30. https://reliefweb.int/report/world/2020-joint-report-multilateral-development-banks-climate-finance.

[2] BloombergNEF (2022). *Energy Transition Investment Trend 2022*. https://about.bnef.com/energy-transition-investment/.

280 GW in 2020 and 295 GW in 2021, with China accounting for 46% of global total. The International Energy Agency (IEA) expects that driven by ambitious renewable energy plans in China, India and the EU, the the new installed capacity of global renewable energy will further grow to 320 GW.

Electric vehicles have led transportation industry into a green transition channel. By the end of 2020, the number of electric vehicles in the world had exceeded 10 million, with a year-on-year increase of 43%[1]. Among them, 4.5 million were in China, ranking first in the world. The sales of electric vehicles in Europe have also showed a considerable growth, stimulated by the subsidy program for this sector.

The green finance market is on a fast track. By the end of 2021, global cumulative issuance of green bonds had exceeded $1.8 trillion, continuing a growth trend for ten consecutive years. Europe, China and the US are the most active markets in the world. The investment strategies of most institutional investors around the world are beginning to tilt towards ESG investments. According to the data from Morningstar Direct[2], global ESG fund assets rose to $2.74 trillion in December 2021, compared with 1.65 trillion at the end of 2020 and $1.28 trillion at the end of 2019.

III. Trend of Global Digital and Green Openness

Since 2021, the pace of economic globalization has continued to be slowed by the COVID-19 pandemic. Digital and green openness have also been affected as never before. In the short term, the challenges cannot be ignored, but in the long run, openness remains an irreversible trend of the times.

1. Trend of global digital openness: Continue to advance, but difficulties will increase

The development of digital economy is booming, but the openness and difficulty of digital trade, digital infrastructure, free flow of data across borders, and rules and standards vary greatly.

---

① IEA (2022). *Global Electric Vehicles Outlook 2021*. https://www.iea.org/reports/global-ev-outlook-2021.

② Morningstar Direct (2022). *Global Sustainable Fund Flows Report*. https://www.morningstar.com/lp/global-esg-flows.

Openness in the field of digital trade is relatively easy. Digital trade liberalization plays an obvious role in promoting a country's economy, and it is the easiest area to reach consensus and realize the highest level of liberalization. In the future, openness in this area is expected to become increasingly wider.

There exist regulations in the field of digital infrastructure. Digital infrastructure connectivity plays a strong supporting role in promoting global digital trade and economic growth. However, since it is usually the carrier of data transmission and storage and digital technology, digital infrastructure is often regulated out of concerns over data leakage and technology spillover.

Cooperation and sharing in digital technology are becoming increasingly difficult. Free flow of data across borders is difficult. Cross-border data flow is an inevitable requirement of trade liberalization, but it is closely related to major issues such as personal privacy protection, data sovereignty and national security, so it attracts extensive attention and receives increasingly strict regulation. Digital technology is the core variable of a new round of technological revolution and industrial transformation, and a key force to boost the economy of all countries in the post-pandemic era. However, due to ever-fiercer technological competition and the emergence of value trade, technological cooperation and sharing among non-allied economies are becoming increasingly difficult, and digital technology gap is deepening. This makes digital technology the least open and most easily decoupled area in the digital domain.

Openness space and difficulty coexist in the field of rules and standards.

a. In the field of digital trade liberalization and facilitation, rules are relatively complete and mature, but still need to be adjusted and enriched in the following aspects. First, the definition of digital products, tariffs collection, reduction and exemption, export control and import restrictions, and other rules all need to be extended to the field of digital trade. In particular, the sustainability of duty-free electronic transmission needs to be explored. Second, with the emergence of the new model, 160 sub-sectors in the existing service commitment table are facing expansion, and service trade openness in the future needs negotiations on the expanded service trade commitment table. Third, digital trade facilitation needs to be further improved. The use and mutual recognition of electronic documents (such as bills of lading, certificates of origin, health inspection and quarantine certificates, etc.), promotion of international templates for electronic invoices, and internationalization of electronic payment systems are all key areas to be promoted.

b. In the area of data development and utilization, rules are becoming more and more perfect, and the space for rules expansion is very big, but the difficulty for this is also big. The difficulties are mainly as follows: first, how to achieve balance between the development of data resources and the protection of personal privacy; second, how to achieve compatibility between security challenges arising from cross-border data flows and different regulatory rules in different countries. The field of data development and utilization can be further subdivided into the following two areas: first, data development and sharing. The construction of rules in the future should be mainly reflected in the areas of data openness, sharing and utilization of individuals, enterprises, industries and governments, data empowerment, asset entry into balance sheets and transaction rules. However, due to the problems of data security, difficulty of empowerment and conflict of interest of data owners, the road to data openness is long. Moreover, as a new production factor, its new characteristics different from traditional factors usually increase the difficulty of data value evaluation and capitalization. As far as cross-border information flow is concerned, it involves cross-border information flow, data localization and offshore data regulation, access and use of the Internet, etc. However, due to huge differences in economic and trade concepts and security concepts of different economies, it is difficult to reach a consensus on cross-border data flow regulation at the international level.

c. In the field of digital governance, only certain agreements such as DEPA , cover part of the digital governance rules. In the future, there will be a lot of room for expansion in digital governance rules and those spillover effects will be great, but they will not pose a big challenge to the domestic system of countries. In view of this, digital governance rules maybe the earliest areas where an agreement can be reached and generate huge welfare effects in the future. They are also important means for a country to empower society and improve the level of digital governance.

2. Prospects of global green openness: Long-term prospects are promising, but short-term challenges should not be ignored

Global green finance and technology cooperation will become more rules-based. The G20 Sustainable Finance Roadmap and the *Common Ground Taxonomy Instruction Report* published at COP26 in 2021 by International Platform on

Sustainable Finance(IPSF) working group co-chaired by China and EU are two important outcomes of global cooperation on green standards, aiming to establish a globally consistent system of sustainable disclosure standards and guide cross-border climate investment and financing activities on a larger scale. The Central Banks and Supervisors Network for Greening the Financial System (NGFS) has been set up by 92 central banks and financial regulators worldwide to promote climate- and environment-related risk management in the financial sector. The Sustainable Banking Network (SBN) consisting of emerging market banking regulators and banking associations was also officially launched in 2019 to advance ESG management and sustainable finance cooperation among financial institutions in emerging markets.

Clean technologies are crucial to the global fight against climate change. In 2015, 24 economies, including the US, Europe and China, launched a global initiative named *Mission Innovation* (MI) at the COP21, aiming to promote scientific and technological investment in clean energy and realize clean energy and technology cooperation on a global scale.

***Green Belt and Road Initiative* will become an important platform to lead international green cooperation.** At present, the "Belt and Road" big data service platform for ecological and environmental protection, the *Belt and Road Green Supply Chain Platform*, the *Green Silk Road Envoy Program*, the *Belt and Road Green Development Coalition* (BRIGC) and other cooperation achievements have been launched, and the *Green Investment Principles* (GIP) for the Belt and Road Initiative have also been signed by many domestic and foreign financial institutions. In May 2022, China issued the "Opinions on Promoting Green Development of the Belt and Road", which stressed that it will promote green "Belt and Road" construction in specific areas such as green infrastructure, green energy, green industry, green trade cooperation, green finance, green technology and green standards.

The pandemic, geopolitical conflicts and extreme weather events will add uncertainty to international green development and cooperation in the future. At present, the impact of the pandemic has not been completely eliminated, and many countries still focus on fighting the pandemic, supporting vulnerable enterprises and guaranteeing people's livelihood, which restricts the scale of green investment. Natural Gas and coal markets also remain tight and volatile, with the European energy crisis at the end of 2021 forcing European utilities to switch to heavily-polluting coal sources.

The Ukraine crisis in 2022 has further added uncertainty to Europe's energy supply, which, added by the US being unable to meet Europe's huge natural gas demand in the short term, may cause Europe to burn more coal and build more pipelines and terminals to import fossil fuels from elsewhere in the short term. Supply chains blocked by the pandemic combined with the geopolitical crisis have also increased supply risks for minerals such as lithium, nickel, palladium, aluminum and platinum needed for key clean energy technologies, and continued high prices for raw materials will also increase the cost of kilowatt-hours of solar PV and wind power.

Extreme weather has exposed the volatility and instability of renewable energy, and with an increasing proportion of new energy sources in the future, energy supply will fluctuate more if no major technological breakthroughs are achieved. Therefore, in the process of green transformation, the risks of replacing old energy with new energy should not be underestimated. This is particularly important for big energy consumers such as China and India. The IEA predicts that global energy demand will grow by another 50-60% by 2030, and energy consumption in Asia in particular will grow by about 6% per year (IEA, 2020). In the backdrop of green transformation, large energy consumers such as China and India need to fundamentally change their energy structure, but due to the high carbon lock-in effect caused by coal-based energy structure, continuing energy demands and emissions reduction pressures from industrialization and urbanization, as well as the huge technological and financial gap, these countries will face very prominent transformation challenges.

In general, the development of digital economy and green economy has become the trend of the times, but the development path is closely related to the policies and institutional settings, development level, social structure, resource endowment and specific environmental pressures of each country, and also is vulnerable to the impact of uncertainties such as the pandemics, wars, extreme weather events and geopolitics. From a general respective, the development of global digital economy and green economy cannot be achieved without the joint participation and open cooperation of all countries.

Chapter 10   High-Level Opening-Up under the New Development Paradigm

In the era of economic globalization, internal and external circulations are deeply integrated and cannot be separated. Profound changes in the domestic and international environment have brought a series of new opportunities as well as new challenges. Only by opening up at a high level can China keep pace with the trend of the times and win the initiative for development. The more China develops, the wider it will be open to the outside. As China opens its door even wider, to promote high-level opening-up is an inevitable choice for it to build a new development pattern.

I. Historic Progress Achieved in Opening-up over the Past Decade

Over the past decade, China has always adhered to the basic state policy of opening-up, implementing a more proactive opening-up strategy and promoting the formation of a new pattern of comprehensive opening-up. The cause of opening-up has made historic strides and changes, and remarkable achievements have been scored. China has gone all out to promote high-quality trade development, integrating the strategies of "bringing in" and "going out", and promoting high-quality Belt and Road cooperation. It has accelerated the building of a network of high-standard free trade areas, and continuously improved its ability to participate in global economic governance, making itself a major stabilizer and driving force of world economic growth.

1. Greater consolidation of the status as a major trading power
Over the past ten years, China has accelerated high-quality development of its

foreign trade, promoted a continuous increase in the scale and quality of foreign trade, promoted its position in the global industrial and supply chains to be stable, and played an important role in the development of the national economy and the recovery of the world economy.

a. Total trade in goods and services rising to the world's largest

From 2012 to 2021, China's total trade in goods and services increased from $4.35 trillion to $6.87 trillion, with the proportion to the world's total increasing from 9.4% to 12.2%, and the ranking in the world rising from the second to the first. Of the total volume, the import and export value in goods increased from $3.87 trillion to $6.05 trillion. Since 2017, China has remained the world's largest country in goods trade for five consecutive years. The import and export value of trade in services increased from $0.48 trillion to $0.82 trillion during the same period, rising from the third to the second place in the world.

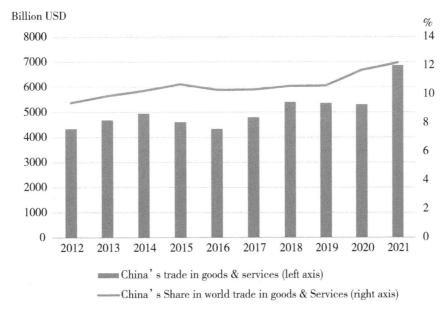

Fig. 10.1   China's trade in goods and services and the share in the world, 2012-2021
Source: WTO.

b. Remarkable results in the high-quality development of trade in goods

The domestic regional layout is more optimized, and the proportion of the central and western regions in exports in 2021 increased by 5.9 percentages compared with 2012. The commodity structure is continuously optimized, and high-tech and high-value-added products such as automobiles and ships have gradually become new growth points. The innovation in trade has achieved remarkable results, and new trade formats and models such as cross-border e-commerce have emerged continuously. The market diversification has achieved positive results, actively expanding emerging markets such as Asia, Latin America and Africa, and signing 19 free trade agreements with 26 countries and regions. The foreign trade business entities are more dynamic, and the number of business entities has increased by 1.7 times during the same period.

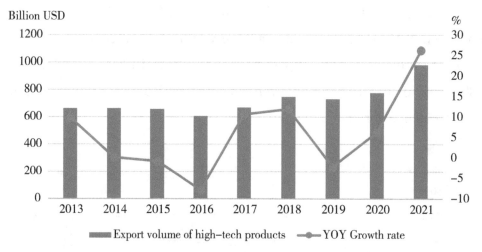

Fig. 10.2   China's high-tech product export and growth rate, 2013-2021

Source: The Ministry of Commerce of China.

c. Innovative development of trade in services

Over the past decade, China's service import and export have increased significantly, with the structure of service trade being optimized at a faster pace, and the development of knowledge-intensive trade in services, such as intellectual property royalties, telecommunications, computers and information services, has in particular accelerated. In 2021, China's import and export of knowledge-intensive services reached 2,325.89 billion yuan, accounting for 43.9% of its total trade in services. In particular, the import and export of intellectual property royalties have increased by 1.5 times over the past decade, with the import increasing from $17.75 billion in 2012 to $37.63 billion in 2021, and the export increasing from $1.04 billion in 2012 to $8.88 billion in 2021.

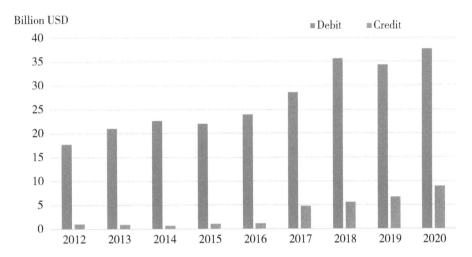

Fig. 10.3   China's Charges for the use of intellectual property, 2012-2020

Source: WTO.

2. A significant increase in the level of two-way investment

Over the past decade, China's two-way investment has grown steadily, the level of both foreign investment utilization and outward foreign direct investment have continuously improved, and an overall balance between the use of foreign investment and OFDI has been achieved. From attaching importance to "bringing in" to attaching importance to both "bringing in" and "going global", China has actively participated in the layout of the global industrial chain and the allocation of global resources.

a. Two-way investment ranks among the largest in the world

Over the past decade, China has fully implemented national treatment for foreign-invested enterprises and worked hard to create a stable, fair, transparent and predictable business environment. As a result, the level of China's foreign investment utilization has continued to improve, ranking second in the world for four consecutive years since 2017, and the amount of foreign investment utilization in 2021 increased by 62.9% compared with 2012. China has also accelerated its pace of going global, promoted steady development of overseas investment and cooperation, and guided more than 40000 enterprises to invest abroad in 189 countries around the world.

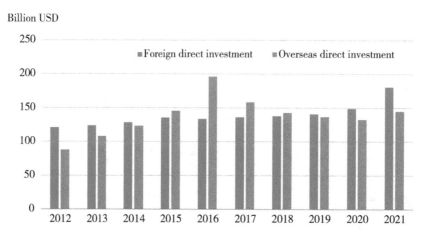

Fig. 10.4   FDI in China and China's ODI, 2012-2021

Source: UNCTAD.

b. Major achievements made in utilizing foreign investment

In the past ten years, China's utilization of foreign capital has expanded from manufacturing to service sector and then converged to high-tech industries. In 2021, the proportion of China's utilized foreign capital in high-tech industries exceeded 30% for the first time, more than doubling from 13.8% in 2012. Foreign direct investment actually used in the service sector increased by 16.7% year-on-year, accounting for 78.9%. China has introduced a series of major opening-up measures in manufacturing, mining, agriculture and finance to attract more foreign companies. The legal system for foreign investment has been further improved, the environment for foreign investment has been much better, and the fair competition treatment for foreign-funded enterprises has been fully guaranteed.

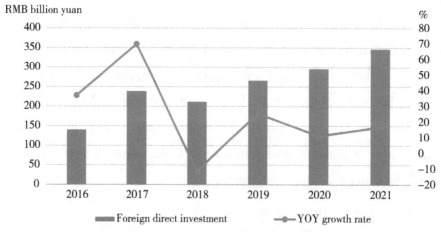

Fig.10.5   Foreign direct investment in China's high-tech industry, 2016-2021

Source: The Ministry of Commerce of China.

c. Growth of outbound investment in a healthy and orderly manner

From 2012 to 2016, China's outward direct investment began to grow rapidly, exceeding $170 billion in 2016. Since 2017, China's outbound investment has developed steadily and international cooperation in green and digital fields has been booming. The construction of new types of infrastructure has been increasing and cooperation areas have been continuously expanded. The pace of transformation of foreign contracted projects has been accelerated, with its business scope extended from traditional civil construction to the whole industrial chain of design, consulting, financing and operation. There have been more projects integrating construction and investment, construction and operation, and positive progress has been made in third-party market cooperation. Overseas economic and trade cooperation zones have been upgraded. By the end of 2021, the total investment in the overseas economic and trade cooperation zones included in the statistics of the Ministry of Commerce of the People's Republic of China had reached $50.7 billion, bringing about evident industrial agglomeration effects. A number of demonstration zones, such as Egypt's Suez Economic and Trade Cooperation Zone and Cambodia's Westport Special Economic Zone, had achieved good cooperation results and obvious radiation effects.

3. Continuous improvement in the new open economic system

Over the past ten years, China has accelerated the building of a new system for open economy, with the door opened to the outside increasingly wider, and opening-up scope and fields increasingly expanded and levels increasingly improved. From coastal areas to inland and border areas, from manufacturing to services, and from opening-up based on the flow of goods and factors of production to opening-up based on rules and other institutions, China's all-round opening-up has reached a new level.

a. Increasing optimization of the regional opening-up layout

Over the past decade, China has accelerated the building of a new pattern of opening-up featuring connectivity between land and sea, and mutual benefits between east and west. Guangdong, Shanghai, Jiangsu, Zhejiang and other provinces or cities have maintained a leading position in foreign investment and foreign trade, and the eastern coastal areas have continued to play a guiding role in opening-up. The successive approval for the establishment of the Xixian New Area in Shaanxi, Gui'an New Area in Guizhou province and other eight new areas, have ushered in accelerated steps of China's inland areas toward opening-up. The regular and large-scale operation of China-Europe freight trains has been achieved and the construction of new land-sea passageways in the western region has been accelerated, driving the opening-up of China's central and western regions. Steady progress has been made in the border (cross-border) economic cooperation zones and key pilot development and opening-up zones along border areas, and initial progress has also been made in building new pivots of opening-up along border areas. From 2012 to 2021, the share of import and export of China's central and western regions increased from 11.1% to 17.7%. In 2021, the central and western regions saw 20.5% and 14.2% actual FDI growth respectively, making them important regions in China for attracting foreign investment.

b. Accelerating institutional opening-up

In 2013, China launched the first negative list for foreign investment in pilot free trade zones, which was extended to the whole country in 2017. From 2017 to 2021, the negative list was reduced for five consecutive years, with the number of restrictions on the national version reduced to 31 and the pilot free trade zone version reduced to 27. In 2021, the negative list for pilot free trade zones was cleared of manufacturing items. In 2021, the first negative list for cross-border service trade was launched in Hainan, which has achieved a major change in the management mode of cross-border trade in services. In 2020, China implemented the new Foreign Investment Law, establishing a basic system for promoting, protecting and managing foreign investment. The laws, regulations and normative documents that are inconsistent with the Foreign Investment Law have been cleared away for three consecutive years. All these mean that the level of China's opening-up to the outside world has significantly risen and its institutional opening-up has been continuously improved.

c. Solid progresses in developing pilot free trade zones and free trade ports

Since the first pilot free trade zone was established in Shanghai in 2013, a total of 21 pilot free trade zones had been established in China by 2021, which has formed a reform and opening-up innovation pattern. Pilot free trade zones have played a leading role in China's opening-up and exploring high-quality development, and a number of pilot experiences have been developed that can be replicated across the country. With less than 0.4% of the national land area, the pilot free trade zones contributed 17.3% of China's imports and exports and 18.5% of its utilized foreign investment in 2021. In 2020, the overall plan for the construction of Hainan Free Trade Port was issued, and the construction of the Hainan Free Trade Port got off to a good start.

4. Fruitful results in international economic and trade cooperation

Over the past decade, China has continued to open up to the outside world, contributing to the recovery of global trade and investment and becoming the biggest engine of world economic growth. While providing high-quality and affordable goods and services to the global market, this has also provided other countries with broader development opportunities and more international public goods. China is not only the "world factory", but also an important participant and contributor to the "world market" and global economic governance.

a. Sound and bigger strides towards co-building of the Belt and Road Initiative

The Belt and Road Initiative has continuously expanded its influence and become a popular international public good and a platform for international cooperation in today's world. From 2013 to 2021, China's trade in goods with Belt and Road countries totaled $11 trillion, and its direct investment in them totaled $164 billion. The contract value and turnover of contracted projects in 24 Belt and Road countries totaled $1.08 trillion and $728.6 billion respectively. Chinese enterprises have built 79 overseas economic and trade cooperation zones in 24 Belt and Road countries, with a total investment of $43.08 billion creating 346,000 local jobs. More than 50,000 China-Europe freight trains have been operated, connecting more than 180 cities in 23 European countries. A number of "small but beautiful" agricultural, medical and poverty reduction projects have been launched, bringing tangible benefits to people in Belt and Road countries. Connectivity ties between China and these countries have been deepened and exchange and cooperation mechanisms have been further improved.

b. An increasingly big "circle of friends" for free trade

Over the past decade, the number of free trade agreements signed by China has nearly doubled, increasing from 10 to 19. At the same time, the share of China's trade with free trade partners increased from 17% to 35% of its total foreign trade volume last year. On January 1, 2022, the Regional Comprehensive Economic Partnership (RCEP) came into force, marking the launch of the world's largest free trade area with the largest population and the largest trade scale. In addition, China has actively promoted its accession to the Comprehensive and Progressive Trans-Pacific Partnership

(CPTPP) and the Digital Economy Partnership (DEPA), taking new steps toward the goal of building high-standard free trade agreements.

c. Continuous improvement in the ability to participate in global economic governance

China has put forward a vision of global governance featuring "extensive consultation, joint contribution and shared benefits", promoting the building of an open world economy, a new type of international relations based on win-win cooperation, and a community with a shared future for mankind. It firmly upholds the multilateral trading system and actively participates in the reform of the WTO. Through the G20 Summit, the BRICS Summit and other platforms, it advocates placing development under the global macro policy framework, puts forward common goals for global economic governance and promotes the formation of a new concept and approach for international development cooperation, contributing Chinese solutions and wisdom to improving global economic governance.

II. Opening-up at A High Level --- A Necessary Part of the New Development Paradigm

Building a new development pattern is a strategic choice made by China under the new circumstances to raise the level of its economic development and create new advantages in international cooperation and competition. In the era of economic globalization, domestic circulation guides external circulation, and external circulation promotes domestic circulation, with the two circulations reinforcing each other and forming a virtuous circle at a higher level of openness.

1. Promoting opening-up at a high level --- the only way to build a new development pattern

The new development pattern is not built on a closed domestic circulation, but on a more open domestic and international "dual circulation". High-level opening-up and the new development pattern go hand in hand and complement each other.

a. Conducive to smooth domestic circulation

The key to building a new development pattern lies in unimpeded economic circulation, especially the effective and unimpeded domestic circulation. China must accelerate the innovation of the supply system and enhance its resilience, make effective supply penetrate the blocking points of the economic circulation, and remove bottleneck constraints, so as to achieve dynamic balance of the economy at a high level. From this perspective, high-level opening-up can not only introduce high-quality factors of production and scarce resources to make up for the needs of domestic production, but can also improve the allocation of domestic factors of production through the alignment of regulations and other rules, increase the efficiency and level of the supply system, and provide effective impetus for unimpeded domestic circulation.

b. Conducive to promoting domestic and international "dual circulation"

The new development pattern is an open domestic and international dual circulation, not a closed domestic single circulation. To build a new development pattern, China needs to give better play to the role of openness while taking domestic circulation as the mainstay, so as to promote a good situation in which domestic circulation can guide international circulation, and international circulation can promote domestic circulation. Therefore, it must pave the way for the interactive development of domestic and international dual circulation through high-level opening-up. On the one hand, China should encourage more high-quality Chinese goods and services to "go global" to stabilize and promote international circulation, and on the other hand, more goods, services, capital and technology should be "brought in" to improve the efficiency and level of domestic circulation. In doing so, it can promote domestic and international circulation to achieve a virtuous circle in terms of market connectivity, industrial integration, innovation promotion, rules integration and other aspects.

2. New connotations of high-level opening-up under the new development pattern

China currently tries to build a new development pattern with domestic circulation as the mainstay and domestic and international circulation mutually reinforcing each other, which raises new and higher requirements for greater opening-up. Against the backdrop of the new development pattern, high-level opening-up takes on new features and changes in terms of mechanisms, advantages, sectors and driving forces.

a. Changing from opening-up based on the flow of factors to one based on institutions

Over the past four decades of reform and opening-up, China has continued to develop an open economy through opening-up based on the flow of goods and factors of production. As foreign cooperation shifts from simple expansion of trade towards diversification in depth and upgrades from paying attention to both "bringing in" and "going out" to building a multi-dimensional and comprehensive network in breadth, the opening-up model based on the flow of goods and elements is no longer able to meet the needs of deepening international cooperation, which requires fundamentally changing the concept of opening-up to the outside world and promoting mutual inclusiveness and integration of China's open economic system with the existing and idealized world system. To build a new development pattern, China should more effectively pool high-quality talents, advanced technologies and other high-end production factors across the world on the supply side, and effectively improve their allocation efficiency in China, so as to gradually optimize domestic circulation. It also requires China to optimize the supply structure in response to the world's high-end demand, so as to promote supply and demand to reach a higher level of balance. Institutional openness is the key to mutual development of domestic and international circulation. The ultimate goal of institutional opening-up is to break all kinds of unreasonable and artificial barriers between domestic and international circulation systems, so that micro subjects inside and outside China can freely transform and combine between domestic and international circulation. Only when the relevant institutional barriers are considerably weakened, can high-quality factors in the international circulation enter domestic circulation smoothly, and the positive spillover effect of the international circulation on the total factor productivity of the domestic circulation be fully realized and finally lead domestic circulation to reach a higher level. This means China must deepen institutional opening-up based on rules and standards, and build a system of rules that is conducive to gathering global factors and leading the upgrading of global economic and trade rules.

Box 10-1　Features of Institutional Openness

The Central Economic Work Conference held at the end of 2018 clearly pointed out that China will promote transition from openness based on the flow of goods and factors of production to openness based on rules and other institutions. This is the first time that China's top authorities put forward the concept of institutional openness.

In the decisions on some major problems made by the Central Committee of the CPC about upholding and improving the system of socialism with Chinese characteristics to promote the modernization of national governance system and governance ability, President Xi Jinping pointed out that "compared to the past, reform and opening-up in the new era has many new connotations and characteristics, a very important point of which is that the weight of institutional construction is heavier", "reform is more about the underlying system and mechanism, which raises higher requirements for the top-level design and stronger requirements for the systematical, holistic and coordinated reform. Accordingly, the task of establishing rules and regulations and building a system is heavier." This marks China's opening-up to the outside world has further advance toward the institutional scope and entered a new stage of institutional opening-up. Institutional opening-up has the following characteristics:

First, following the rules of market economy

Under the target frame of building the socialist market economy system, some basic rules of market economy should always be taken as the principles to be followed in the reform of the foreign-related economic system, including the rule of law economy, fair competition, the combination of market regulation and macro-control, etc. Under the conditions of openness, it is necessary to follow and participate in the coordination of various rules and practices of international interests.

Second, providing institutional guarantee for an open economy

The essence of institutional opening-up is to create an institutional environment for an open economy. Institutional openness is the only way to improve the rule of law-based economy. To promote the continuous improvement of the rules of market operation and market activities, it is necessary to promote economic development by relying on laws and regulations, and changing from administrative management to the governance based on the law and regulations. It is also necessary to keep in line with international high standards of investment and trade rules to build a fair, open, competitive and orderly institutional system according to internationalized, legalized and marketized requirements in terms of resource allocation mechanism, the market economy environment, the economic operation and management mode, the international macroeconomic policy coordination mechanism, the government management function, and the international economic governance structure, etc.

Third, displaying obvious phased features and fitting in with the open economic development

China's open economy is characterized by distinct stages, and correspondingly, the content of institutional reform and the key rules that are abided by in different stages also have their own emphasis. Institutional opening-up before the Third Plenary Session of the 18th CPC Central Committee coincided with the process of domestic reform from the planned economy system to the one in which the planned economy system dominates but market regulations also play a role, and then to the one that the market plays a dominant role. It meets the needs of China transiting from local pilot opening-up to full and active integration into the global economy. With the proposal put forward by the Third Plenary Session of the 18th CPC Central Committee that a new open economic system will be built. China began to take "the construction of a new higher level of open economy system" as a main content of the economic system reform at the present or for some time in the future, which not only adapts to the "from big to strong development" transition of China's open economy and helps enhance China's status and role in the global rule system, but also is in line with accelerating the improvement of the socialist market economy in the new era.

b. Changing from opening-up advantages based on factor supply to ones based on market environment

Since the reform and opening-up, China has seized strategic opportunities brought by the international industrial transfer, and by relying on low-cost labor, land and other factors, attracted capital and technology inflow of multinational corporations from developed countries, and built an open economic model based on "the import of raw materials, production at home and export to the international market". At present, under the changed conditions in both the international market and its comparative advantages, such kind of economic model is unsustainable, and China should give full play to its market scale and environmental advantages and take advantage of its domestic circulation to attract global commodities and resource factors, to build its new advantages in international cooperation and competition. In the context of its effort to build a new development pattern, China should continue to improve the quality of factor supply, leverage its advantages in market size, optimize the international business environment, cultivate new comparative advantages, and achieve high-level opening-up. On the one hand, the construction of a unified domestic market in China is conducive to enhancing the advantages of its local market size, promoting innovation through the expansion of domestic demand, and thus fostering higher quality production factors. At the same time, it can also attract global quality production factors to promote domestic industrial and supply chains to advance toward a higher level and integrate to the international market and international circulation with greater advantages, and enhance and improve China's position in international division of labor. On the other hand, the expanding scale and openness of the domestic market will promote mutually reinforcing of domestic and international "dual circulation", make better use of the two markets and two kinds of resources, cultivate new advantages of the market environment to participate in the division of global factors, and better serve China's bid to build a new development pattern.

c. Shifting from manufacturing openness to high-level two-way openness of the service sector

After the reform and opening-up, China mainly focused on the opening of manufacturing, effectively boosting the development vitality of the sector and becoming the world's largest manufacturing country. At present, there is a big gap between China's service industry and that of developed countries, and in order to further open up, it is urgent for China to shift opening-up from manufacturing to service industry. Opening-up under the new development pattern is a two-way process that includes both opening-up to the outside and opening-up to the inside. This means that to promote the opening of the service industry to the outside world, China should ease access restrictions on services, promote the orderly opening of financial, education, culture, healthcare and other services, relax foreign investment access thresholds in children nurturing and old-age care, architectural designing, accounting audit, trade logistics, e-commerce and other services, realize mutual promotion and development of domestic and international dual circulation. At the same time, it should attach importance to the opening of the service sector at home, adhere to the principle of competition neutrality and unified market access system, ensure all kinds of market players can equally enter the opening areas in accordance with the law, and in particular lift restrictions on private capital investment and promote gradual opening of the monopoly service industries to the private economy, to release more market vitalities and promote the development of domestic circulation.

d. Shifting from passive follow-through and integration to actively leading the way in opening-up motivations

In the past, China's opening-up was always accompanied by international "pressure", which was mainly a follow-through opening-up, and external pressure has been constantly transformed into a driving force of further opening-up. However, with the deepening of reform and opening-up, China's voice in international rule-making has gradually increased and its position in the world has become more and more important. Follow-through opening-up can no longer meet the needs of China's long-term development. Under the new development pattern, domestic and international development will promote each other, and rules, regulations, management and standards will be more interconnected. The shift from follow-through opening-up to active opening-up has become an essential part of China's high-level opening-up under the new development pattern. At present, China is actively preparing to join the CPTPP, the DEPA and other high standard international economic and trade agreements, and the driving force behind China's high-level opening-up has undergone fundamental changes. On the one hand, China goes all out to deepen international cooperation in a more pragmatic and flexible manner. It supports an open, transparent, inclusive and non-discriminatory multilateral trading system, promotes trade and investment liberalization and facilitation, and advances economic globalization in a more open, inclusive, balanced, and win-win direction. On the other hand, China has actively participated in various cooperation mechanisms and taken an active part in the reform and development of the global governance system. Making full use of various international platforms will effectively promote economic, trade and investment cooperation, and participation in the formulation or modification of relevant international trade and investment rules will continuously enhance China's narrative in the reform of rules. In this light, the initiative to open up is an inevitable choice for China to promote high-level opening-up under the new development pattern.

III. High-Level Opening-Up Helps Foster A New Pattern of Development

As the dual circulation based on opening-up both at home and abroad, the new development pattern puts forward higher requirements for the level and quality of opening-up. To promote opening-up at a high level in the context of a new development pattern, China should work harder in exploring a new opening-up system, cultivating new advantages of open development, opening new prospects for international cooperation, and building a solid opening-up safety net.

1. Improving the new system for opening-up

To promote opening-up at a high level under the new development pattern, China needs to improve the quality and level of its participation in the international circulation under the new situations. While consolidating the achievements of opening-up based on the flow of goods and factors of production, it should continuously strengthen institutional opening-up, remove institutional barriers to linking China and the world, and build a new system for an open economy at a higher level.

a. Further promoting opening-up of goods and factors of production

The new development pattern calls for China better integrating into the international circulation and further promoting the opening-up of goods and factors of production. It requires China to optimize the commodity structure and deepen the optimization of import and export, reduce import tariffs and institutional costs, increase imports of high-quality consumer goods, advanced technologies, important equipment, energy and resources, and promote high-end and refined imports and exports to build the "Chinese brand" of goods. China should optimize the supply of factors for opening-up and development, actively explore policy and institutional innovations in the entry, exit and residence of high-end overseas talents, facilitation of cross-border investment and financing, and orderly opening of data and information, and facilitate the employment of talents, cross-border capital flow, and secure and orderly flow of data.

b. Continuously expanding market opening

China has continuously eased market access for foreign investment and better integrated it into the national economic circulation. It has further reduced the negative list for market access for foreign investment, continuously opened up manufacturing, services and agriculture, allowed foreign capital to hold shares or independently operate in more sectors, and actively introduced advanced technology, management expertise and business models. It has promoted the opening-up of key areas, such as advancing the openness of relevant businesses in telecommunications, Internet, education, culture and medical care in an orderly manner. It has improved the catalog of industries that encourage foreign investment, supporting foreign investment in areas such as medium- and high-end manufacturing, new and high technologies, transformation and upgrading of traditional manufacturing, modern services as well as in central and western regions, supported foreign-funded enterprises in setting up global and regional headquarters and research and development centers, and encouraged foreign investment to actively participate in the construction of new types of infrastructure.

c. Accelerating institutional opening-up

China has further reformed domestic institutions and mechanisms, fully implemented the management system of pre-establishment national treatment plus a negative list, advanced investment and trade liberalization and facilitation, and continuously improved the market-oriented, law-based and international business environment. It has advanced the development of pilot free trade zones and free trade ports with high standards and high quality, and carried out comprehensive trials to open more services to the outside world. It has improved the system of pilot tasks for independent and open platforms, and explored the innovative linkage between pilot free trade zones, free trade ports, comprehensive trials for greater openness in the service sector and service trade innovation, comprehensive pilot zones for cross-border e-commerce, pilot policies launched by various departments. It has given full play to the role of open platforms and worked hard to establish an institutional system in line with the prevailing rules of international investment and trade.

2. Fostering new opening-up and development advantages

Under the new development pattern, to participate in the international market through opening-up at a high standard, China should promote better connectivity between domestic and international markets, promote coordinated development and positive interaction between domestic and external demands, and drive economic development in a stronger and more sustainable manner.

a. Adhering to integrated development of domestic and foreign trade

To promote opening-up at a high level, China should promote integrated development of domestic and foreign trade, and plays its key role in unblocking domestic and international "dual circulation". First of all, it is necessary to promote the integration of domestic and foreign trade subjects, cultivate large circulation enterprises with international competitiveness, promote the foreign trade enterprises to expand the domestic market, create a platform for integrated development of domestic and foreign trade, and build bridges between domestic and foreign trade. Second, it is necessary to promote the building of a unified domestic market, establish unified market systems and rules nationwide, promptly clean up and abolish policies that hinder the unified market and fair competition in various regions, break down local protection and market segmentation, and promote the smooth flow of commodity factors and resources in a wider area. Finally, the country should unify domestic and foreign trade standards, actively carry out the transformation of domestic and international standards, promote the same assembly line, standards and quality to domestic and foreign products, improve the quality and brand of products, and cultivate new opening-up advantages.

b. Expanding high-level two-way investment

China should make efficient use of global resources, factors and market space through high-level two-way investment, and improve the guaranteeing mechanism of industrial and supply chains, to raise its industrial competitiveness. Greater efforts should be made to attract and utilize foreign capital, comprehensively optimize foreign investment services, strengthen foreign investment promotion and protection, give play to the exemplary role of major foreign investment projects, support greater foreign investment in medium- and high-end manufacturing, new and high technologies, transformation and upgrading of traditional manufacturing, and modern services, as well as in the central and western regions, support foreign-funded enterprises in setting up research and development centers and participating in national science and technology planning projects, and encourage profits reinvestment of foreign-funded enterprises. The country should innovate outbound investment methods, optimize the structure and distribution of outbound investment, and improve its ability to improve returns from outbound investment. It should improve the network and distribution system for overseas production and services, accelerate the international development of producer services such as finance, consulting, accounting and law, and promote Chinese products, services, technologies, brands and standards to go global. At the same time, it should support enterprises to integrate into global industrial and supply chains, and enhance their capacity and level of transnational operations. It should guide enterprises to strengthen compliance management and prevent, improve the ability to prevent risks and defuse overseas political, economic and security risks.

Practical measures should also be taken to advance the building of multilateral and bilateral investment cooperation mechanisms, improve the policy and service systems for promoting and guaranteeing outbound investment, and advance legislation on outbound investment.

c. Promoting innovation and upgrading of open platforms

The China International Import Expo, the China Import and Export Fair (Canton Fair), the China International Trade Fair in Services and the China International Consumer Goods Expo are all the major decisions taken by China to open up its market and serve as the important windows for China to share its big market and the important links for it to connect with the rest of the world. China should give full play to such important exhibition platforms, promote sustainable and healthy development of the platform economy, enlarge comprehensive effects, and increase imports of high-quality products, to share China's large market with the rest of the world. It should not only "bring in" global new products, new technologies, and new services, but also should encourage capable and reputable Chinese enterprises to "go out", constantly promoting more pragmatic cooperation to meet the needs of industrial upgrading and people's yearning for a better life.

3. Opening new scenarios for international cooperation

International economic connectivity and exchanges are the objective requirement of world economic development. In the new stage of development, China should adhere to high-level opening-up and actively cooperate with the countries, regions and enterprises that are willing to cooperate with China, so as to form a new scenario of all-dimensional, multi-tiered and diversified opening-up and cooperation.

a. Promoting high-quality Belt and Road cooperation

China should adhere to the principle of "extensive consultation, joint construction and shared benefits", uphold the principle of "green, open and clean governance", deepen practical economic and trade cooperation, make trade more unimpeded, improve the quality of investment cooperation, strengthen international cooperation, and tell Chinese stories well. It should work together with other countries to strengthen the convergence of trade and investment rules, reduce non-tariff barriers, increase the transparency of technical trade measures, and enhance trade and investment facilitation. It should actively promote cooperation on digital technology innovation, dovetail with the needs of different regions, countries and partners, and take an active part in building a regional platform for the development of digital economy and a new framework for digital rules governance. At the same time, it should actively promote the green development of Belt and Road countries, and enhance the ability of small and medium-sized enterprises to participate in the green construction of the Belt and Road.

b. Advancing regional, multilateral and bilateral economic and trade cooperation

China should promote the building of an open world economy, uphold multilateralism and free trade, firmly oppose protectionism, unilateralism and hegemonism of all kinds, and promote market connectivity. It should accelerate the implementation of the strategy of upgrading free trade areas, continue to negotiate with relevant countries on high-level free trade agreements, investment agreements and various forms of preferential trade arrangements, optimize the network of free trade areas, and expand the scale of plurilateral trade agreements. It should promote the China-GCC, China-Israel, China-Norway, China-Ecuador, and China-Japan-ROK free trade agreement talks, jointly build free trade areas with more countries, improve and upgrade the established free trade agreements, promote the signing of the China-EU investment agreement, speed up the China-Japan-ROK FTA negotiation process, actively launch the effort to join the CPTPP and DEPA, etc, to build a global network of high-standard FTAs, forge peaceful, innovative and civilized partnerships, and create new opportunities for international cooperation.

c. Actively participating in the reform of the global governance system

Only when the global governance system adapts to new requirements and changes in the international economic landscape can it provide institutional guarantee for the global economy. Therefore, China should actively advocate a new vision of international cooperation featuring mutual benefit and win-win cooperation, place equal emphasis on opening-up to both developed and developing countries, and increase the voice and representation of the emerging markets and developing countries in global economic governance. It should focus on maintaining the existing reasonable order and international norms and reforming the old imperfect and unreasonable rules, and advocate and participate in the formulation of new rules that are inclusive and just. It should also strengthen international cooperation against the pandemic to promote an early recovery of the global economy, support the necessary reform of the WTO, support the development of platforms such as the Shanghai Cooperation Organization, BRICS and G20, and increase the research and formulation of standards in digital trade, cross-border e-commerce and mobile payment, to contribute "Chinese solutions" to the formulation of international economic and trade rules.

4. Strengthening the safety net of opening-up

To build a new development pattern and promote high-level opening-up, China needs to strike a balance between openness and security, improve the security guarantee system for opening-up, and enhance its ability to dynamically safeguard security in an open environment.

a. Firmly fostering the concept of secure development

To advance high-level opening-up, China needs to firmly adopt the concept of secure development. The more it opens, the more it must attach importance to security and give priority to security issues. It should not only open windows, but also install screen windows, and balance development and security, to well handle the strength, progress and depth of opening-up and actively respond to traditional and non-traditional risks.

b. Establishing a mature guarantee system

China should speed up the study and formulation of laws and regulations that adapt to the new domestic and international situations, fill in institutional gaps and make up for institutional weaknesses, improve the system for secure development and legal guarantee, so that all aspects and links of opening-up have rules to follow. In accordance with laws, regulations and international rules, and to meet the needs of high-level opening-up, China should establish and improve the systems of foreign investment security review, anti-monopoly review, and the list of unreliable entities. It should enrich trade adjustment assistance, trade remedy and other policy tools to properly address economic and trade frictions. It should also strengthen guarantee cooperation on international supply chain and establish a system for overseas interests protection and risks early-warning and precaution.

c. Enhancing the capacity for safe opening-up

China should strive to enhance its industrial competitiveness and opening-up supervision and risks prevention capabilities, to provide a better protective fence for opening-up. It should enhance its rule-making capacity, pursue multilateral, regional and bilateral approaches, and safeguard free trade and multilateralism. It should improve its talents guarantee ability, actively cultivate international talents in the fields of economy, law and management, and build a diversified and open mechanism for attracting and employing talents.

Chapter 11   Giving Full Play to the Role of CIIE as A Demonstration Window

The China International Import Expo (CIIE), which was planned, proposed, deployed and promoted by General Secretary Xi Jinping in person, is China's major decision to promote a new round of high-level opening-up and a major initiative to open up to the world. For the past five years, the international influence of the CIIE has been increasing, making it a window of China's new development pattern, a carrier of China's high-level opening-up and a stage of multilateralism. Through truly achieving "global buying, global selling and global benefiting", it has contributed Chinese wisdoms to the recovery of the global economy, the in-depth development of economic globalization, and the improvement of the global economic governance system in the post-pandemic era.

I. Achieving More Positive Outcomes

In the World Trade Report 2021, the World Trade Organization pointed out that international economic cooperation is crucial to economic resilience in the context of the COVID-19 pandemic. The holding of the CIIE as scheduled for five years in a row has turned China's big market into a big opportunity for the world, sending a positive signal that China will open wider to the outside world and strengthen international cooperation, and demonstrating China's responsibility to share market opportunities with the world and promote world economic recovery.

1. Advancing against headwinds in the turbulent world economy

In 2021, the world economy further recovered, global trade in goods remained strong, and trade in services returned to the pre-pandemic level, with total global trade reaching $28.5 trillion, up 25% year-on-year and 13% higher than the pre-pandemic level in 2019. However, due to the cyclical slowdown of global trade growth before the pandemic, the risk of global trade contraction intensified in 2022. Rising interest rates, debt problems and the withdrawal of stimulus measures may also have a negative impact on trade growth.

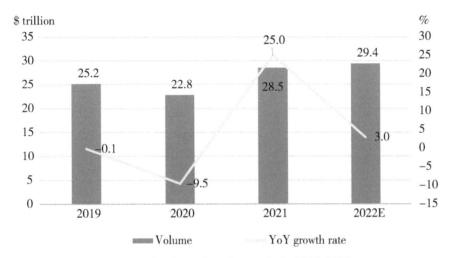

Fig. 11.1   Global trade trends in 2019-2022

Sources: WTO and World Bank.

Since the outbreak of the pandemic, China has taken effective prevention and control measures to keep industrial and supply chains relatively stable, and its imports from trading partners have remained generally stable. Against the backdrop of the cancellation of most international exhibitions and international buyers and investors getting mired in a dilemma, the CIIE has been held as scheduled, building a bridge between the Chinese market and the world, giving full play to the role of China's super-large market as a "stabilizer" for world economic development, and injecting strong impetus into global economic recovery. In the 4th CIIE, more than 2,900 enterprises from 127 countries and regions participated and the exhibition area reached a new high of 366,000 square meters; More than 280 of the top 500 companies or leading companies in their respective areas participated in the exhibition, and on-site transactions were fruitful, with one-year intended turnovers amounting to $70.72 billion.

Table 11.1   Top 20 countries by imports and their growth rates in 2020-2021

Ranking	2020			2021		
	Country	Import ($ trillion)	YoY growth rate, %	Country	Import ($ trillion)	YoY growth rate
1	United States	2.41	-6.3	United States	2.93	21.8
2	China	2.06	-0.7	China	2.67	29.9
3	Germany	1.17	-5.5	Germany	1.42	21.4
4	Japan	0.63	-11.9	Japan	0.77	21.7
5	United Kingdoms	0.63	-8.4	United Kingdoms	0.69	8.9
6	Netherlands	0.60	16.0	Netherlands	0.62	4.1
7	France	0.57	-11.5	India	0.57	0.2
8	South Korea	0.47	-7.0	Italy	0.56	19.2
9	Italy	0.42	-11.0	Mexico	0.51	19.8
10	Canada	0.41	-10.6	Canada	0.49	20.8
11	Belgium	0.40	24.1	Spain	0.43	7.7
12	Singapore	0.33	-8.3	Belgium	0.34	4.7
13	Spain	0.32	-13.3	Poland	0.34	3.2
14	Switzerland	0.29	5.5	Switzerland	0.32	10.6
15	Poland	0.26	4.1	Turkey	0.27	5.5
16	Russia	0.23	-6.3	Australia	0.26	13.0
17	Turkey	0.22	4.5	Malaysia	0.24	8.6
18	Thailand	0.21	-3.8	Brazil	0.23	12.4
19	Australia	0.20	-8.2	Czech	0.21	3.0
20	Malaysia	0.19	-7.4	Sweden	0.19	-1.4

Sources: WTO, UN Comtrade Database.

2. Continuously playing its role as a comprehensive and open platform for global sharing

Adhering to its positioning as a global public product and integrating exposition, forum, diplomacy, and people-to-people exchanges, the CIIE continues to play the role of the four major platforms of international procurement, investment promotion, people-to-people exchanges, and openness and cooperation. It has become a bridge and bond linking China to the rest of the world and put up an international public platform for supporting economic globalization and safeguarding the multilateral trading system.

a. An international procurement platform connecting supply and demand efficiently

The 4th CIIE brought together 39 trading groups and 599 trading sub-groups from all over the country attending the exhibition. Among them were 98 trading sub-groups of the Central Enterprise Trading Group with a generally stronger purchasing power. The number of purchasers with an annual import capacity of more than $100 million exceeded 1,300. The 5th CIIE will continue to promote supporting activities and service innovation, continue to give full play to the CIIE's "global buying, global selling" function, and open the procurement demand of foreign enterprises at the Chinese market.

Box 11-1　Innovating International Procurement Supporting Facilities and Services at the 5th CIIE

On April 18, 2022, a 200-day countdown to the opening of the 5th CIIE, the CIIE Bureau released the intended demands of buyers for the first time. Over the past five years, the CIIE has always adhered to the "comprehensive exhibition, professional organization", and constantly innovated ways to improve the professionalism and precision of supply and demand connection, to actively create conditions for meeting the needs of exhibitors and buyers.

The 5th CIIE has released 4 batches of trade groups' intended purchase demands, covering all 6 exhibition areas, involving 66 categories and nearly 600 products from 20 trading groups including those from Central enterprises, the National Health Commission, Beijing, Zhejiang, Jiangxi, Gansu and so on. It is hoped that exhibitors can actively pay attention to relevant information, display their new achievements, expand new channels and inject new momentum through the CIIE as a broad platform.

The release of the buyer's intended demands is a new attempt to better play the role of the CIIE international procurement platform. It can not only help exhibitors find new business opportunities more efficiently and promote new cooperation, but also help supply and demand parties more precisely find "connection points" and achieve mutual promotion and common progress.

b. An investment promotion platform to promote the introduction of investment

The CIIE is committed to "turning exhibitors into investors", and more and more global enterprises are taking the CIIE as a window to accelerate deep engagement in the Chinese market. In addition to official events, the CIIE also dovetails with China's policies and measures such as the Catalogue of Industries of Encouraging

Foreign Investment, to further carry out a series of activities involving "CIIE going to local regions". During the preparation of the 4th CIIE, two events were organized --- "CIIE Comes to Sichuan" and "CIIE Comes to Liaoning", promoting more than 320 foreign-funded enterprises to connect with the parks, enterprises and institutions of Sichuan and Liaoning, providing strong support for high-level opening-up and high-quality development of respective localities. The 5th CIIE will continue to carry out such activities to promote "CIIE Comes to Jiangxi or other places" and assist in local investment attraction.

c. A people-to-people exchange platform to enhance cultural integration

At the CIIE, more and more brands and enterprises make their debut appearance in the world and more and more enterprises customize products based on Chinese consumer culture, realizing mutual promotion of the economy, trade and culture. The number of booths for "cultural exchange activities" at the 4th CIIE exceeded that of the previous event, with an exhibition area of over 30,000 square meters. More than 100 cultural exchange activities and more than 300 booth activities were held, and 261 intangible cultural heritage items and 104 "time-honored Chinese brands" were displayed. Over the past four years, the CIIE has increasingly become a bridge and bond for people-to-people exchanges and mutual trust, building a "rainbow bridge" of exchanges and mutual learning among different civilizations.

Box 11-2   A people-to-people exchange platform to promote local cultures to the world

At the 4th CIIE, Shandong organized 69 time-honored brands and intangible cultural heritage enterprises to participate in its cultural exchange activities, and set up two exhibition areas, or the Shandong Time-honored Brands and Intangible Cultural Heritage Cultural Experience Hall, and Zhicheng Shandong-Boshan National Cultural Export Base, to showcase the excellent culture and ingenuity products planted in the Qilu land to guests from home and abroad. Through the cultural exchange platform of the CIIE, the excellent Qilu culture has been displayed and spread to the world, which has helped tell the stories of Shandong well, and enhanced the brand influence of Shandong's time-honored brands and intangible cultural heritage enterprises. During the exhibition, the passenger flow in the exhibition area exceeded 100,000 person-times, the on-site sales value reached 6.3176 million yuan, and the intended order value was 62.35 million yuan.

Zhejiang's National Pedestrian Street exhibition area was full of highlights at the 4th CIIE, with five major sections of "Zhejiang Silk", "Zhejiang Craftsmanship", "Zhejiang Exhibition", "Zhejiang Health" and "Zhejiang Taste" to exhibit local exquisite silk products, craftsmen's skills, special snacks, fascinating traditional performances, which highlighted the inclusiveness and diversity of Zhejiang culture and its leisure and colorful life, and narrated the thousands-year-long profound and unique cultural connotations of Zhejiang, as well as Zhejiang people's humanistic spirit of wisdom, diligence and courage.

d. An open platform to promote win-win cooperation

The CIIE showcases China's ideas and practices of opening-up and cooperation with the world, and embodies the broad consensus of "promoting cooperation through opening-up and pursuing development through cooperation". The CIIE is committed to organizing and carrying out a series of supporting activities such as supply and demand matching meetings, talks and investment fairs according to the development needs of participating countries, especially developing countries and the least developed countries. By participating in the CIIE, participating countries can accumulate experience in international exhibitions and improve their enterprises' ability to engage in international economic competition and cooperation.

Box 11-3   The 4th CIIE facilitates China's opening-up and cooperation with Central and Eastern Europe, Africa and other regions

The 4th CIIE brought in a total of nearly 50 overseas exhibition organizations from 41 countries and regions, with an exhibition area of 43,000 square meters and more than 1,200 enterprises, mainly small and medium-sized enterprises, covering a wide range of industries and a variety of products. In addition, it provided free booths to nearly 30 least developed countries. In the preparatory stage, the CIIE Bureau, together with overseas business organizations, overseas exhibition organizing agencies and partners, organized 21 online promotion sessions, including special sessions for Central and Eastern Europe, Middle East, Latin America, Africa and other regions.

For the implementation of economic and trade fruits reached at the Summit of

China and Central and Eastern European Countries, the 4th CIIE set up a special food zone for Central and Eastern European countries, where nearly 60 local food enterprises with a total exhibition area of nearly 1,500 square meters were brought by exhibition groups from Poland, Serbia, Greece and Hungary, forming a new beautiful scenery in the food and agricultural products exhibition area.

e. Supporting activities to enlarge the functions of the four platforms

At the 4th CIIE, a total of 100 on-site activities with rich content and various forms were held, including policy interpretation, contract docking, new product display, investment promotion and other categories. The organizers were high-level. influential international organizations such as the United Nations Industrial Development Organization (UNIDO), the International Trade Center (ITC) and the World Intellectual Property Organization (WIPO) held several high-end international forums; The Ministry of Commerce, the Ministry of Industry and Information Technology, the Ministry of Culture and Tourism, the People's Bank of China, the State Administration for Market Regulation, the National Food and Drug Administration, the National Healthcare Security Administration and other central government departments held several special events. Based on its theme positioning, the authority and professionalism of the CIIE's on-site supporting activities have been continuously enhanced over the past four years, and international organizations, national ministries and commissions, local governments, industry organizations, research institutions, purchasers, exhibitors and other parties have extensively participated, boosting the CIIE's role as the "four platforms" of international procurement, investment promotion, people-to-people exchanges, and opening-up and cooperation.

Box 11-4   Content richness of large trade and investment matchmaking events and new product launches

The 4th CIIE continued to hold large-scale trade and investment matchmaking fairs, most of which showcased greater professionalism through centering on five investment promotion themes, focusing on six industrial fields, improving online negotiation services and strengthening transactions docking and matching. A total of 640 exhibitors and 766 buyers from 55 countries participated in the online and offline events and 273 cooperation intentions were reached. At the same time, 17 investment promotion meetings were held to further help "exhibits become commodities, exhibitors become investors".

In the New Product Launch Zone of the 4th CIIE, 62 internationally renowned enterprises released 123 new products and services, which, mostly launched the first time in the world, exhibited the first time in Asia, and debut shows in China, attracted numerous media reports. The event was broadcast live on the China Media Group News Special Program and broadcast online on all platforms. According to incomplete statistics, the number of views reached 33 million, attracting extensive attention.

3. Adding new drivers to the digital economy

As new technologies such as big data, cloud computing and artificial intelligence are gradually integrated into production and life, the digital economy is booming and becoming a new driving force of high-quality economic development in China and the world at large. The CIIE has exhibited a large number of digital products, technologies and solutions, promoted relevant investment, and made use of digital technologies to carry out institutional innovation, thus adding new impetus to the development of the digital economy.

a. Providing digital transformation application scenarios and solutions

The CIIE has become a big platform for the new products, technologies and solutions of the digital economy to be launched for the first time in China and even in the world. It has set a good example for the digital transformation of the global economy. The CIIE offers a window for the world to experience the latest trends and dynamics of digital transformation.

Box 11-5   A large number of digital schemes showcased at the 4th CIIE

An European enterprise enables digital construction with innovation

A century-old European brand was once again invited to enter the technical equipment exhibition area. In the display field, the enterprise concentrated on displaying capacitor touch blackboard, electronic class plate, touch conference machine, E Ink two-in-one display, OLED portable display, Mini LED display, 4K 144Hz e-sports display and other cutting-edge video products and application solutions, through the creation of six application scenarios of smart education, smart transportation, smart medical treatment, smart retail, smart office and smart home. The enterprise was able to lead the industry trend with its strength and enable digital construction with its innovative technology.

Digitally enabling smart education

In the 4th CIIE's exhibition area of smart education, an 86-inch infrared touch smart education blackboard was displayed on site, which can provide 4K high-definition visual effects, clearer and more beautiful pictures for teachers and students, and improve students' concentration in class. Infrared touch technology makes writing smooth and improves the efficiency of blackboard writing. The 86-inch educational tablet not only realizes multi-screen remote teaching interaction, but also makes boring classes full of fun. Electronic class cards with functions such as attendance recording and face recognition can meet the needs of classroom space application in normal teaching.

The offer of "smart cars"

An American automobile enterprise moved its Shanghai Gigafactory to the CIIE, for the first time displaying physical products such as body in white, stamping parts, batteries and motors. In the form of workshop live video and intensive reading display boards, the enterprise provided a panoramic analysis of the intelligent production and manufacturing process of its Shanghai Gigafactory's motor, battery, die casting, stamping, welding, painting and final assembly workshops. Walking around the booth, the audience was like having a complete tour of its Shanghai Gigafactory, feeling the "intelligent manufacturing" logic behind the car.

b. Cross-border e-commerce accelerates "turning exhibits into commodities"

The CIIE actively uses facilitation measures of cross-border e-commerce to promote the sales of commodities on display. According to the Customs Facilitation Measures to Support the 4th China International Import Expo 2021, and the Notes on Customs Clearance for the 4th China International Import Expo 2021, the imported exhibits included in the list of imported commodities of cross-border e-commerce retail were allowed to enter the special customs supervision area or bonded logistics center of the 4th CIIE after the exhibition. Those who meet the conditions could be sold according to the mode of bonded retail imported commodities purchased by cross-border e-commerce network. Cross-border e-commerce companies have moved CIIE exhibits from their booths to the Internet, greatly broadening the sales channels of CIIE exhibits and enhancing their brand influence.

Box 11-6   Shanghai Customs Helps Turn 4th CIIE Exhibits into Cross-border E-Commerce Commodities

On November 19, 2021, a batch of cosmetics imported from France to the 4th CIIE entered Qingpu Comprehensive Bonded Area after completing the carry-over procedures at the customs authorities, and was put on the shelves of Greenland Global Commodity Trade Port as a cross-border e-commerce new business form --- Greenland Global Flash Purchase, which was sold according to the preferential tax rate of cross-border e-commerce.

In Hongqiao Import Commodity Exhibition and Trade Center, CIIE exhibitors relied on the adjacent Hongqiao Business District Bonded Logistics Center to realize the mutual transfer of exhibits and commodities, turning exhibits into commodities in the form of bonded exhibition or cross-border e-commerce sales, and realizing the integration of online, offline, and bonded warehousing, and sales through cross-border e-commerce retail import channels.

c. Exploring new models of digital trade

The CIIE is committed to building a digital trading platform to promote economic and trade development. The four CIIEs all adopted the "online plus offline" model, giving a strong boost to the development of digital trade. At the CIIE, the online exhibition halls provided a more convenient channel for people to visit CIIE commodities and experience the culture and products of different countries without leaving home. The Customs also committed to using digital technologies to innovate trade management and facilitate rapid entry of CIIE goods into the Chinese market.

Box 11-7   Entry of Exhibits: "Second Release" by Shanghai Customs

On September 27, 2021, the first batch of imported exhibits of the 4th CIIE, a hydrogen energy racing model car, was flown from Luxembourg to Shanghai by air and cleared customs after being cleared by Shanghai Customs. Under the new operation mode and facilitation measures of "direct inspection" from ports to exhibition halls, these CIIE exhibits have been upgraded from "paperless customs clearance" to "instantaneous release". All these are due to the special module of the big data platform for cross-border trade management, or the "Special window for CIIE", created by Shanghai Customs.

4. Enabling global sustainable development

a. Leading green and low-carbon consumption

In 2020, China put forward the goal of carbon emission peaking and carbon neutrality. Therefore, several exhibition areas of the 4th CIIE added special zones for energy conservation and environmental protection, with some exhibitors demonstrating cutting-edge "double carbon" technologies and concepts, and introducing "zero carbon" new products, leading the trend of low carbon consumption.

Box 11-8   A gust of "green wind" blown by the 4th CIIE, with low-carbon products being in the spotlight

Cycling printer

An enterprise showcased low-power printers that can be powered to do its job using the power generated by a person's ride. Using cold printing technology, the inkjet printer consumes about 90% less energy than conventional solutions. A person riding at a constant speed for less than a minute can run a commercial A4 inkjet printer with just 12 watts of power.

Variable compression ratio turbocharged engine new car

Along with the new energy vehicles, a Japanese enterprise also showcased the world's first mass-produced turbocharged engine with variable compression ratio, which can switch intelligently from 8:1 (high performance) to 14:1 (high efficiency). It planned to introduce nine electric models to the Chinese market by 2025, including the new all-electric crossover SUV and six models with its e-power technology.

---

b. Green intelligence empowers global supply chains

Under the "double carbon" goal, the supply chain pattern urgently needs to be reconstructed. The CIIE, which brings together the world's latest technologies, products and solutions, is also contributing green wisdom to the global supply chain. The 4th CIIE showcased technologies and solutions on green energy, building energy conservation and environmental governance, covering traditional energy, new energy, new materials, electricity, water treatment and other fields, providing enterprises with cutting-edge technologies and sustainable solutions in clean energy transformation.

Box 11-9   Contribution of Green Wisdom by 4ᵗʰ CIIE Exhibitors

Continuing to exhibit sustainable experience and digital technology

In the 4ᵗʰ CIIE's newly-established energy, low-carbon and environmental protection technology zone, the advanced ideas, solutions and consulting services of green energy management and green intelligent manufacturing exhibited by a French enterprise not only invited extensive attention, but also gained a large number of intended orders, covering many industries such as new energy, chemical oil and gas, iron and steel metallurgy, biopharmaceutical, cement and building materials, real estate and so on.

Launching intelligent cloud platform for digital carbon management

At the 4ᵗʰ CIIE, an American enterprise launched the industry's first dual-standard S-Carbon digital carbon management intelligent cloud platform. The platform is dedicated to providing a solution to help companies manage the KPI fulfillment in the overall carbon emission reduction and carbon neutrality goals of complex supply chains and large suppliers. In addition, the platform can also monitor and analyze suppliers' performance under carbon emission reduction KPIs, provide executive summaries and reports, and promote enterprises to participate in global carbon target projects such as the Science Based Targets Initiative (SBTi), and enhance enterprises' green financing capacity in the international market.

Green "Smart Warehouse"

An American enterprise's "Smart Warehouse" provided a one-stop intelligent warehousing solution, which enabled efficient and accurate cargo flow and order selection through the process of item selection, delivery and automatic storage and retrieval. While realizing the transformation and upgrading of traditional warehousing logistics to digital intelligent logistics, it can reduce energy consumption.

II. Creating A "Demonstration Window" for New Development Pattern

Opening-up is a distinctive symbol of China in the new era. Over the past five years, the CIIE has become an important occasion for China to announce its opening-up initiatives and witness the implementation of China's high-level opening-up measures. As an important window for the world to perceive China's commitment to opening-up at a high level, the CIIE is becoming an important platform for market connectivity, industrial integration, innovation promotion and rules matching, setting a good example for China to achieve opening-up at a high level and build a new development pattern.

1. Market connectivity: Buy the world, benefit the world, better link domestic and international supply and demand

To build a new development pattern, China needs to smooth the flow of both domestic and international markets and resources, turn the Chinese market into a global market and a shared market, and meet the needs of both Chinese and global consumers. The CIIE actively complies with the upgrading trend of domestic consumption market, provides markets and opportunities for global enterprises in the surging anti-globalization international environment, and enhances the adaptability of the supply system to domestic demand. The CIIE brings high-quality overseas goods and services to China, enables more countries and enterprises willing to carry out international economic and trade cooperation with China to learn about the Chinese market, enter the Chinese market and cultivate the Chinese market. This will help China form a high-level dynamic equilibrium in which demand leads supply and supply creates demand.

2. Industrial integration: Promote investment, promote upgrading and facilitate high-quality economic development

The CIIE has played an active role in driving trade and investment, pushing "exhibitors to become investors". More and more global enterprises now are taking the CIIE as a window to accelerate their deep cultivation in China. In the 4th CIIE, the re-participation rate of the world's top 500 enterprises and industrial leading enterprises exceeded 80%, the number of exhibitors exceeded that of the last one, and the number of overseas small and medium-sized enterprises organized to participate increased by 30%. Located near the Expo venue, Hongqiao Pinhui added new functions to serve the investment of overseas SMEs. Since 2021, more than 600 foreign companies have entered China through investment in Hongqiao Pinhui. With the attraction of the huge domestic market, the CIIE has tightened bond between global enterprises and the

Chinese market, enhanced connections between domestic and international industrial chains, hedged adverse factors such as supply chain obstruction under the pandemic, and further smoothed the dual circulation of the domestic and international markets.

3. Innovation promotion: Gather dynamism, stimulate vitality and foster new engines of innovation-driven development

The CIIE plays an important role in innovation achievements sharing and deep integration of science, technology and the economy. It quickly and efficiently opens the channels between domestic market demand and international market supply, and promotes the sharing and flow of domestic and international innovation resources. The CIIE actively promotes the cooperation of cutting-edge technology enterprises in the fields of automation, intelligence, medical care and high-end manufacturing in the Chinese market, introduces advanced international production factors, builds the innovation ecosystem, and releases the huge potential of innovation-driven high-quality economic development.

Box 11-10   An European enterprise's research and development ecology breeds innovation, benefiting China and the whole world

The 4th CIIE opened its doors wider and provided a high-quality platform for all parties to display their innovation achievements and promote common development through mutual learning, win-win cooperation and sharing. The enterprise's Global R&D China Center, officially opened in October 2021, made its second appearance at the CIIE and demonstrated its latest progress and planning. The enterprise's latest layout in the field of rare diseases was also unveiled at the same time, and a series of cooperation and contracts in the field of rare diseases would be reached in the next few days, accelerating scientific research and development and the availability of cooperation outcomes.

Through independent research and development and cooperative development, the enterprise brought with it innovative drugs covering the most urgent diseases for Chinese patients, such as respiratory, oncology, cardiovascular, metabolic, digestive, kidney and rare diseases. Through the CIIE platform, the enterprise also continued to introduce high-quality drugs at home and abroad, and continuously increased cooperation in pharmaceutical equipment, benefiting the vast number of Chinese patients. At the 4thCIIE, the enterprise signed a strategic cooperation intention with other enterprises to jointly seek cooperation opportunities in the areas of increasing the frequency of anemia detection in patients with chronic kidney disease (CKD) and managing the whole course of kidney diseases.

4. Rules matching: Promote openness and tighten the bond of win-win cooperation

While opening wider to the outside world, China has taken an active part in improving global economic governance and aligning itself with high-standard international economic and trade regulations, to which the CIIE has made important contributions. The CIIE is an announcement platform and an important window for China to reduce the negative list for foreign investment access. For four consecutive CIIEs, the Chinese government has issued a negative list for foreign investment access across the country and in pilot free trade zones, and expanded opening-up measures in the financial, telecommunications, medical and other sectors in an orderly manner, taking the CIIE as a window to take the lead in implementing them. For example, after the Negative List of Cross-border Service Trade of Hainan Free Trade Port was released in July 2021, the 4th CIIE carried out online investment roadshow activities in time for purchasers and related enterprises in its service trade exhibition area, effectively expanding radiation effects of the new measures.

III. Practicing True Multilateralism

"China will not change its determination to open up to a higher level, to share development opportunities with the rest of the world, or to make economic globalization more open, inclusive, balanced and beneficial to all", just as President Xi Jinping said. True multilateralism is about upholding the vision of open, inclusive and shared development, and maintaining the international system with the United Nations at its core and the multilateral trading system with the WTO as its cornerstone. The CIIE is a crystal demonstration of China's firm commitment to globalization and true multilateralism.

1. Starting from the common good of mankind

The CIIE has always adhered to the philosophy of a community with a shared future for mankind, demonstrating China's commitment and determination to share development opportunities with other countries in the world. China has strengthened discussions with participating countries via the CIIE on such topics as trade and investment, digital economy, green and low-carbon, sanitation and health, and promoted unimpeded trade and innovative implementation of key COVID-19 products and medical solutions. It takes an active part in addressing climate change, safeguarding global food and energy security, and continues to provide more assistance to other developing countries within the framework of South-South cooperation. At a time when the COVID-19 pandemic still spreads at a high level, the CIIE has sent a signal that the world needs exchanges, integration, cooperation and solidarity more than ever, sparking resonance across the world.

2. Firmly upholding the multilateral order

The CIIE unswervingly upholds the global governance concept of "extensive consultation, joint contribution and shared benefits", safeguards the international system with the United Nations at its core and the multilateral trading system with the WTO as its cornerstone, and strives to promote the reform of the global economic governance system. It has maintained a sound cooperation mechanism with multilateral international organizations such as the WTO, G20, APEC and Shanghai Cooperation Organization. The leaders of the United Nations Industrial Development Organization, the United Nations Global Compact, the International Trade Center, the World Intellectual Property Organization and other international organizations attended and addressed each of the CIIEs and sent delegations to participate in its exhibitions. In addition, the CIIE is committed to helping developing countries, especially the least developed countries, integrate into the multilateral trading system and promote the reform of the global economic governance system by encouraging developing countries to participate in international economic and trade activities.

3. Contribution of "Hongqiao Wisdom" to the world

Closely focusing on the core theme of "global openness" and the positioning of "international public goods", and concentrating on hot topics in the field of global openness, Hongqiao International Economic Forum strives to build a high-end dialogue platform for guests from domestic and foreign political, business and academic circles, and contribute "Hongqiao wisdom" to the open development of the world. Under the theme of "World Economy under A Century of Changes: Global Economic Cooperation in the Post-Pandemic Era", the fourth Hongqiao Forum held hold sub-forums on hot topics such as green development, health, digital economy, intelligent manufacturing and consumption trends. The Forum has been warmly received at home and abroad, and China's attitude and proposals, such as actively promoting international cooperation against the pandemic, expanding imports and opening to the outside world, promoting sustainable development and unswervingly upholding the common interests of the world, have drawn wide attention.

Box 11-11   Guests from all Walks of Life Play "Hongqiao Symphony" at the Fourth Hongqiao Forum

The Fourth Hongqiao International Economic Forum, titled "World Economy under A Century of Changes: Global Economic Cooperation in the Post-Pandemic Era", held one top-level forum, 12 sub-forums and one international seminar, and more than 150 government officials, representatives of international organizations, diplomatic envoys, renowned scholars at home and abroad, and the representatives of the world's top 500 enterprises or other leading enterprises addressed online or offline, attracting the interactions of nearly 3,000 representatives from all walks of life.

Participants of the sub-forums discussed hot topics in frontier areas. At the Green Development Sub-Forum, ITC Executive Director Pamela Coke-Hamilton and others discussed the impact of green development on global economic and trade development in the context of climate change, shared the advanced experience and practice of green development, and looked forward to the new prospect of international trade and investment development. At the Sub-forum on health, Zhong Nanshan, academician of the Chinese Academy of Engineering, and other health professionals held in-depth discussions, contributing their wisdom to international cooperation on public health, building a Global Community of Health for All, and realizing high-quality development centered on people's health. At the Digital Economy Forum, Li Yong, Director-General of the United Nations Industrial Development Organization, Christopher Pissarides, Nobel Laureate in Economics, and other guests discussed the major challenges that countries need to jointly address, such as the cross-border flow of data, data openness and intellectual property protection, and the digital divide. At the Intelligent Technology Sub-forum, Li Dongsheng, chairman of TCL, pointed out that AI, 5G, cloud computing, Internet of Things and other digital infrastructure and technology solutions continue to become matured, and intelligent technology will unleash strong innovation potentials to boost the construction of a new global ecosystem of intelligent value chain. At the Regional Financial Sub-Forum, Governor of the Central Bank of the Philippines Benjamin Diokno, Governor of the National Bank of Cambodia Chea Chanto and other participants focused on the role of the Regional Comprehensive Economic Partnership (RCEP) in promoting regional economic development and discussed how to contribute to global economic recovery.

IV. Promoting High-quality Development of the CIIE

Based on the new development stage, the CIIE should implement the new development concept, make continuing contributions to the building of a new development pattern, organically connect the major measures of China's opening-up with its holding, and actively explore institutional innovation, to contribute to China's institutional opening-up and take solid steps toward high-quality development.

1. Boosting its brand value as "China's opening-up window"

The CIIE should continue to serve as a demonstration window for fulfilling China's commitment to high-level opening-up and further enhance its brand value. China should optimize the communication channels, adopt the integration of traditional media and new media, make good use of international communication platforms and enhance its communication power, to further enhance the brand value of the CIIE and increase its attraction to overseas exhibitors and investors.

2. Continuously promoting institutional innovation of the CIIE

China should continue to improve the mode of holding the CIIE. Support policies for the CIIE should be further improved and optimized, normalized and institutionalized, the policy toolbox should continue to be enriched, policy expectations should be stabilized, support measures should be innovated, and quality services should be provided to exhibitors and trade groups. The CIIE should optimize the investment attraction mechanism, carry out precise investment attraction in the industrial chain in key areas such as green development and digital economy, promote two-way contact between supply and demand, and improve the investment motivation and influence of buyers. It should continue to optimize the setting of the exhibition area and further improve its degree of specialization. It should promote the internationalization and specialization of Hongqiao International Economic Forum, make it better serve the core theme of "global openness" and its positioning as an "international public good", and expand its influence, to make the forum an exchange platform, an important bridge and an ideological plateau for the theories and best practices of global openness.

3. Coordinating with China's regional opening-up strategy

China should promote the coordination of the CIIE with the opening-up policies of the Yangtze River Delta and Pearl River Delta regions, the central and western regions and border areas, and continue to strengthen the role of the CIIE in promoting the country's regional opening-up. It should strive to push for the interactive development of the CIIE and the Yangtze River Delta region, optimize Shanghai's city security coordination mechanism, continuously improve exhibition participation and supporting services, and raise the level of trade matching and investment promotion, to make all kinds of display trading platform become a very important channel for the Yangtze River Delta region to link with the international market. At the same time, China should accelerate the coordinated development of the CIIE with the Pearl River Delta region, the central and western regions and open border areas, intensify efforts to encourage exhibitors to carry out supporting activities in relevant provinces and cities and improve CIIE warming-up, investment negotiation and matching activities, to further expand cooperation space, and timely copy and promote the experience.

Chapter 12　Chinese Solution and Contribution to Global Openness and Cooperation

As globalization encounters headwinds, instability and uncertainties in global economic and social development are on the rise, so are global development and governance deficits. A number of challenges are pushing the global economy to the brink of what could be its "toughest test since World War II"[1]. In the era of globalization, the economy and security of all countries mutually interconnect and influence each other. No country can achieve its own development in isolation, nor can it meet global challenges on its own. Peace and development remain the theme of the times, and genuine global cooperation is needed to overcome global challenges. China is committed to opening-up and promoting global openness and cooperation through the Belt and Road Initiative and the Global Development Initiative, contributing Chinese wisdom and solution to improving global governance.

I. Contribution of Belt and Road to multilateral development and international cooperation

Since proposed in 2013, the Belt and Road Initiative has gained momentum and become a popular international public good and platform for cooperation. Especially against the backdrop of the COVID-19, Belt and Road cooperation, through extensive and in-depth international cooperation, has achieved fruitful results in the fight against theCOVID-19, economic recovery, green development, and global poverty reduction, making new contributions to the building of a community with a shared future for mankind.

---

[1]　Remarks made by Kristalina Georgieva, managing director of the International Monetary Fund, at an offline meeting of the World Economic Forum.

1. Benefiting the global fight against the COVID-19

As early as 2015, China issued the Three-Year Implementation Plan on Advancing Health Exchanges and Cooperation along the Belt and Road (2015-2017). In 2016, Chinese President Xi Jinping put forward the "Silk Road of Health" in Uzbekistan, officially making health an important part of the Belt and Road Initiative, and injecting new vitality into global public health cooperation. Over the past years, China has worked with Belt and Road countries and relevant international organizations to deepen health policy coordination, develop the "Belt and Road Hospital Alliance", build the overseas centers of traditional Chinese medicines, and implement the China-ASEAN Public Health Personnel Training Program and China-Africa Public Health Cooperation Program, all of which have achieved positive results.

As the pandemic continues to spread, the international community has a strong demand in the field of healthcare[1]. China attaches great importance to strengthening health cooperation with the international community, and has made it clear that in the Belt and Road cooperation, it will give priority to the healthcare sector. China will work with Africa to implement the "Health Action" within the framework of the Forum on China-Africa Cooperation, give full play to the role of the Belt and Road Alliance of International Science organizations, promote scientific research cooperation among its members, learn from each other and share experience in fighting the COVID-19, and scientifically deploy medical resources and important materials.

China attaches great importance to the pandemic in developing countries and calls on the international community to pay more attention to them. Developing countries face the greatest pressure in the global pandemic and the "vaccine gap" has become a pain for them to fight the COVID-19 pandemic. According to the United Nations, 75% of the world's COVID-19 vaccines are controlled by 10 countries. As of May 2022, more than 11 billion doses of COVID-19 vaccine had been used in the world, with Africa only accounting for about 5% of the total. In his speeches on many international occasions, such as the World Health Assembly and the Global Health Summit, President Xi Jinping put forward China's proposals and opinions on international cooperation to fight theCOVD-19. China has paid close attention to the fight against

---

[1] Zhao, L. (2020). Building a silk road of health contributes to a community of human health. *Guangming Daily*, October 19, page 16.

the pandemic in developing countries and fulfilled its commitments with concrete actions to make vaccines a global public good.

Traditional Chinese Medicine (TCM) has gained wider international recognition in international cooperation against thepandemic. According to incomplete statistics, China has introduced TCM diagnosis and treatment programs to more than 150 countries and regions, provided TCM products to more than 10 countries and regions in need, and sent TCM experts to 29 countries and regions to help guide their fight against the pandemic. In the report of the WHO Expert Assessment Meeting on TCM Treatment for COVID-19 released at the end of March, the WTO affirmed the safety and effectiveness of TCM treatment for COVID-19. Accelerating the joint construction of the "Silk Road of Health" is of positive significance to strengthening global confidence in the fight against the pandemic and promoting the building of a Global Community of Health for All, and it is also an important pillar for global economic recovery[1].

Box 12-1   China's proposals on global cooperation against COVID-19

Since the outbreak of the COVID-19, China has put forward a series of proposals to promote global cooperation.

In order to promote global cooperation in the fight against the pandemic, President Xi Jinping announced China's five measures to support global solidarity in his address entitled "Solidarity and Cooperation to Defeat the Pandemic and Build a Global Community of Health for All" at the opening video conference of the 73rd World Health Assembly in May 2021: (1) China will provide $2 billion in international assistance in the next two years to support the fight against theCOVID-19, economic recovery and social and development in the countries affected by the pandemic, especially developing countries; (2) China will work with the United Nations to set up global humanitarian emergency warehouses and hubs in China to ensure supply chains for COVID-19 supplies, and establish green channels for transportation and customs clearance; (3) China will set up 30 China-Africa cooperation hospitals, and speed up the

---

[1]   Wang, Y. (2020). Building a silk road of health that benefits people around the world. *Guangming Daily*, June 22, page 7. https://epaper.gmw.cn/gmrb/html/2020-06/22/nw.D110000gmrb_20200622_6-07.htm.

building of the headquarters of the African Center for Disease Control and Prevention, to help Africa improve its capacity for disease prevention and control; (4) When China's COVID-19 vaccine is developed and put into use, it will be used as a global public good to make China's contribution to the accessibility and affordability of vaccines in developing countries; (5) China will work with other G20 members to implement the Debt Repayment Suspension Initiative for the poorest Countries, and is ready to work with the international community to increase support for countries particularly affected by the pandemic and under particular pressure to help them overcome the current difficulties.

At the Global Health Summit on May 21, President Xi Jinping put forward five proposals on promoting global anti-pandemic cooperation and announced five major measures to support global cooperation in the fight against the pandemic, including: to set up an international forum for COVID-19 vaccine cooperation, where vaccine manufacturing and R&D countries, enterprises and stakeholders will work together to promote fair and equitable distribution of vaccines around the world; to provide an additional $3 billion in international assistance in the next three years to support developing countries in fighting the COVID-19 and restoring economic and social development. By the end of 2021, China had provided more than 360 billion masks, more than 4 billion protective suits, more than 7 billion testing kits, and more than 300,000 ventilators to 150 countries and 13 international organizations, sent 37 medical teams to 34 countries, and provided about 2 billion doses of vaccine to 111 countries and international organizations, more than any other country. "Made in China" vaccines have won high praise from the international community. In war-torn areas such as Afghanistan and Syria, China has been the first to provide COVID-19 vaccine assistance, bringing hope to the local people. At the Forum on China-Africa Cooperation, President Xi Jinping also announced that China will provide Africa with another 1 billion doses of vaccine the next year, of which 600 million does will be free and 400 million does will be jointly produced by China and Africa. At the summit marking the 30th anniversary of China-ASEAN dialogue relations, China expressed willingness to provide an additional $1.5 billion in development assistance in the next three years to help ASEAN countries fight the pandemic and recover their economies.

Mankind is a community with a shared future, and solidarity and cooperation are the most powerful weapons to defeat the pandemic. The COVID-19 does not differ according to race, ethnicity, nationality or wealth, and the success of a country's pandemic prevention and control is closely related to the success of the global pandemic prevention and control. Only by working together can the international community finally defeat the pandemic and promote global economic recovery at an early date.

2. Contributing to global economic recovery

An open China serves as a stabilizer of the world economy. Over the past decade, China's contribution to world economic growth has remained at around 30%. After the outbreak of the COVID-19, China quickly brought it under control at home, and while adhering to the "dynamic clearing" policy, it also introduced a combination of measures to stabilize the economy, which laid a solid foundation for the global fight against the pandemic and domestic economic recovery, and also made China the only major economy to achieve positive growth in 2020.

Against the backdrop of the complex international situation and the pandemic, the Chinese economy has shown strong resilience and risk-resisting capability, providing a strong driving force for world economic growth. In 2021, China's economic aggregate exceeded 110 trillion yuan, and the scale of investment it attracted hit a record high, up 14.9% from the previous year, further consolidating China's position as a "stabilizer" and "powerhouse" of the world economy. The overlapping of the recurrent COVID-19 outbreaks and rising global inflation in 2022 has put downward pressure on world economic growth. China's economy is also facing risks and challenges brought about by the recurrence of the pandemicand external shocks, but the fundamentals of its steady and long-term growth remain unchanged, with strong resilience, great potential and ample room for maneuvering. In the first half of 2022, China continued to leverage its industrial, market and policy advantages and withstood the pressure of repeated outbreaks of the pandemicto realize GDP growth of 2.5% year-on-year, and imports and exports of goods continued to grow at a high rate, making its due contribution to global economic recovery.

In the course of jointly building the Belt and Road, China has strengthened economic and trade cooperation with relevant countries and made positive contributions to the economic development of countries along the Belt and Road.

In particular, after the outbreak of the pandemic, the global industrial and supply chain circulation was disrupted, the shipping capacity continued to be strained, the air transport capacity remained insufficient, the freight costs rose sharply, and the problem of containers shortage occurred from time to time. In this context, the joint construction of the Belt and Road has demonstrated its strong resilience and vitality, and the advantages of the China-Europe freight trains remain prominent in their safety, reliability and price stability. In 2021, the China-Europe Line operated 15,000 freight trains, with a total carrying capacity of 1.46 million TEUs, up 22% and 29% year-on-year, respectively. The trains opened 78 routes and reached 180 cities in 23 countries.

The Belt and Road Initiative has enabled co-building countries, especially developing countries, to share developing opportunities from China's quick development. It has created more jobs, increased tax revenue and enhanced local capacity for independent development. For example, China-ASEAN trade and investment has bucked the trend despite the pandemic and played an important role in economic stability and recovery of ASEAN countries. In 2021, trade in goods between China and the ASEAN reached $878.2 billion, up 28.1% year-on-year, making the ASEAN China's largest trading partner for the second consecutive year. In the same year, China's direct investment in the ASEAN reached $14.35 billion.

According to the World Bank report, the Belt and Road Initiative can increase the trade of the world and participating countries by 6.2% and 9.7%, respectively, and is expected to increase the real income of low-income countries and regions by 1.2-3.4%. Thanks to the Initiative, emerging and developing economies saw an increase in their share of global GDP by 3.6 percentage points from 2012 to 2021.

Box 12-2   Eight years of fruitful Belt and Road cooperation

Since proposed in 2013, the Belt and Road Initiative has adhered to the principle of "extensive consultation, joint contribution and shared benefits", continuously deepened economic and trade cooperation, and achieved substantial and fruitful results[1]. The

---

[1] The State Council press conference gave a briefing on how the country has adhered to the "stability" as the top priority to promote high-quality development of commerce, see the China Government Website. http://www.gov.cn/xinwen/2022-03/03/content_5676592.htm; Jointly building the Belt and Road: Promoting mutual benefit and win-win cooperation among countries, International Business Daily. https://www.comnews.cn/content/2022-05/23/content_8840.html.

fruitful results the Initiative has yielded in deepening unimpeded trade, strengthening investment cooperation, advancing project construction and improving institutional platforms has given a strong boost to mutual benefit and win-win cooperation between participating countries.

The Belt and Road Initiative has significantly improved its market position in promoting unimpeded trade. From 2013 to 2021, the annual trade volume between China and Belt and Road countries expanded from $1.04 trillion to $1.8 trillion, an increase of 73%. While rapidly expand the scale, the quality of trade has also been improving. In terms of investment cooperation, the integration of industrial and supply chains has also improved significantly. From 2013 to 2021, China's direct investment in Belt and Road countries totaled $161.3 billion, and these countries set up 32,000 enterprises in China, with an actual cumulative investment of $71.2 billion. The overseas economic and trade cooperation zones built by Chinese enterprises have paid $6.6 billion in taxes and fees to host countries and created 392,000 local jobs.

In terms of project construction, the level of connectivity has been significantly improved. From 2013 to 2021, the total value of new projects signed by Chinese companies in Belt and Road countries reached $1.08 trillion, with a turnover of $728.6 billion, covering transportation, power and other sectors. A number of major cooperation projects have been completed and implemented: The whole line of China-Laos Railway has been put into operation, the Budapest-Belgrade Railway has been progressing in an orderly manner, the construction of the ballast track on the main line of the Jakarta-Bandung high-speed railway in Indonesia has officially started, and the Piraeus port is operating well. In the next, the Initiative will focus on agriculture, healthcare and poverty reduction, so as to bring tangible benefits to the people of Belt and Road countries.

As to institutional platforms, the efficiency of exchanges and cooperation has been significantly improved. Bilateral economic and trade mechanisms have continuously been improved, and more than 100 mechanisms for unimpeded trade, investment cooperation, trade in services and e-commerce have been established. Open platforms represented by major exhibitions and forums have been flourishing.

3. Promoting global green development

Climate change threatens global development and security, and green development is an important concern of all countries. As President Xi Jinping pointed out, "sustainable development is an area where the best interests of all parties converge and where they can cooperate", "China is committed to promoting green development and building a beautiful homeland where man and nature coexist in harmony", "We will forge a closer partnership for green development, strengthen cooperation in green infrastructure, green energy and green finance, and improve multilateral cooperation platforms such as the BRI International Green Development Coalition and the Belt and Road Green Investment Principles, so as to make 'green' the foundation of Belt and Road cooperation".

China is an important participant and contributor to the construction of global ecological civilization. While actively implementing the Paris Agreement, making high-standard carbon emission commitments to the international community and promoting its own green development, China has cosisitently stressed the concept of green development in the process of jointly building the Belt and Road. It has set up the BRI International Green Development Coalition, launched the Belt and Road Green Supply Chain Platform, and held a series of themed exchange activities such as the Belt and Road International High-level Dialogue on Ecology and Environmental Protection to jointly build a green Belt and Road.

The Green Belt and Road Initiative emphasizes the balance between economic development and ecological protection, advocates the construction of a new pattern of resource conservation and environmental protection in accordance with the principles of balanced population, resources and environment, and unified economic, social and ecological benefits, and promotes the transformation and upgrading of industrial structure and the transformation of production and living styles. The Green Belt and Road Initiative focuses on resource conservation, clean energy, energy efficiency and low-carbon technologies. It is an important part of global environmental and climate governance and provides impetus for green, low-carbon and sustainable development.[1]

---

[1]   Xu, Q. (2021). Joint hands to build green Belt and Road. *People's Daily*, January 20. https://www.gmw.cn/xueshu/2021-01/20/content_34557686.htm.

China and other Belt and Road countries have taken concrete actions to promote green infrastructure, green investment and green finance, and built more environment-friendly projects with high standards, so as to jointly promote the further development of the green Belt and Road. For example, the Karot Hydropower Station, the fifth largest hydropower station built by a Chinese company in Pakistan, is the first hydropower investment project in the China-Pakistan Economic Corridor that will provide 3.2 billion KWH of cheap and clean electricity every year, which can meet the electricity demand of about 5 million people, and will effectively alleviate the contradiction between power supply and demand in Pakistan. With the support of the Asian Infrastructure Investment Bank (AIIB) and other multilateral development banks, Maldives has established the first sustainable regional solid waste disposal system. In October 2020, China Power International, Electricity Power, the AIIB, European Bank for Reconstruction and Development (EBRD), and Industrial and Commercial Bank of China (ICBC) officially signed the financing agreement for Zhanatas Wind Power Project in Kazakhstan. The International Platform on Sustainable Finance (IPSF), jointly launched by China and the European Union, by making full use of the Belt and Road Green investment and financing cooperation and multilateral and bilateral platforms such as the China-EU, China-UK and China-France High-Level Economic and Financial Dialogue, has contributed to the realization of the Paris Agreement on Climate Change and the UN 2030 Agenda for Sustainable Development[1].Thanks to the joint efforts of relevant countries and international institutions, cooperation projects in environmental protection technologies and green industries have been continuously launched along the Belt and Road, giving a strong boost to the green development of Belt and Road countries.

4. Advancing global poverty reduction

The huge changes in current world situations never seen in a century and the COVID-19 pandemic have brought about global challenges, disrupting world economic recovery and development. The Human Development Index has dropped for the first time in 30 years, some developing countries have returned to poverty and chaos caused

---

[1] Yu, Y., zhu, D., Lv, Q., Liu, G., Zhang, M., & Lin, R. (2020). Jointly build a green Belt and Road. *People's Daily*, http://finance.people.com.cn/n1/2020/1126/c1004-31944855.html.

by the pandemic, and even many people in developed countries are getting stuck in living difficulties. According to the 2021 Sustainable Development Goals Report of the United Nations[①], 119 million to 124 million people around the world returned to extreme poverty in 2020, and the number of people suffering starvation increased significantly. Inequalities already existing both within and between countries have been exacerbated by the pandemic. Affected by multiple factors, global food and energy prices have risen sharply, and developing countries, especially the least developed countries, are facing increased food security crises and poverty risks. The global poverty reduction process has once again encountered a chill.

China's success in poverty reduction is the biggest contribution to global poverty reduction. In 2021, China declared an overall victory in the battle against poverty. As the largest developing country, China has lifted more than 850 million people out of poverty since reform and opening-up, contributing more than 70% to global poverty reduction.

The Belt and Road Initiative is committed to promoting poverty reduction in countries along the Belt and Road, making participating countries share China's development opportunities and helping them create more jobs, increase tax revenue, and enhance the capacity for independent development. Development is the fundamental way to eradicate poverty. According to the white paper issued by China in 2021 titled "Poverty Alleviation: China's Experience and Contribution", the Belt and Road Initiative is aimed to promote broader, higher-level and deeper regional economic and social development cooperation, and support and help relevant countries to better achieve poverty reduction and development. Over the past decade, while devoting to poverty eradication itself, China has carried out extensive cooperation on poverty alleviation with countries in Africa, Latin America, ASEAN and other countries along the Belt and Road, signed poverty alleviation cooperation agreements, and actively supported and helped developing countries, especially the least developed countries, to eradicate poverty. So far, China has established more than 20 economic and trade cooperation zones and over 100 industrial parks in Africa, making positive contributions to Africa's industrialization, job creation and export growth. According

---

①   UNDESA (2021). *The Sustainable Development Goals Report 2021*. https://www.un.org/en/desa/sustainable-development-goals-sdgs.

to incomplete statistics, these economic and trade cooperation zones alone have created about tens of thousands of jobs and paid more than $1 billion in taxes for the host countries. According to the World Bank, by 2030, the Belt and Road Initiative will generate $1.6 trillion in annual benefits for the world, accounting for 1.3% of global GDP. It will lift 7.6 million people out of absolute poverty and 32 million out of moderate poverty between 2015 and 2030.

II. GDI builds Global Consensus on Development

In following the trend of the times for peace and development, the Global Development Initiative (GDI) has gained broad support from the international community and gradually become an international consensus. As the initiative moves from consensus to practice, it will be of great significance to the global realization of the Sustainable Development Goals.

1. Meeting the needs of the times

At present, the international situation still remains complex and severe, and global challenges continue to cast a shadow on world economic development. Developing countries, in particular, face even greater risks and challenges.

On September 21, 2021, President Xi Jinping put forward the Global Development Initiative at the general debate of the 76th session of the United Nations General Assembly. The Initiative mainly includes development first, people-centered, inclusive, innovation-driven, harmonious coexistence between man and nature under the action-oriented approach. President Xi called on the international community to strengthen cooperation in such areas as poverty reduction, food security, anti-pandemic and vaccines, financing for development, climate change and green development, industrialization, digital economy and connectivity. Since then, it has been mentioned on many important international occasions, such as the commemoration of the 50th anniversary of the restoration of the lawful seat of the People's Republic of China in the UN, the G20, the Forum on China-Africa Cooperation, and the High-Level Dialogue on Global Development.

At the APEC CEO summit on November 11, 2021, China further enriched the Global Development Initiative, pointing out that China is willing to continue to play its role as a responsible power, promote global cooperation on poverty reduction, food security and financing for development, implement the UN 2030 Sustainable Development Agenda, to build a global community with a shared future for development.

The Global Development Initiative was put forward against the backdrop of the huge changes in the world situation and the pandemic both never seen in a century, the accelerating restructuring of industrial and supply chains, the widening development gap between countries, and the growing difficulties in global sustainable development. The Initiative reflects the common aspirations of the international community, developing countries in particular, builds consensus for global development cooperation, and charts the course for world economic development.

2. Adding new connotations to international cooperation

Rooted in China's own development experience, the Global Development Initiative draws on China's profound understanding and theoretical distillation of the concept of development, and enriches and innovates the concept of global development.

Development is the fundamental solution to major global issues. Only through development can the people's yearning for a better life be met. The Global Development Initiative aims to encourage the international community to give priority to development in the global macro policy framework, and provide more powerful and targeted support to developing countries. It has drawn up a blueprint for national development and international development cooperation, and charted the course for advancing global development.

The Global Development Initiative follows a people-centered approach to development. The people-centered development philosophy reflects the value pursuit and governance concept of the Chinese government of putting people first, governing for the people and benefiting the people. Development is meaningful only when it is for the people, and only by relying on the people to promote development can development have lasting impetus. The core value of development is that the fruits are shared by the people. People-centered development will help make global development more equitable and inclusive and alleviate major issues such as the global wealth gap and development gap. In today's world, there is still a large development gap between the emerging markets and developing countries and developed countries. For the vast number of underdeveloped countries and regions, only the common prosperity of all countries can be called true prosperity, and only through inclusiveness can benefits be delivered to the people of all countries. Chinese leaders have publicly expressed their readiness on many international occasions to work with all parties to implement the Global Development Initiative and ensure that no country is left behind.

The Global Development Initiative is committed to promoting stronger, greener and healthier development and promoting more balanced, coordinated and inclusive development. The Initiative regards the world as a whole, focuses on the comprehensive and sustainable development of man, adheres to the ecological philosophy of dialectical unity between man and nature, and seeks to achieve harmonious coexistence between man and nature.

The Global Development Initiative is innovation-driven. At present, a new round of scientific and industrial revolution is gaining momentum, and innovation is becoming an underlying driving force of global development. To promote global innovation-driven development, a non-discriminatory and fair development environment conducive to innovation must be created and institutional barriers to innovation be removed to enable science and technology to truly serve global development.

3. From consensus to practice

The Global Development Initiative is highly responsive to the needs of all parties and has thus won broad international consensus. Thanks to the positive response of many parties, the Initiative has been included in important outcome documents such as the Foreign Ministers' Meeting between China and Pacific Island Countries, the Summit Commemorating the 30th Anniversary of China-ASEAN Dialogue Relations, the Eighth Ministerial Meeting of the Forum on China-Africa Cooperation, and the Third Ministerial Meeting of the Forum on China and Latin American and Caribbean States.

The UN is an important platform for promoting cooperation on the Global Development Initiative. In January 2022, the inaugural meeting of the Group of Friends of the Global Development Initiative was held at the UN headquarters in New York, and more than 100 countries and many international organizations, including the UN, expressed their positive support for the Initiative. So far, 60 countries have joined the Group.[①] UN Secretary-General Antonio Guterres believes that the Global Development Initiative is of great significance to promoting the realization of the UN 2030 Sustainable Development Goals and addressing the issue of inequality and imbalance in global development.

Adhering to an action-oriented approach, the Global Development Initiative has been translated from word into action. Through docking in key areas, docking the demands of all countries, docking cooperation mechanisms, and docking partners from all walks of life, the Initiative has advanced pragmatic cooperation in eight key areas --- poverty reduction, food security, anti-pandemic and vaccine, financing for development, climate change and green development, industrialization, digital economy, and interconnectivity, pooled a strong power for achieving the 17 UN Sustainable Development Goals on schedule, and brought new hope to developing countries for leapfrog development.

> ### Box 12-3　Global Development Initiative: China is taking action
>
> China has taken a series of concrete actions to promote the implementation of the Global Development Initiative, demonstrating its responsibility as a major power.
>
> At the general debate of the 76th session of the UN General Assembly, China proposed a series of practical measures, including enhancing the synergy and efficiency of multilateral development cooperation and accelerating the implementation of the UN 2030 Agenda for Sustainable Development; supporting developing countries, especially vulnerable countries in great difficulties, through debt relief and development assistance; creating an open, fair, just and non-discriminatory environment for scientific and technological development; vigorously supporting green and low-carbon development of developing countries.
>
> At the summit marking the 30th anniversary of China-ASEAN dialogue relations, China expressed its willingness to provide an additional $1.5 billion in development assistance to ASEAN countries in the next three years for their fight against the COVID-19and economic recovery, carry out international development cooperation with the ASEAN and launch negotiations on relative agreement , support the establishment of a

---

① Wang, Y. (2022). Global Development Initiative has been well received by the international community. May 19. http://new.fmprc.gov.cn/web/wjbzhd/202205/t20220519_10689605.shtml.

China-ASEAN development knowledge network, strengthen exchanges and cooperation in poverty reduction, and promote balanced and inclusive development.

At the Eighth Ministerial Conference of the Forum on China-Africa Cooperation, China announced that it would provide another 1 billion doses of vaccine to Africa, assist in the implementation of 10 medical and health projects in the continent, send to it 1,500 medical personnel and public health experts, assist in the implementation of its 10 poverty reduction and agriculture projects, and dispatch to it 500 agricultural experts. In early 2022, China put forward the "Vision for Peaceful Development in the Horn of Africa", adding a new footnote to the implementation of the Global Development Initiative in Africa.

At the 2022 High-Level Dialogue on Global Development, China called on all parties to create a development pattern featuring balanced, coordinated, inclusive, win-win cooperation and common prosperity for all, and announced a series of important measures to implement the Global Development Initiative, including the establishment of the fund for global development and South-South cooperation, greater input into the China-UN peace and development fund, and the establishment of the global development promotion center.

III. Contributing More Chinese Wisdom to Global Openness and Cooperation

The Belt and Road Initiative and the Global Development Initiative are both China's important practice to actively participate in global development governance and build a community with a shared future for mankind. Looking ahead, China will continue to promote high-quality Belt and Road cooperation and implement the Global Development Initiative, and will make greater contribution to global openness and cooperation.

1. Contributing more public goods and platforms to international cooperation

At present, the functions of the UN, the WTO and other international governance platforms have been weakened, and the global governance deficit, trust deficit, peace deficit and development deficit are on the rise. As the largest developing country, China strives to provide developing countries with more equitable, non-discriminatory, inclusive international public goods and platforms conducive to international cooperation and development.

The Belt and Road Initiative is an active attempt by China to provide international public goods. Both the Initiative itself and the concept are multilateral[1]. Under the Belt and Road international cooperation framework, China has promoted the establishment of the AIIB, the Silk Road Fund and the CIIE as public platforms with international influence. The Global Development Initiative is another important public good China has provided to the international community following the Belt and Road Initiative. To implement the Global Development Initiative, China has hosted the High-Level Dialogue on Global Development and the World Youth Development Forum, established the Global Development and South-South Cooperation Fund, set up the Global Development Promotion Center, and established a global development knowledge network, all of which have contributed to building consensus on and injecting impetus into global development cooperation.

In the future, China will provide more international cooperation platforms and public goods to the world, support and expand the representation and voice of developing countries in international affairs, and welcome all countries to hitch a ride on the express train of China's development and provide new opportunities for the world with China's new development.

2. Contributing more practical solutions to addressing global problems

At present, the global economic recovery is disrupted, the steps toward dealing with climate change are sluggish, and the implementation of the UN 2030 Agenda for Sustainable Development encounters great difficulties. China has always been committed to resolving global issues through cooperation and dialogue, and has offered new practical solutions to global issues through Belt and Road cooperation and the implementation of the Global Development Initiative.

China has initiated the Belt and Road Initiative to promote policy communication, infrastructure connectivity, trade, financial and people-to-people exchanges with other participating states, and build a road of peace, prosperity, openness, green, innovation

---

[1] Wang, H. (2022). Promoting multilateralization and international of the Belt and Road Initial. *Chinese Social Sciences Net*. https://baijiahao.baidu.com/s?id=1724432148085583363&wfr= spider&for=pc.

and civilization to better meet the needs of all parties and win broad trust. The Global Development Initiative has systematically proposed solutions to global development issues. By "refocusing" on development issues, it has charted a "roadmap" for narrowing the North-South divide and addressing development imbalance, and pooled a strong power for achieving more robust, green and sound global development.

In the future, China will push the Belt and Road Initiative and the Global Development Initiative to take sound and bigger steps forward. With an action-oriented approach, China will make greater efforts to promote global carbon emissions peaking and carbon neutrality with its commitment to green and low-carbon development, and steadily advance the UN 2030 Agenda for Sustainable Development with its strong and sound development.

3. Contributing more Chinese wisdom to building a community with a shared future for mankind

In today's world, there are over 200 countries and regions and over 2,500 ethnic groups, and their different histories, national conditions and customs have given birth to a colorful world. China respects the diversity of world civilizations, respects the will of other countries to pursue independent development paths, upholds the interests of developing countries, practices true multilateralism, and stands on the side of human progress.

From the Belt and Road Initiative to the Global Development Initiative, China has always stood for resolving differences through dialogue, strengthening solidarity and cooperation, and working with the international community to jointly address global threats. China has actively participated in global development governance, calling for returning peace and development as the theme of the times to the core of global governance, and promoted a more fair and reasonable system of global governance by putting forward Chinese solutions, winning extensive recognition and response from the international community. China upholds the common values of peace, development, fairness, justice, democracy and freedom for all mankind, advocates exchanges and mutual learning among civilizations, and promotes mutual respect and harmonious coexistence among them.

Through the Belt and Road Initiative and the Global Development Initiatives, China will promote all countries to foster the consciousness of the community with a shared future for mankind, in which "I am apart of you, and you are a part of me", cultivate the idea of win-win cooperation in the "big family", reject ideological debate, transcend the "clash of civilization" trap, and make the diversity of the world a driving force of human social progress and a colorful natural form of human civilization.

Appendix

I. Ranking of World Openness Index Since 2008
（Sorted by the ranking in 2020; G20 Member States in bold）

	2020	2019	2018	2017	2016	2015	2014	2013	2012	2011	2010	2009	2008
Singapore	1	1	1	1	1	1	2	2	2	2	2	2	2
Germany	**2**	**2**	**3**	**3**	**3**	**4**	**4**	**4**	**4**	**4**	**4**	**3**	**3**
Hong Kong, China	3	3	2	2	2	2	3	3	3	3	3	4	4
Ireland	4	4	4	4	4	6	5	7	7	8	8	9	11
Switzerland	5	6	5	6	5	8	6	5	5	6	7	7	10
Netherlands	6	7	9	8	8	7	9	8	8	7	10	8	8
Canada	**7**	**9**	**8**	**11**	**10**	**11**	**10**	**9**	**10**	**9**	**9**	**11**	**7**
Malta	8	10	10	14	12	12	12	12	12	11	6	6	6
France	**9**	**8**	**7**	**9**	**9**	**10**	**11**	**10**	**11**	**10**	**11**	**10**	**9**
United Kingdom	**10**	**5**	**6**	**5**	**6**	**9**	**7**	**6**	**6**	**5**	**5**	**5**	**5**
Belgium	11	12	12	15	14	15	14	14	15	14	14	17	16
South Korea	**12**	**14**	**15**	**17**	**19**	**22**	**19**	**28**	**36**	**41**	**43**	**50**	**51**
Luxembourg	13	20	31	7	15	5	8	11	9	27	23	15	41
Hungary	14	25	26	26	21	26	25	26	26	26	27	27	26
New Zealand	15	28	24	23	25	25	26	25	25	25	25	13	14
Czech	16	19	18	19	20	21	24	24	23	23	24	26	27
Australia	**17**	**16**	**14**	**12**	**11**	**14**	**17**	**18**	**21**	**22**	**22**	**25**	**25**
Austria	18	23	20	22	24	23	22	19	19	18	20	21	21
Cyprus	19	15	16	28	32	32	30	51	40	19	18	19	19
Denmark	20	24	23	24	23	24	23	23	20	21	21	24	23
Italy	**21**	**11**	**11**	**13**	**13**	**13**	**13**	**13**	**13**	**13**	**13**	**14**	**15**
Sweden	22	17	21	21	22	20	18	20	18	17	17	20	22
United States	**23**	**22**	**19**	**10**	**7**	**3**	**1**	**1**	**1**	**1**	**1**	**1**	**1**
Estonia	24	27	25	27	28	27	27	22	24	24	28	29	29
Israel	25	13	13	16	16	17	16	15	14	15	15	18	17
Japan	**26**	**21**	**28**	**25**	**26**	**16**	**15**	**16**	**16**	**12**	**12**	**12**	**12**
Lithuania	27	31	30	30	36	50	47	47	52	45	42	39	37

(Continued)

	2020	2019	2018	2017	2016	2015	2014	2013	2012	2011	2010	2009	2008
Spain	28	18	17	18	17	19	20	21	22	20	19	22	20
Greece	29	49	51	55	55	56	33	32	30	32	33	33	33
Latvia	30	29	27	29	27	29	28	29	28	30	31	35	36
Costa Rica	31	30	29	31	30	33	59	43	43	43	59	57	58
Portugal	32	33	34	35	33	34	31	31	31	31	30	30	30
Norway	33	26	22	20	18	18	21	17	17	16	16	16	13
Finland	34	32	32	32	31	31	29	27	27	29	29	28	28
Chile	35	35	33	36	40	37	37	36	33	28	26	23	18
Nicaragua	36	36	36	38	37	36	44	42	41	42	39	40	40
Macao, China	37	37	40	43	48	47	42	44	50	44	44	46	48
Slovakia	38	42	41	42	41	40	40	38	39	39	41	41	47
China	**39**	**40**	**42**	**41**	**42**	**43**	**43**	**45**	**47**	**53**	**58**	**61**	**62**
Georgia	40	44	47	58	58	60	56	58	62	99	99	87	78
Bahrain	41	41	39	40	38	38	34	30	29	40	38	37	39
Peru	42	39	35	37	47	46	53	49	49	51	61	58	60
Malaysia	43	48	46	48	46	44	39	55	56	58	55	42	24
Poland	44	43	44	45	44	45	58	57	57	57	54	56	57
Uruguay	45	34	37	39	39	39	36	33	32	35	34	31	31
Mexico	**46**	**54**	**54**	**53**	**54**	**55**	**52**	**50**	**48**	**48**	**46**	**43**	**42**
Panama	47	38	38	34	35	30	35	37	37	34	36	36	34
Guatemala	48	46	43	46	43	41	51	48	51	49	45	45	46
Trinidad and Tobago	49	45	45	44	29	28	38	35	34	36	40	47	49
Slovenia	50	55	57	57	57	57	55	54	54	50	47	44	38
Iceland	51	50	49	49	62	78	73	73	76	75	79	80	83
Oman	52	47	48	47	45	42	45	41	44	47	50	51	52
Croatia	53	52	53	56	56	58	54	56	58	59	56	52	53
Bulgaria	54	51	52	33	34	35	32	34	35	33	32	34	35
Jordan	55	57	55	52	50	49	41	40	38	38	37	32	32
Cambodia	56	53	50	50	49	48	57	59	60	64	68	76	81
Mauritius	57	58	58	51	53	52	49	52	45	37	35	38	44
El Salvador	58	59	59	59	60	59	61	60	59	56	51	48	43
Antigua and Barbuda	59	56	56	54	52	53	50	53	53	52	52	67	71
Romania	60	63	63	64	64	65	63	67	67	67	72	72	77
Guyana	61	62	61	62	51	51	48	46	42	46	48	55	55
Kuwait	62	60	60	61	63	62	62	61	68	69	67	66	72
Botswana	63	61	62	63	61	61	60	63	55	55	49	53	59
Vietnam	64	75	75	72	76	80	81	82	84	87	86	88	90
Colombia	65	65	65	67	69	81	90	98	103	102	102	100	92

(Continued)

	2020	2019	2018	2017	2016	2015	2014	2013	2012	2011	2010	2009	2008
Mongolia	66	69	70	69	70	70	72	71	70	80	83	86	80
Zambia	67	70	69	68	67	67	64	62	61	61	63	63	66
Dominican Rep.	68	71	68	70	78	75	70	70	65	62	60	73	76
Paraguay	69	72	72	74	72	74	76	75	74	71	69	60	61
Argentina	**70**	**66**	**71**	**76**	**80**	**87**	**88**	**89**	**90**	**78**	**78**	**77**	**79**
Saudi Arabia	**71**	**68**	**67**	**66**	**65**	**63**	**68**	**65**	**66**	**66**	**65**	**68**	**64**
Thailand	72	83	83	83	85	85	85	86	87	90	96	93	82
Armenia	73	79	80	79	81	69	67	68	69	68	70	65	68
Russia	**74**	**64**	**64**	**60**	**59**	**54**	**46**	**39**	**46**	**54**	**57**	**62**	**69**
North Macedonia	75	77	78	75	74	73	77	77	73	77	77	71	73
Ecuador	76	67	66	65	66	64	87	88	86	84	62	54	54
Barbados	77	74	73	77	71	76	82	81	82	82	88	96	100
Uganda	78	73	74	71	75	71	71	72	71	73	74	75	74
Honduras	79	78	77	81	83	84	91	90	93	91	91	79	56
Albania	80	81	81	80	82	82	83	80	75	76	87	99	102
Philippines	81	80	79	78	77	77	75	94	92	96	93	85	88
Indonesia	**82**	**76**	**76**	**82**	**79**	**79**	**79**	**78**	**79**	**85**	**66**	**70**	**67**
Jamaica	83	87	87	85	68	66	65	66	63	63	64	59	50
Gambia	84	85	86	84	84	83	80	79	81	83	81	81	86
Kyrgyz	85	89	91	91	91	108	104	104	97	74	73	74	70
Ukraine	86	86	85	98	98	104	107	106	106	106	108	109	99
Morocco	87	88	88	88	89	91	92	91	91	92	90	91	93
Lebanon	88	93	92	90	88	89	69	69	72	72	71	64	63
Cabo Verde	89	104	105	120	128	128	128	128	128	128	127	127	126
Moldova	90	94	94	94	93	96	98	115	118	119	117	112	107
Turkey	**91**	**91**	**93**	**73**	**73**	**72**	**74**	**76**	**77**	**81**	**80**	**83**	**85**
Lesotho	92	98	99	102	101	106	105	102	107	104	101	101	106
India	**93**	**84**	**84**	**87**	**86**	**86**	**86**	**85**	**89**	**89**	**89**	**92**	**94**
South Africa	**94**	**90**	**89**	**95**	**95**	**94**	**93**	**92**	**94**	**94**	**94**	**89**	**91**
Belize	95	95	95	93	92	92	94	95	95	95	100	105	105
Egypt	96	92	90	89	105	103	103	100	83	60	53	49	45
Bolivia	97	97	96	96	90	88	84	83	85	88	85	78	75
Kenya	98	96	97	92	94	90	89	87	88	86	84	84	87
Papua New Guinea	99	82	82	86	87	68	66	64	64	65	76	82	89
Azerbaijan	100	103	104	99	97	100	101	101	102	103	112	116	101
Sudan	101	108	109	109	122	122	121	124	125	127	128	129	125
Samoa	102	101	103	105	106	105	109	109	109	107	107	106	109
Bosnia and Herzegovina	103	106	100	103	102	99	97	84	80	70	82	90	84

(Continued)

	2020	2019	2018	2017	2016	2015	2014	2013	2012	2011	2010	2009	2008
Kazakhstan	104	109	111	107	110	113	112	111	113	113	116	111	112
Tunisia	105	100	101	100	99	95	95	93	96	98	92	97	96
Fiji	106	110	107	106	104	102	100	96	100	101	103	103	103
Brazil	**107**	**99**	**98**	**97**	**96**	**93**	**78**	**74**	**78**	**79**	**75**	**69**	**65**
Laos	108	102	102	101	100	101	99	103	104	110	113	117	119
Namibia	109	113	113	114	113	112	113	112	114	115	109	114	118
Zimbabwe	110	105	108	104	103	98	114	117	99	93	97	115	117
Mozambique	111	107	106	108	107	111	106	105	105	114	114	110	114
Belarus	112	114	114	113	114	120	123	116	116	117	118	118	115
Bangladesh	113	111	110	110	108	107	108	107	108	105	105	104	104
Nigeria	114	112	112	111	109	109	102	99	101	100	98	98	98
Algeria	115	115	115	112	111	110	110	108	110	108	104	102	108
Congo, Rep. of	116	121	121	119	119	118	122	122	122	121	121	119	120
Madagascar	117	116	116	115	116	97	96	97	112	111	111	95	97
Pakistan	118	119	117	116	115	114	111	110	111	109	106	107	110
Sri Lanka	119	120	120	118	117	116	117	119	98	97	95	94	95
Mali	120	117	118	117	112	115	116	113	117	118	115	113	113
Tanzania	121	124	124	122	118	117	115	114	115	116	119	120	116
Ghana	122	118	119	124	121	119	120	121	120	112	110	108	111
Ethiopia	123	123	123	123	123	123	118	118	119	120	120	121	122
Malawi	124	122	122	121	120	121	119	120	126	125	125	124	123
Côte d'Ivoire	125	125	125	126	125	125	125	123	121	122	122	122	121
Nepal	126	126	126	125	124	124	124	127	123	123	123	123	130
Gabon	127	128	128	128	127	127	127	126	127	126	126	126	127
Burundi	128	127	127	127	126	126	126	125	124	124	124	125	124
Central African Rep.	129	129	129	129	129	129	129	129	129	129	129	128	128

II. World Openness Index: 129 Economies, Selected Years Since 2008

(Sorted by the index in 2020 from top to bottom; G20 members in bold)

		2020	2019	2018	2017	2016	2015	2014	2013	2012	2008
1	Singapore	0.8900	0.8646	0.8630	0.8536	0.8501	0.8557	0.8587	0.8571	0.8546	0.8438
2	**Germany**	**0.8591**	**0.8552**	**0.8508**	**0.8394**	**0.8352**	**0.8350**	**0.8365**	**0.8350**	**0.8259**	**0.8243**
3	Hong Kong, China	0.8442	0.8503	0.8580	0.8467	0.8471	0.8494	0.8579	0.8542	0.8486	0.8221
4	Ireland	0.8386	0.8371	0.8249	0.8266	0.8276	0.8272	0.8196	0.8054	0.7978	0.7802
5	Switzerland	0.8078	0.8133	0.8173	0.8100	0.8111	0.8071	0.8047	0.8078	0.8084	0.7814
6	Netherlands	0.8039	0.7997	0.7865	0.7916	0.7939	0.8072	0.7920	0.8000	0.7870	0.7856
7	**Canada**	**0.7998**	**0.7953**	**0.7867**	**0.7878**	**0.7848**	**0.7846**	**0.7896**	**0.7888**	**0.7864**	**0.7874**

(Continued)

		2020	2019	2018	2017	2016	2015	2014	2013	2012	2008
8	Malta	0.7971	0.7838	0.7809	0.7748	0.7751	0.7731	0.7849	0.7738	0.7745	0.7921
9	**France**	**0.7953**	**0.7986**	**0.7985**	**0.7904**	**0.7877**	**0.7862**	**0.7872**	**0.7864**	**0.7837**	**0.7848**
10	**United Kingdom**	**0.7952**	**0.8171**	**0.8080**	**0.8147**	**0.8026**	**0.8054**	**0.8036**	**0.8055**	**0.8063**	**0.7998**
11	Belgium	0.7878	0.7777	0.7765	0.7706	0.7711	0.7679	0.7701	0.7704	0.7652	0.7618
12	**South Korea**	**0.7862**	**0.7718**	**0.7695**	**0.7630**	**0.7577**	**0.7549**	**0.7572**	**0.7406**	**0.7279**	**0.6928**
13	Luxembourg	0.7850	0.7667	0.7503	0.7925	0.7675	0.8289	0.8013	0.7856	0.7868	0.7115
14	Hungary	0.7810	0.7632	0.7597	0.7537	0.7574	0.7530	0.7521	0.7479	0.7443	0.7374
15	New Zealand	0.7777	0.7622	0.7624	0.7568	0.7538	0.7537	0.7518	0.7484	0.7470	0.7656
16	Czech	0.7774	0.7668	0.7661	0.7591	0.7575	0.7562	0.7543	0.7501	0.7491	0.7367
17	**Australia**	**0.7765**	**0.7681**	**0.7722**	**0.7855**	**0.7761**	**0.7685**	**0.7643**	**0.7567**	**0.7500**	**0.7397**
18	Austria	0.7736	0.7664	0.7644	0.7582	0.7561	0.7548	0.7561	0.7552	0.7505	0.7459
19	Cyprus	0.7716	0.7696	0.7681	0.7527	0.7418	0.7420	0.7399	0.7065	0.7216	0.7481
20	Denmark	0.7708	0.7662	0.7634	0.7563	0.7566	0.7547	0.7546	0.7536	0.7501	0.7424
21	**Italy**	**0.7704**	**0.7814**	**0.7805**	**0.7754**	**0.7725**	**0.7729**	**0.7734**	**0.7728**	**0.7674**	**0.7618**
22	Sweden	0.7693	0.7674	0.7643	0.7583	0.7571	0.7565	0.7580	0.7550	0.7513	0.7453
23	**United States**	**0.7687**	**0.7666**	**0.7653**	**0.7904**	**0.7985**	**0.8370**	**0.8607**	**0.8681**	**0.8628**	**0.9328**
24	Estonia	0.7685	0.7628	0.7621	0.7528	0.7498	0.7499	0.7487	0.7546	0.7472	0.7296
25	Israel	0.7675	0.7772	0.7746	0.7672	0.7654	0.7646	0.7662	0.7654	0.7653	0.7575
26	**Japan**	**0.7673**	**0.7666**	**0.7593**	**0.7554**	**0.7533**	**0.7647**	**0.7677**	**0.7643**	**0.7631**	**0.7782**
27	Lithuania	0.7669	0.7568	0.7568	0.7475	0.7383	0.7220	0.7172	0.7131	0.7095	0.7202
28	Spain	0.7664	0.7669	0.7668	0.7611	0.7585	0.7577	0.7569	0.7546	0.7494	0.7466
29	Greece	0.7643	0.7300	0.7275	0.7163	0.7139	0.7116	0.7372	0.7351	0.7328	0.7243
30	Latvia	0.7641	0.7610	0.7595	0.7493	0.7502	0.7440	0.7427	0.7390	0.7375	0.7220
31	Costa Rica	0.7625	0.7595	0.7589	0.7458	0.7445	0.7413	0.6963	0.7217	0.7167	0.6868
32	Portugal	0.7597	0.7495	0.7485	0.7411	0.7400	0.7382	0.7383	0.7373	0.7325	0.7286
33	Norway	0.7571	0.7632	0.7635	0.7585	0.7582	0.7579	0.7567	0.7581	0.7564	0.7666
34	Finland	0.7570	0.7523	0.7501	0.7442	0.7441	0.7421	0.7427	0.7434	0.7398	0.7321
35	Chile	0.7527	0.7485	0.7491	0.7404	0.7351	0.7359	0.7342	0.7307	0.7320	0.7535
36	Nicaragua	0.7514	0.7459	0.7455	0.7380	0.7377	0.7365	0.7225	0.7218	0.7199	0.7122
37	Macao, China	0.7509	0.7456	0.7428	0.7322	0.7243	0.7250	0.7251	0.7192	0.7102	0.7038
38	Slovakia	0.7507	0.7413	0.7397	0.7328	0.7315	0.7288	0.7266	0.7246	0.7228	0.7071
39	**China**	**0.7507**	**0.7420**	**0.7392**	**0.7349**	**0.7299**	**0.7268**	**0.7248**	**0.7188**	**0.7107**	**0.6768**
40	Georgia	0.7484	0.7373	0.7345	0.7131	0.7107	0.6987	0.6984	0.6971	0.6797	0.6610
41	Bahrain	0.7477	0.7417	0.7431	0.7364	0.7376	0.7356	0.7368	0.7389	0.7347	0.7123
42	Peru	0.7450	0.7423	0.7456	0.7394	0.7250	0.7251	0.7113	0.7125	0.7104	0.6826
43	Malaysia	0.7447	0.7336	0.7361	0.7277	0.7261	0.7260	0.7289	0.6995	0.6944	0.7422
44	Poland,	0.7442	0.7380	0.7376	0.7298	0.7282	0.7255	0.6965	0.6973	0.6941	0.6876
45	Uruguay	0.7434	0.7488	0.7454	0.7365	0.7358	0.7355	0.7351	0.7345	0.7325	0.7274
46	**Mexico**	**0.7431**	**0.7222**	**0.7242**	**0.7192**	**0.7161**	**0.7123**	**0.7128**	**0.7117**	**0.7106**	**0.7114**
47	Panama	0.7426	0.7427	0.7440	0.7417	0.7389	0.7426	0.7362	0.7274	0.7273	0.7237

(Continued)

		2020	2019	2018	2017	2016	2015	2014	2013	2012	2008
48	Guatemala	0.7396	0.7357	0.7387	0.7294	0.7284	0.7272	0.7129	0.7127	0.7100	0.7073
49	Trinidad and Tobago	0.7356	0.7368	0.7375	0.7312	0.7469	0.7441	0.7307	0.7310	0.7315	0.6964
50	Sloveniaf	0.7323	0.7219	0.7211	0.7131	0.7115	0.7090	0.7057	0.7023	0.6997	0.7162
51	Iceland	0.7296	0.7296	0.7320	0.7241	0.6953	0.6614	0.6650	0.6675	0.6622	0.6547
52	Oman	0.7275	0.7356	0.7330	0.7294	0.7277	0.7272	0.7224	0.7231	0.7156	0.6923
53	Croatia	0.7261	0.7257	0.7246	0.7150	0.7118	0.7081	0.7057	0.6991	0.6940	0.6923
54	Bulgaria	0.7249	0.7261	0.7252	0.7433	0.7397	0.7375	0.7379	0.7333	0.7301	0.7232
55	Jordan	0.7249	0.7197	0.7217	0.7197	0.7234	0.7221	0.7260	0.7238	0.7235	0.7273
56	Cambodia	0.7213	0.7248	0.7280	0.7223	0.7236	0.7242	0.6981	0.6934	0.6888	0.6563
57	Mauritius	0.7201	0.7137	0.7141	0.7216	0.7161	0.7177	0.7153	0.7041	0.7117	0.7092
58	El Salvador	0.7183	0.7119	0.7137	0.7045	0.7023	0.7007	0.6856	0.6854	0.6900	0.7101
59	Antigua and Barbuda	0.7172	0.7204	0.7212	0.7177	0.7191	0.7172	0.7150	0.7030	0.7021	0.6659
60	Romania	0.7075	0.6980	0.6959	0.6878	0.6859	0.6827	0.6815	0.6769	0.6743	0.6614
61	Guyana	0.7064	0.7000	0.7030	0.6941	0.7224	0.7195	0.7160	0.7169	0.7169	0.6915
62	Kuwait	0.7060	0.7039	0.7050	0.6974	0.6943	0.6892	0.6853	0.6828	0.6742	0.6658
63	Botswana	0.6997	0.7012	0.7029	0.6888	0.6981	0.6944	0.6932	0.6808	0.6949	0.6853
64	Vietnam	0.6943	0.6704	0.6700	0.6659	0.6616	0.6583	0.6560	0.6530	0.6511	0.6414
65	Colombia	0.6859	0.6940	0.6946	0.6790	0.6732	0.6574	0.6392	0.6227	0.6189	0.6379
66	Mongolia	0.6823	0.6813	0.6797	0.6705	0.6706	0.6680	0.6693	0.6717	0.6724	0.6573
67	Zambia	0.6768	0.6798	0.6799	0.6750	0.6775	0.6735	0.6806	0.6820	0.6852	0.6687
68	Dominican Rep.	0.6766	0.6796	0.6810	0.6693	0.6599	0.6631	0.6714	0.6720	0.6774	0.6631
69	Paraguay	0.6759	0.6746	0.6736	0.6658	0.6652	0.6641	0.6637	0.6650	0.6637	0.6800
70	**Argentina**	**0.6758**	**0.6880**	**0.6787**	**0.6643**	**0.6590**	**0.6432**	**0.6442**	**0.6424**	**0.6382**	**0.6578**
71	**Saudi Arabia**	**0.6754**	**0.6818**	**0.6827**	**0.6811**	**0.6823**	**0.6843**	**0.6728**	**0.6797**	**0.6766**	**0.6715**
72	Thailand	0.6742	0.6546	0.6565	0.6524	0.6499	0.6491	0.6508	0.6463	0.6486	0.6552
73	Armenia	0.6737	0.6631	0.6637	0.6614	0.6573	0.6707	0.6734	0.6746	0.6728	0.6681
74	**Russia**	**0.6725**	**0.6947**	**0.6953**	**0.7016**	**0.7069**	**0.7153**	**0.7223**	**0.7241**	**0.7113**	**0.6678**
75	North Macedonia	0.6724	0.6666	0.6669	0.6646	0.6638	0.6652	0.6637	0.6607	0.6644	0.6653
76	Ecuador	0.6711	0.6873	0.6891	0.6852	0.6821	0.6838	0.6444	0.6445	0.6489	0.6920
77	Barbados	0.6676	0.6708	0.6731	0.6643	0.6658	0.6624	0.6544	0.6540	0.6559	0.6153
78	Uganda	0.6666	0.6719	0.6714	0.6661	0.6638	0.6664	0.6711	0.6692	0.6695	0.6650
79	Honduras	0.6661	0.6634	0.6672	0.6584	0.6560	0.6544	0.6382	0.6361	0.6344	0.6913
80	Albania	0.6598	0.6624	0.6630	0.6595	0.6564	0.6553	0.6533	0.6542	0.6632	0.6140
81	Philippines	0.6582	0.6630	0.6645	0.6631	0.6611	0.6621	0.6642	0.6322	0.6357	0.6461
82	**Indonesia**	**0.6563**	**0.6668**	**0.6696**	**0.6571**	**0.6592**	**0.6587**	**0.6614**	**0.6586**	**0.6585**	**0.6681**
83	Jamaica	0.6537	0.6483	0.6493	0.6506	0.6755	0.6790	0.6791	0.6792	0.6782	0.6936
84	Gambia	0.6527	0.6518	0.6523	0.6515	0.6511	0.6548	0.6577	0.6543	0.6564	0.6497
85	Kyrgyz	0.6514	0.6430	0.6439	0.6386	0.6392	0.6122	0.6174	0.6166	0.6243	0.6662
86	Ukraine	0.6505	0.6491	0.6528	0.6287	0.6269	0.6180	0.6159	0.6139	0.6144	0.6156

(Continued)

		2020	2019	2018	2017	2016	2015	2014	2013	2012	2008
87	Morocco	0.6418	0.6471	0.6470	0.6445	0.6414	0.6375	0.6348	0.6335	0.6374	0.6325
88	Lebanon	0.6417	0.6400	0.6422	0.6389	0.6417	0.6413	0.6723	0.6723	0.6684	0.6729
89	Cabo Verde	0.6410	0.6215	0.6225	0.5899	0.5569	0.5560	0.5577	0.5568	0.5585	0.5564
90	Moldova	0.6400	0.6385	0.6403	0.6337	0.6363	0.6267	0.6260	0.6022	0.6013	0.6051
91	**Turkey**	**0.6391**	**0.6420**	**0.6415**	**0.6658**	**0.6646**	**0.6658**	**0.6649**	**0.6628**	**0.6606**	**0.6498**
92	Lesotho	0.6371	0.6329	0.6344	0.6220	0.6200	0.6148	0.6165	0.6176	0.6139	0.6064
93	**India**	**0.6359**	**0.6524**	**0.6537**	**0.6450**	**0.6452**	**0.6476**	**0.6499**	**0.6507**	**0.6435**	**0.6256**
94	**South Africa**	**0.6342**	**0.6422**	**0.6458**	**0.6337**	**0.6329**	**0.6318**	**0.6339**	**0.6333**	**0.6323**	**0.6401**
95	Belize	0.6339	0.6382	0.6394	0.6361	0.6369	0.6367	0.6311	0.6292	0.6292	0.6070
96	Egypt	0.6331	0.6410	0.6448	0.6441	0.6179	0.6189	0.6201	0.6202	0.6542	0.7084
97	Bolivia	0.6319	0.6355	0.6361	0.6336	0.6398	0.6418	0.6526	0.6513	0.6495	0.6642
98	Kenya	0.6312	0.6358	0.6352	0.6364	0.6361	0.6386	0.6427	0.6452	0.6461	0.6465
99	Papua New Guinea	0.6304	0.6583	0.6607	0.6453	0.6449	0.6727	0.6756	0.6806	0.6776	0.6437
100	Azerbaijan	0.6294	0.6245	0.6249	0.6276	0.6290	0.6236	0.6215	0.6193	0.6193	0.6142
101	Sudan	0.6278	0.6166	0.6168	0.6134	0.5856	0.5831	0.5856	0.5801	0.5722	0.5629
102	Samoa	0.6273	0.6258	0.6253	0.6176	0.6172	0.6152	0.6115	0.6099	0.6086	0.6024
103	Bosnia and Herzegovina	0.6270	0.6180	0.6293	0.6219	0.6194	0.6236	0.6271	0.6509	0.6583	0.6525
104	Kazakhstan	0.6257	0.6163	0.6159	0.6144	0.6109	0.6054	0.6068	0.6051	0.6053	0.5982
105	Tunisia	0.6227	0.6283	0.6271	0.6267	0.6238	0.6285	0.6311	0.6329	0.6266	0.6252
106	Fiji	0.6226	0.6160	0.6213	0.6149	0.6183	0.6198	0.6218	0.6242	0.6230	0.6126
107	**Brazil**	**0.6189**	**0.6284**	**0.6348**	**0.6303**	**0.6325**	**0.6348**	**0.6632**	**0.6660**	**0.6604**	**0.6704**
108	Laos	0.6182	0.6246	0.6264	0.6228	0.6213	0.6216	0.6225	0.6175	0.6185	0.5907
109	Namibia	0.6176	0.6129	0.6148	0.6065	0.6046	0.6061	0.6067	0.6039	0.6033	0.5917
110	Zimbabwe	0.6166	0.6214	0.6203	0.6185	0.6186	0.6263	0.6039	0.5981	0.6233	0.5923
111	Mozambique	0.6160	0.6170	0.6218	0.6144	0.6163	0.6100	0.6161	0.6154	0.6147	0.5975
112	Belarus	0.6119	0.6095	0.6117	0.6067	0.6043	0.5848	0.5839	0.5999	0.6027	0.5932
113	Bangladesh	0.6100	0.6155	0.6167	0.6128	0.6115	0.6138	0.6139	0.6113	0.6088	0.6097
114	Nigeria	0.6036	0.6144	0.6150	0.6118	0.6112	0.6116	0.6206	0.6205	0.6198	0.6172
115	Algeria	0.6036	0.6074	0.6075	0.6079	0.6107	0.6106	0.6094	0.6105	0.6083	0.6033
116	Congo, Rep. of	0.6008	0.5961	0.5947	0.5960	0.5933	0.5944	0.5854	0.5827	0.5815	0.5848
117	Madagascar	0.5994	0.6058	0.6056	0.6051	0.6028	0.6264	0.6297	0.6230	0.6058	0.6184
118	Pakistan	0.5983	0.6042	0.6052	0.6040	0.6032	0.6040	0.6070	0.6062	0.6073	0.6009
119	Sri Lanka	0.5942	0.5983	0.5980	0.5988	0.5997	0.6007	0.5967	0.5933	0.6241	0.6254
120	Mali	0.5927	0.6045	0.6040	0.6012	0.6048	0.6032	0.6037	0.6038	0.6013	0.5981
121	Tanzania	0.5926	0.5867	0.5869	0.5857	0.5987	0.5965	0.6038	0.6029	0.6031	0.5930
122	Ghana	0.5864	0.6045	0.6017	0.5829	0.5879	0.5873	0.5858	0.5847	0.5898	0.6008
123	Ethiopia	0.5852	0.5885	0.5894	0.5851	0.5848	0.5821	0.5917	0.5946	0.5904	0.5822
124	Malawi	0.5830	0.5909	0.5917	0.5898	0.5890	0.5848	0.5892	0.5885	0.5676	0.5777
125	Côte d'Ivoire	0.5804	0.5843	0.5828	0.5735	0.5754	0.5749	0.5793	0.5804	0.5819	0.5823

(Continued)

		2020	2019	2018	2017	2016	2015	2014	2013	2012	2008
126	Nepal	0.5791	0.5785	0.5813	0.5784	0.5793	0.5789	0.5810	0.5661	0.5755	0.3132
127	Gabon	0.5706	0.5709	0.5705	0.5676	0.5679	0.5679	0.5676	0.5692	0.5659	0.5555
128	Burundi	0.5683	0.5723	0.5720	0.5710	0.5697	0.5690	0.5716	0.5729	0.5728	0.5671
129	Central African Rep.	0.5500	0.5508	0.5500	0.5488	0.5513	0.5491	0.5504	0.5519	0.5489	0.5470

III. Brief Introduction to World Openness Index

This section includes the following contents: concept and theory of opening-up to the outside world, indicator system, weight setting and sources of data, and nondimensionalization of indicators.

1. Concept and Theory of Opening-up to the Outside World

The basic meaning of "opening-up to the outside world" is clear and consistent, that is, the specific entities of at least two economies carry out exchanges at the economic, social and cultural levels to lead to the flow of goods, services, personnel, capital, information, knowledge, and technology. The subject of "opening-up to the outside world", mentioned in this report, mainly refers to the macro-level economy, that is, a specific economy. This means that the openness index takes the entire economy as the basic unit of observation.

The openness index measures cross-border economic openness and the related cross-border social openness and cross-border cultural openness.

In the field of economic openness, cross-border exchanges undoubtedly have the longest history, including, but not limited to, cross-border trade. Economic opening-up has long been dominated by the opening-up of cross-border trade, and cross-border trade has long been dominated by goods. In recent decades, the proportion of services has gradually increased, and it has almost become predominant in some economies. Foreign trade in goods has long been dominated by primary and final products, although the intermediate products have accounted for an increasing proportion and even become the main part of cross-border trade in some economies. Cross-border trade is actually a direct manifestation or extension of a country's endowment of resources (including natural resources and human resources) and production technology endowments. This is exactly the basic principle discussed in the classical theory of international trade. Therefore, this report uses the cross-border trade theory as a starting point to construct a theoretical model of opening-up to the outside world.

Based on the summary of various frontier mainstream cross-border trade models by Costinot & Rodríguez-Clare (2014)[1], price of a product of economy i in economy j can be expressed as function of a number of variables, including those directly related to cross-border opening-up, such as the fixed and variable costs of entry of one economy into another. Those costs and the areas of cross-border opening-up that influence the costs are as follows:

— Variable trade costs: variable trade costs for export of final products are mainly influenced by trade opening-up policies of the importing economy, and variable trade costs for imports of intermediate goods are mainly influenced by trade opening-up policies of the importing economy.

— Productivity of production enterprises is subject to influence of the host economy's investment opening-up policies.

— Fixed costs of enterprises' exports and cross-border investments are subject to influence of financial opening-up policies.

— Total factor productivity is subject to influence of cross-border diffusion of knowledge and technology.

— The variable costs of corporate decisions are influenced by the quality of institutions, such as contractual improvement and property rights protection.

Accordingly, the areas affecting cross-border trade and economy can be put in the following three categories: First, it is economic openness, mainly trade openness, investment openness, and financial openness. Second, it is social openness, mainly tourism, studying abroad, and immigration opening-up. Third, it is cultural opening-up, mainly cultural trade and cultural exchange. Those three types of openness all include the opening-up of corresponding systems.

To highlight cross-border institutional openness, cross-border openness is divided into cross-border openness performance and complimentary openness policies, each covering economic, social and cultural openness.

---

[1] Costinot. A., & Rodríguez-Clare, A. (2014). Trade theory with numbers: Quantifying the consequences of globalization, *Handbook of international economics, 4,* 197-261.

2. Indicator System, Weight Setting and Data Sources

a. Indicator system

The indicator system of external openness measurement is the core content of constructing the world openness index, and its setting principles follow the following principles: 1). scientific principle, including the two-way openness balance, the objectivity of openness data, and the heterogeneity of openness contents. 2). the principle of representativeness, including the representativeness of openness areas and the representativeness of openness subject. 3). the principle of sustainability, characterized by high data accessibility, stable data sources, high quality of data, and broad prospects for expansion and application.

Based on the above-mentioned concepts, theories and principles, the indicator system constituting the world openness index is divided into four levels, among which the details of the indicators of the second, third and fourth levels are shown in the table below.

Compared with other openness indicators, the world openness index, based on the aforementioned indicator system has the following characteristics. First, it measures economic openness and social and cultural openness that is intertwined with economic openness. Second, it focuses on both internal openness and external openness. Third, it focuses on both openness performance and openness policy.

b. Weight setting

The weight setting the indicator system at each level is based on expert survey. Based on a questionnaire survey of 41 Chinese experts in international economics, the weight setting of the indicator system is shown in the table below.

c. Sources of data

Sources of underlying indicator data include the World Bank, World Trade Organization, International Monetary Fund, United Nations Conference on Trade and Development, World Tourism Organization, UNESCO, United Nations Department of Economic and Social Affairs, World Intellectual Property Organization (WIPO), among others. The detailed breakdown is shown in the following table.

Indicators, weightings and sources of underlying data

Secondary indicator	Tertiary indicator	Tier-4 indicator	Weighting	Source of underlying data
Openness policy (0.518)	Economic openness policies	Weighted applied tariff rate	0.3390	WB
		Number of non-tariff trade barrier imposed by reporting economy	0.2590	WTO
		Inbound openness of concerned free trade agreement(s)	0.0510	WTO
		Outbound openness of concerned free trade agreement(s)	0.0510	WTO
		Inbound openness of concerned international investment agreement(s)	0.0500	UNCTAD
		Outbound openness of concerned international investment agreement(s)	0.0500	UNCTAD
		Financial openness policy	0.1000	Chinn-Ito Index
	Social openness policy	Cross-border visa openness policy	0.1000	Henley & Partners
	Cultural openness policy	(*Applicable at the appropriate time*)		
Openness performance (0.482)	Economic openness performance (0.69)	Import of goods	0.1690	IMF/WB
		Export of goods	0.1690	IMF/WB
		Import of services	0.1610	IMF/WB
		Export of services	0.1610	IMF/WB
		Foreign direct investment	0.1410	IMF/WB
		Outbound direct investment	0.1410	IMF/WB
		Portfolio investment inflows	0.0290	IMF/WB
		Portfolio investment outflows	0.0290	IMF/WB
	Social openness performance (0.17)	Inbound tourists	0.1896	World Tourism Organization/WB
		Outbound tourists	0.1896	World Tourism Organization/WB
		Inbound students	0.2150	UNESCO
		Outbound students	0.2150	UNESCO
		Immigrants	0.0954	UN DESA
		Emigrants	0.0954	UN DESA
	Cultural openness performance (0.14)	Import of IPR services	0.1830	IMF/WB
		Export of IPR services	0.1830	IMF/WB
		Patent application by residents of other economies	0.1710	WIPO
		Overseas patent application by residents of reporting economy	0.1710	WIPO
		International citations of science documents	0.1100	SCImago
		Cultural goods import	0.0910	UNESCO
		Cultural goods export	0.0910	UNESCO

Note: Numbers in parentheses are the weights of the indicators at the corresponding level. The weights of indicators on social openness performance are different from those in *World Openness Report 2021* (Page 49), which was wrong for typesetting error.

Despite the above sources, some values of some underlying indicators remain missing. The following approach was adopted to make up for those missing values.

— When an economy has a value for only one year in the entire sample period, this value is used for all other years.

— When an economy has a value for more than one uninterrupted year in the whole sample period, the data for the other years are taken in accordance with the principle of proximity. For example, if only values of 2011 and 2012 are available, then the value of 2011 is used for the year before 2011 and the value of 2012 is used for the year after 2012.

— For an economy that has a value in more than one year during the whole sample period and there is an interruption, the values between the two interrupted years are taken according to the principle of proximity (e.g., when only 2011 and 2014 have values, the value of 2011 is taken for 2012 and that of 2014 is taken for 2013); when the values are missing for an odd number of years, the value of the middlemost year is taken as the average of the two values at the two ends (e.g., when only values of 2011 and 2015 are available, the value of 2011 is taken for 2012, the value of 2015 is taken for 2014, and the average of the values of 2011 and 2015 is taken for 2013).

— For a country that has no values during the entire sample period, another country that is most similar to it in terms of economic development, social and cultural conditions, institutional characteristics, and geographical features should be picked so that the values of that country can be taken for the country with missing values.

3. Dimensionless treatment of indicators

a. Principles

Dimensionless treatment is a necessary step for underlying index data processing. It should abide by the following principles: the designing of the treatment method should be based on the economics principle of supply and demand.

Opening-up to the outside world is a two-way process. First, it is inward opening-up. That is, economy A opens its market to other economies to meet A's own needs, which is reflected by economy A importing goods, capital, technology, and personnel from other economies. Second, it is outward opening-up of other economies. That is, other economies open themselves to economy A to meet their own needs, which is reflected by economy A exporting goods, capital, technology, and personnel to those economies.

Such a principle is, in essence, to make the openness indicators dimensionless based on market supply and demand conditions. First, if the value of economy A on certain inward opening-up indicator is an absolute one, it should be divided by the total value of this indicator for economy A. Second, if the value of the economy A on one certain outward opening-up indicator is an absolute one, it should be divided by the global value of the indicator after deducting the value of economy A. In this report, it is stipulated that the "corresponding aggregate indicator" for the openness indicator in the economic value category is GDP, and the "corresponding aggregate indicator" for the openness indicator in the headcount category is total population, and the rest can be deduced in the same vein.

b. Specific methods

1) Outflow measured by value

Such an indicator system includes six indicators, namely, export of goods, export of services, outbound direct investment, outbound portfolio investment, export of IPR services, and cultural product export.

It is calculated as follows:

$$y_{it} = \frac{x_{it}}{\sum_{j \neq i} GDP_{jt}}$$

In the equation, y_{it} is the final value of the indicator of Economy i during Period t; x_{it} is the original value of the indicator, and $\sum_{j \neq i} GDP_{jt}$ is the *GDP* summation of all the other economies in the world.

2) Inflow measured by value

Such an indicator system includes six indicators, namely, import of goods, import of services, foreign direct investment, foreign portfolio investment, import of IPR service, and cultural product import.

It is calculated as follows:

$$y_{it} = \frac{x_{it}}{GDP_{it}}$$

In the equation, y_{it} is the final value of of the indicator of Economy i during Period t; x_{it} is the original value of the indicator.

3) Outflow measured by headcount

Such an indicator system includes three indicators, namely, outbound tourists, outbound students, and emigrants.

It is calculated as follows:

$$y_{it} = \frac{x_{it}}{\sum_{j \neq i} POP_{jt}}$$

In the equation, y_{it} is the final value of the indicator of Economy i during Period t; x_{it} is the original value of the indicator; and $\sum_{j \neq i} GDP_{jt}$ is the summation of population of all the other economies in the world.

4) Inflow measured by headcount

Such an indicator system includes three indicators, namely, inbound tourists, inbound students, and immigrants.

It is calculated as follows:

$$y_{it} = \frac{x_{it}}{POP_{it}}$$

In the equation, y_{it} is the final value of the indicator of Economy i during Period t; x_{it} is the original value of the indicator; and POP refers to population.

5) Patent application

It includes two indicators: residents applying for patents abroad (patex) and non-residents applying for patents within the reporting economy (patim).

Patex is calculated as follows:

$$patex_{it} = \frac{abroad_{it}}{\sum_{j \neq i}(resi_{jt} + nonr_{jt})}$$

In the equation, $abroad_{it}$ refers to the number of patent applications of Economy i filed in other countries in Year t; $\sum_{j \neq i}(resi_{jt} + nonr_{jt})$ refers to the total number of patent applications approved by countries other than Economy i (*resi* refers to residents and *nonr* refers to non-residents).

patim is calculated as follows:

$$patim_{it} = \frac{nonr_{it}}{resi_{it} + nonr_{it}}$$

In the equation, $nonr_{it}$ is the number of patent applications by non-residents (those from abroad) in Economy i; $resi_{it} + nonr_{it}$ is the total number of patent applications in Economy i.

6) Cross-border citations of science papers

It is calculated as follows:

$$paper_{it} = \frac{Citations_{it} - Selfcitations_{it}}{\sum_{j} Documents_{jt}}$$

In the equation, $Citations_{it}$ refers to total citations of science papers of Economy i in Year t; $Selfcitations_{it}$ refers to self-citations; and $\sum_j Documents_{jt}$ is the total number of science papers of all the other economies except Economy i.

7) External openness based on international trade and investment agreements

There are two indicators and It is calculated as follows:

$$T_{it} = \sum_p T_{ipt} \frac{GDP_{pt}}{\sum_{j \neq i} GDP_{jt}}$$

In the equation, T_{it} is openness of Economy i in Year t, based on trade or investment agreements; GDP_{pt} is the GDP of the contracting partner; $\sum_{j \neq i} GDP_{jt}$ is the total GDP of all the other economies except Economy i; T_{ipt} is a dummy variable; it takes 1 when the agreement is effective for Economy i and p in Year t; otherwise it takes 0.

8) Internal openness of concerned international trade and investment agreements

There are two indicators and It is calculated as follows:

$$T_{it} = \frac{GDP_{it}}{\sum_p T_{ipt} \times GDP_{pt}}$$

In the equation, T_{it} is the openness of Economy I in Year t, based on trade or investment agreements; GDP_{it} is GDP of Economy i; GDP_{pt} is the GDP of the contracting partner; T_{ipt} is a dummy variable; it takes 1 when the agreement is effective for Economy i and p in Year t; otherwise it takes 0.

9) Non-tariff trade barrier

It is calculated as follows:

$$X_{it} = ntb_{it} \times hs_{it}$$

In the equation, X_{it} refers to non-tariff barriers imposed by Economy i in Year t; ntb_{it} refers to number of non-tariff measures; hs_{it} refers to quantity of concerned products.

10) Indicators not requiring additional treatment

They include three indicators, namely, weighted tariff rate, financial openness index, and passport convenience index.

c. Centralized treatment of indicators

To achieve consistency in standard indicator dimensions, indicators have been processed as follows:

$$y_{it} = \frac{x_{it} - min(x)}{max(x) - min(x)}$$

In the equation, y_{it} is indicator of Economy I in Year t after the centralization process; x_{it} is the pre-centralization indicator; $max(x)$ and $min(x)$ are the maximum value and minimum value, respectively, of indicator x during the entire sample period.

For some inverse indicators, such as weighted tariff rate and non-tariff measures, the larger the value is, the lower the level of openness; it is calculated as follows:

$$y_{it} = 1 - \frac{x_{it} - min(x)}{max(x) - min(x)}$$

This calculation method projects all indicators on [0, 1].

IV. Groupings of Economies Gauged by World Openness Index
(Sorted by alphabetical name of economies)

	Economy	Grouping by region							Grouping by income				Others						
		North America	East Asia & Pacific	Latin America & Caribbean	South Asia	Europe & Central Asia	Sub-Saharan Africa	Middle East & North Africa	High income	Upper Middle Income	Lower Middle Income	Low income	Belt and Road economies[1]	Advanced economies	EU	EA	G20	G7	BRICS
		1	2	3	4	5	6	7	8	9	10	11	12	13	14	15	16	17	18
1	Albania					√				√			√						
2	Algeria							√		√			√						
3	Antigua and Barbuda			√					√				√						
4	Argentina			√						√			√				√		
5	Armenia					√				√			√						
6	Australia		√						√					√			√		
7	Austria					√			√				√	√	√	√	√		
8	Azerbaijan					√				√			√						
9	Bahrain							√	√				√						
10	Bangladesh				√						√		√						
11	Barbados			√					√				√						
12	Belarus					√				√			√						
13	Belgium					√			√					√	√	√			
14	Belize			√						√									
15	Bolivia			√							√		√						
16	Bosnia and Herzegovina					√				√			√						
17	Botswana						√			√			√						
18	Brazil			√						√							√		√
19	Bulgaria					√				√			√		√				
20	Burundi						√					√	√						
21	Cabo Verde						√				√		√						

(Continued)

		Grouping by region							Grouping by income				Others						
	Economy	North America	East Asia & Pacific	Latin America & Caribbean	South Asia	Europe & Central Asia	Sub-Saharan Africa	Middle East & North Africa	High income	Upper Middle Income	Lower Middle Income	Low income	Belt and Road economies①	Advanced economies	EU	EA	G20	G7	BRICS
		1	2	3	4	5	6	7	8	9	10	11	12	13	14	15	16	17	18
22	Cambodia		√								√		√						
23	Canada	√							√					√			√	√	
24	Central African Rep.						√					√	√						
25	Chile			√					√				√						
26	China		√							√			√				√		√
27	Colombia			√						√									
28	Congo, Rep. of						√				√		√						
29	Costa Rica			√						√			√						
30	Côte d'Ivoire						√				√		√						
31	Croatia					√			√				√		√				
32	Cyprus					√			√				√	√	√	√			
33	Czech					√			√				√	√	√				
34	Denmark					√			√					√	√				
35	Dominican Rep.			√						√			√						
36	Ecuador			√						√			√						
37	Egypt							√			√		√						
38	El Salvador			√							√		√						
39	Estonia					√			√				√	√	√	√			
40	Ethiopia						√					√	√						
41	Fiji		√							√			√						
42	Finland					√			√					√	√	√			
43	France					√			√					√	√	√	√	√	
44	Gabon						√			√			√						
45	Gambia						√					√	√						
46	Georgia					√				√			√						
47	Germany					√			√					√	√	√	√	√	
48	Ghana						√				√		√						
49	Greece					√			√				√	√	√	√			
50	Guatemala			√						√									
51	Guyana			√						√			√						
52	Honduras			√							√								
53	Hong Kong, China		√						√					√					

(Continued)

	Economy	Grouping by region							Grouping by income				Others						
		North America	East Asia & Pacific	Latin America & Caribbean	South Asia	Europe & Central Asia	Sub-Saharan Africa	Middle East & North Africa	High income	Upper Middle Income	Lower Middle Income	Low income	Belt and Road economies[①]	Advanced economies	EU	EA	G20	G7	BRICS
		1	2	3	4	5	6	7	8	9	10	11	12	13	14	15	16	17	18
54	Hungary					√			√				√		√				
55	Iceland					√			√					√					
56	India				√						√						√		√
57	Indonesia		√								√		√				√		
58	Ireland					√			√					√	√	√			
59	Israel							√	√					√					
60	Italy					√			√				√	√	√	√	√	√	
61	Jamaica			√						√			√						
62	Japan		√						√					√			√	√	
63	Jordan							√		√									
64	Kazakhstan					√				√			√						
65	Kenya						√				√		√						
66	South Korea		√						√				√	√			√		
67	Kuwait							√	√				√						
68	Kyrgyz					√					√		√						
69	Laos		√								√		√						
70	Latvia					√			√				√	√	√	√			
71	Lebanon							√		√			√						
72	Lesotho						√				√		√						
73	Lithuania					√			√				√	√	√	√			
74	Luxembourg					√			√				√	√	√	√			
75	Macao, China		√						√					√					
76	Madagascar						√					√	√						
77	Malawi						√					√							
78	Malaysia		√							√			√						
79	Mali						√					√	√						
80	Malta							√	√				√	√	√	√			
81	Mauritius						√			√									
82	Mexico			√						√							√		
83	Moldova					√					√		√						
84	Mongolia		√								√		√						
85	Morocco							√			√		√						
86	Mozambique						√					√	√						
87	Namibia						√			√			√						
88	Nepal				√							√	√						
89	Netherlands					√			√					√	√	√			

(Continued)

	Economy	Grouping by region							Grouping by income				Others						
		North America	East Asia & Pacific	Latin America & Caribbean	South Asia	Europe & Central Asia	Sub-Saharan Africa	Middle East & North Africa	High income	Upper Middle Income	Lower Middle Income	Low income	Belt and Road economies①	Advanced economies	EU	EA	G20	G7	BRICS
		1	2	3	4	5	6	7	8	9	10	11	12	13	14	15	16	17	18
90	New Zealand		√						√				√	√					
91	Nicaragua			√							√		√						
92	Nigeria						√				√		√						
93	North Macedonia					√				√			√						
94	Norway					√			√					√					
95	Oman							√	√				√						
96	Pakistan				√						√		√						
97	Panama			√					√				√						
98	Papua New Guinea		√								√		√						
99	Paraguay			√						√									
100	Peru			√						√			√						
101	Philippines		√								√		√						
102	Poland					√			√				√		√				
103	Portugal					√			√				√	√	√	√			
104	Romania					√				√			√		√				
105	Russia					√				√			√				√		√
106	Samoa		√							√			√						
107	Saudi Arabia							√	√				√				√		
108	Singapore		√						√				√	√					
109	Slovakia					√			√				√	√	√	√			
110	Slovenia					√			√				√	√	√	√			
111	South Africa						√			√			√				√		√
112	Spain					√			√					√	√	√			
113	Sri Lanka				√					√			√						
114	Sudan						√				√		√						
115	Sweden					√			√					√	√				
116	Switzerland					√			√					√					
117	Tanzania						√					√	√						
118	Thailand		√							√			√						
119	Trinidad and Tobago			√					√				√						
120	Tunisia							√			√		√						
121	Turkey					√				√			√				√		
122	Uganda						√					√	√						

(Continued)

	Economy	Grouping by region							Grouping by income				Others						
		North America	East Asia & Pacific	Latin America & Caribbean	South Asia	Europe & Central Asia	Sub-Saharan Africa	Middle East & North Africa	High income	Upper Middle Income	Lower Middle Income	Low income	Belt and Road economies①	Advanced economies	EU	EA	G20	G7	BRICS
		1	2	3	4	5	6	7	8	9	10	11	12	13	14	15	16	17	18
123	Ukraine					√					√		√						
124	United Kingdom					√			√					√			√	√	
125	United States	√							√					√			√	√	
126	Uruguay			√					√				√						
127	Vietnam		√								√		√						
128	Zambia						√				√		√						
129	Zimbabwe						√				√		√						
	Subtotal	2	19	23	5	43	25	12	49	39	30	11	98	36	27	19	19	7	5
	Global Total②	3	37	42	8	58	48	21	80	54	54	28	149	40	27	19	19	7	5

Note: ① The list of the economies along the "the Belt and Road" is as of August 27, 2022. ② The number of global economies is 216 in the *World Development Indicators* of the World Bank and 196 in the *World Economic Outlook* of the International Monetary Fund, respectively.

Source: (i) The groupings by region or by income from the World Bank, see https://data.worldbank.org/country;

(ii) The list of WTO members from the World Trade Organization, see https://www.wto.org/english/thewto_e/whatis_e/tif_e/org6_e.htm;

(iii) The list of economies along the "Belt and Road" from the official website of China's Belt and Road network, see

https://www.yidaiyilu.gov.cn/info/iList.jsp?cat_id=10037;

(iv) The members of Advanced economies. European Union (EU), European Area (EA) or Group of Seven (G7) from the International Monetary Fund, see https://www.imf.org/en/Publications/WEO/weo-database/2022/April/select-country-group;

(v) The list of Group of Twenty (G20) from the G20 Summit (Indonesia, 2022), see https://g20.org/about-the-g20/#about.

Acknowledgements

The *World Openness Report 2022* is the flagship publication of the Hongqiao International Economic Forum, which was prepared under the general responsibility and guidance of the following editors: ZHANG Yuyan, the Director and Senior Fellow of Institute of World Economics and Politics (IWEP) at Chinese Academy of Social Sciences (CASS), and GU Xueming, the Directors of Research Center for Hongqiao International Economic Forum.

Special thanks give to the contributors of this report as follows: BAI Jie, DONG Yan, GUO Ruonan, HAN Yonghui, LI Ruizhe, LI Xiaoxue, LIN Meng, LIU Dongmin, LIU Jianping, LIU Shiguo, LU Hongyan, LU Yuan, REN Lin, SONG Wei, SUN Ming, TIAN Huifang, WANG Ning, WANG Wenhai, YANG Zirong, YE Xin, YU Zirong, ZANG Chengwei, ZHANG Dan, ZHANG Han, ZHANG Lin, ZHANG Tao, and ZHU Cong.

The editors thank GAO Lingyun, GU Baozhi, HUANG Tao, Simon Evenett, SONG Hong, WANG Xinkui, and YAO Yang for their insightful comments and suggestions, together with YANG Dan, ZHANG Di, YANG Wenxiu and XU Xiaohui for data collection and processing.

Thanks are devoted to WANG Yin, China Social Sciences Press, who guided and coordinated the publication of this report; BAI Tianshu, ZHANG Bingjie, and XIN Chen of China Social Sciences Press, and Mengdi Turbutt-Cai of Paths International Ltd., who edited the report; LI Ping, who typeset the report; and Paths International Ltd. for the printing process and invaluable logistics coordination.

Any inquiries please contact the author at liusg@cass.org.cn.

This book is the result of a co-publishing agreement between China Social Sciences Press and Paths International Ltd (UK)

This report is supported by National Institute for Global Strategy of Chinese Academy of Social Sciences.

Title: World Openness Report 2022
By Institute of World Economics and Politics, CASS
Research Center for Hongqiao International Economic Forum
Hardback ISBN: 978-1-84464-770-5
Paperback ISBN978-1-84464-771-2
Ebook ISBN 978-1-84464-772-9

Paths International Ltd
www.pathsinternational.com
Published in the United Kingdom